Web Mapping Illustrated

Tyler Mitchell

O'REILLY®

Beijing · Cambridge · Farnham · Köln · Paris · Sebastopol · Taipei · Tokyo

Web Mapping Illustrated
by Tyler Mitchell

Copyright © 2005 O'Reilly Media, Inc. All rights reserved.
Printed in the United States of America.

Published by O'Reilly Media, Inc., 1005 Gravenstein Highway North, Sebastopol, CA 95472.

O'Reilly books may be purchased for educational, business, or sales promotional use. Online editions are also available for most titles (*safari.oreilly.com*). For more information, contact our corporate/institutional sales department: (800) 998-9938 or *corporate@oreilly.com*.

Editor:	Simon St.Laurent
Production Editor:	Mary Anne Weeks Mayo
Cover Designer:	Ellie Volckhausen
Interior Designer:	David Futato

Printing History:

June 2005:	First Edition.

 This book uses RepKover™, a durable and flexible lay-flat binding.

ISBN: 0-596-00865-1
[C]

Table of Contents

Foreword

For novices and geospatial experts alike, mapping technologies are undergoing as significant a change as has been seen since mapping first went digital. The prior introduction of Geographic Information Systems (GIS) and other digital mapping technologies transformed traditional map making and introduced an era of specialists in these new geographic technologies. Today, an even newer set of technological advancements are bringing an equally massive change as digital mapping goes mainstream. The availability of Global Positioning Systems (GPS), broadband Internet access, mass storage hard drives, portable devices, and—most importantly—web technologies are accelerating the ability to incorporate geographic information into our daily lives. All these changes have occurred simultaneously and so quickly that the impact of only a fraction of the full potential of spatial technologies has yet been felt.

In parallel with the exciting opportunities that modern technologies are providing the digital geospatial universe, a less broadly known but perhaps far more important phenomenon has emerged: a new world of open source collaboration. Open source development and user communities, along with a healthy commitment from industry, are filling the growing need and demand for spatial technologies for making better decisions and providing more information to the growing mapping needs of technology users. In a multidimensional world, geography forms a common framework for disseminating information. The open source community and industry is filling that need at a growth rate unmatched in the industry.

In an age when web technologies have erased the distances between peoples of different continents and nationalities, this book and the technologies behind it remind us of the continued importance of place in the world in which we live. Mapping has always highlighted the differences and variations that occur over space; but at the same time it has reminded us that we share this world with our neighbors, and our actions have impact beyond ourselves. Hopefully, web mapping technologies will help to bring this powerful information to all of us for our common future good.

If you are reading this book without ever having heard of Geographic Information Systems or Remote Sensing, you are not alone. It is for you that the publishing of this book is so timely; it is now that mapping technologies are for the first time becoming readily accessible to the broader IT world. The incredible wealth of information provided in this book will allow you to interact with the open source mapping community as so many have already done, and will one day allow you to help the many others that will follow.

I hope that this book will, if nothing else, engage you in understanding the power that mapping information can bring to your web presence and other IT needs—regardless of whether you are with an NGO, a small or large corporation, or a government organization. The importance of this book cannot be overstated. It comes at a critical stage, when two phenomena with tremendous momentum are coming together: the emergence of Open Source mapping technology, and the availability of technologies enabling digital mapping to become accessible by the masses.

—Dave McIlhagga
President, DM Solutions Group

Preface

What is it about maps? For some of us, maps are intriguing no matter where we are. I've spent hours poring over them learning about foreign places. There is a sense of mystery surrounding maps. They contain information that can only be revealed through exploration.

Digital maps allow a user to explore even further by providing an *interactive* experience. Most maps have traditionally been static. Now digital maps allow users to update information and customize it for their particular needs.

Youthful Exploration

For me, map-based exploration started at a young age. I remember the thrill of finding our Scout camp on a topographic map. Part of the map is shown in Figure P-1. I found my home town, local roads, and even greenhouses. It was hard to believe that someone bothered to map the streets I used to play on or the tobacco fields I worked in during summer vacation. Yet there they were, drawn on this fascinating map that hangs on my office wall 20 years later.

These maps opened the door to planning hiking adventures and bicycle trips. I blame maps for luring me further and further away from home—to see what a map symbol or town looked like on the ground.

When I wasn't exploring, I was often on the computer learning more about the *digital* world. My combined interest in computers and exploration naturally led me to the field of computerized mapping and geographic information systems (GIS). It never occurred to me that my enjoyment of maps and computers would become a career.

Whether showing a friend where you live or displaying the path of a pending hurricane, maps play an important role in lives of people everywhere. Having the tools

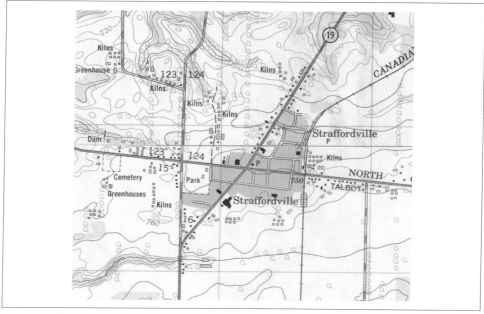

Figure P-1. Part of the topographic map of my home town in southern Ontario, Canada; my home was located at the X symbol. Portions of NTS map sheets 40l/15c and 10c/15c ©2005. Produced under licence from Her Majesty the Queen in Right of Canada, with permission of Natural Resources Canada.

and ability to map the world you live in is incredibly powerful. The following quote is from the Mayan Atlas:

> Maps are power. Either you will map or you will be mapped. If you are mapped by those who desire to own or control your land and resources, their map will display their justifications for their claims, not yours.

Having open access to mapping tools further enables mapping efforts. Being able to share those maps with the world through web mapping makes the effort all the more worthwhile.

The Tools in This Book

The tools in this book are the results of a handful of open source projects. They are a critical set of tools in my professional data management toolbox. From visualizing map data to converting between formats, I have come to depend on many of them daily. They are also an important part of my future goals for mapping and data management.

These tools are a subset of what is available today, both in the mainstream commercial market and in the open source realm. Because these are open source, they are free for you to use and adopt as you see fit. Many of them are pushing the envelope of what even the commercial products can do.

I began using many of these tools shortly after finishing university. My day job was in mapping and geospatial data analysis, and I had access to some of the latest commercial tools. However, when I wanted to pursue projects at home on my own time, the traditional tools were simply not available. The licensing restrictions and costs forced me to find alternatives; eventually, the open source tools took over. Any gaps in my array of tools will likely be filled within a year of this book being published.

There is a lot of active development going on across the spectrum of open source mapping and GIS projects. Many projects use the latest open standards for interoperability and tend to implement them much faster than the commercial products.

My initial motivation for writing was to fill in the gaps of existing documentation and answer the new user's common questions. I hope it does this and more. I hope you become as excited about these tools as I am. Years of programming have given us a powerful toolkit for mapping, data management, and even youthful exploration.

What This Book Covers

This book introduces several concepts and tools. They can be grouped into the following four categories:

- Mapping and data-management concepts
- Command-line data-management tools
- Command-line and web-based mapping tools
- Spatial database management

You will study the following tools:

Geospatial Data Abstraction Library (GDAL) with OGR
> This tool includes application programming interfaces (APIs) and command-line utilities for raster and vector data. GDAL's web site is *http://www.gdal.org*.

OpenEV
> For basic desktop GIS and imagery analysis; includes tools to draw new map features for use in other programs.

UMN MapServer
> This tool includes command-line tools to build CGI web applications and uses the MapServer API, called MapScript, to custom-script mapping applications.

PostGIS
> This tool is an extension to the PostgreSQL database management system that allows you to store and manipulate spatial data alongside tabular data.

Organization of This Book

This book is organized into 14 chapters and 2 appendixes:

Chapter 1, *Introduction to Digital Mapping*
> This chapter introduces digital mapping, including web mapping, and presents some of the barriers to using the technology. It also includes a list of web sites providing web mapping services and outlines the technology required to do web mapping.

Chapter 2, *Digital Mapping Tasks and Tools*
> This chapter outlines the goals of digital mapping and the common types of tasks involved including viewing, analysis, creating/manipulating, conversion, and sharing.

Chapter 3, *Converting and Viewing Maps*
> This chapter introduces the concepts of raster and vector data types, and the main tools used in this book: OpenEV, MapServer, GDAL, OGR, and PostGIS.

Chapter 4, *Installing MapServer*
> In this chapter, we walk through the main components of MapServer applications. You'll find detailed instructions for installing binaries or compiling MapServer from source. The chapter also provides a list of MapServer support contacts.

Chapter 5, *Acquiring Map Data*
> This chapter discusses how to assess your data needs and acquire data to meet those needs. It provides a list of resources for finding free mapping data.

Chapter 6, *Analyzing Map Data*
> This chapter covers setting up the FWTools package and using GDAL/OGR utilities for examining raster and vector datasets. Here you'll find examples that combine these utilities with command-line text processing tools to produce customized reports and summaries.

Chapter 7, *Converting Map Data*
> This chapter shows how to convert raster and vector data between formats using GDAL/OGR utilities. You'll learn how to convert between formats such as ESRI shapefiles, GML, DGN, and PostGIS formats.

Chapter 8, *Visualizing Mapping Data in a Desktop Program*
> This chapter provides a list of desktop mapping programs. It also introduces OpenEV as a desktop mapping program and walks through common tools in OpenEV. Here, you'll find examples of color-theming and preparing 3D views.

Chapter 9, *Create and Edit Personal Map Data*
> This chapter discusses what to consider when preparing to create your own data. You'll use OpenEV to digitize and draw new features into a shapefile.

Chapter 10, *Creating Static Maps*

In this chapter, you'll use command-line MapServer programs to create map images, scalebars, and legends. You'll use configuration files—a.k.a. map files—to create color-themed and labeled maps.

Chapter 11, *Publishing Interactive Maps on the Web*

This chapter studies how to set up MapServer for use with a web server. It builds on Chapter 10, making the mapping application available through a web page. You'll learn how to add HTML components for zooming, layer control, and reference maps.

Chapter 12, *Accessing Maps Through Web Services*

This chapter introduces the concept of web services and the Open Geospatial Consortium (OGC) specifications. It focuses on Web Map Service (WMS) and Web Feature Service (WFS). You'll find manual URL creation and MapServer configuration examples.

Chapter 13, *Managing a Spatial Database*

This chapter introduces the PostGIS extension to the PostgreSQL database. Here, you find installation guidelines and resources for Windows, Linux, and Mac operating systems. It also describes loading data into a PostGIS database, creating queries using SQL, and adding PostGIS data sources into MapServer applications.

Chapter 14, *Custom Programming with MapServer's MapScript*

In this chapter, you'll find out how to install or compile MapScript for various languages. The chapter introduces the main MapScript objects and provides examples of MapServer map files and Python code for drawing maps. It also includes examples of code in several languages.

Appendix A, *A Brief Introduction to Map Projections*

This appendix discusses coordinate systems and projections and introduces the main classes of projections and their use. It also explains EPSG codes and provides visual examples of several projections and associated MapServer map file syntax.

Appendix B, *MapServer Reference Guide for Vector Data Access*

This appendix describes different types of vector data sources and presents a comprehensive guide to 15 vector data formats MapServer can use. Here, you'll find map file syntax for native MapServer formats and for those accessed through the OGR library.

Conventions Used in This Book

Italic is used for:

- New terms where they are defined
- Emphasis in body text

- Pathnames, filenames, and program names; however, if the program name is also the name of a Java class, it is written in constant width font, like other class names
- Host and domain names (e.g., *http://www.maptools.org*)

`Constant width` is used for:

- Code examples and fragments
- Anything that might appear in an XML document, including element names, tags, attribute values, entity references, and processing instructions
- Anything that might appear in a program, including keywords, operators, method names, class names, utilities, and literals

`Constant width bold` is used for:

- User input
- Emphasis in code examples and fragments

`Constant width italic` is used for:

- Replaceable elements in code statements

 This icon indicates a tip, suggestion, or general note.

 This trap icon indicates a warning or caution.

Case-sensitive filenames and commands don't always allow authors to adhere to standard English grammar. It is usually possible to rewrite the sentence so the two don't conflict, and when possible I have endeavored to do so. However, on rare occasions when there is simply no way around the problem, I let standard English come up the loser.

Finally, many of the examples used here are designed for you to follow along with. I hope you can use the same code examples, but for reasons beyond my control, they might not work. Please feel free to reuse them or any parts of them in your own code. No special permission is required. As far as I am concerned, they are in the public domain (though the same isn't true of the explanatory text).

Safari Enabled

 When you see a Safari® Enabled icon on the cover of your favorite technology book, it means the book is available online through the O'Reilly Network Safari Bookshelf.

Safari offers a solution that's better than e-books. It's a virtual library that lets you easily search thousands of top technology books, cut and paste code samples, download chapters, and find quick answers when you need the most accurate, current information. Try it for free at *http://safari.oreilly.com*.

Comments and Questions

Please address comments and questions concerning this book to the publisher:

> O'Reilly Media, Inc.
> 1005 Gravenstein Highway North
> Sebastopol, CA 95472
> (800) 998-9938 (in the United States or Canada)
> (707) 829-0515 (international or local)
> (707) 829-0104 (fax)

There's a web page for this book that lists errata, examples, and any additional information. You can access this page at:

> *http://www.oreilly.com/catalog/webmapping*

To comment or ask technical questions about this book, send email to:

> *bookquestions@oreilly.com*

For more information about our books, conferences, Resource Centers, and the O'Reilly Network, see our web site at:

> *http://www.oreilly.com*

Acknowledgments

Several fellow passengers on this writing roller coaster deserve special mention. This project would never have happened without the support and patience of my editor, Simon St.Laurent. He helped me through several proposals, refining and focusing the content of this book.

Regardless of a successful book proposal, I would never have pursued this project without the support of my loving wife. Her encouragement, patience, and enthusiasm kept me going to the end.

Technical reviewers for this book helped catch my mistakes and improve the content substantially. Thank you very much to all of them: Bart van den Eijnden, Darren Redfern, Jeff McKenna, Paul Ramsey, and Tom Kralidis. A handful of others helped answer my endless stream of questions. If you helped with even a yes/no question, it was appreciated.

I'm thankful for the support and encouragement I received from Dave McIlhagga and DM Solutions Group in general. It was a continual reminder that this book was necessary.

The developers of these tools deserve special recognition for their contributions to open source GIS and mapping. Without them, there wouldn't be much to write to about! I would also like to acknowledge the long-term support of the University of Minnesota and their willingness to let the MapServer community grow beyond their borders.

A significant amount of documentation already exists for MapServer. Without the efforts of many companies and volunteers, I would never have learned as much as I have about these great tools. Thank you, fellow authors. In no way does this book mean to downplay your efforts.

Several friends and colleagues have helped encourage me over the years. Without their encouragement to think outside the box and strive for something better, I doubt I'd be writing this today.

I spent way too many hours on IRC channels picking the brains of other chatlings. When email was just too slow, this help was much appreciated and allowed real-time assistance from the broader community.

## CHAPTER 1

Introduction to Digital Mapping

Not long ago, people drew and colored their maps by hand. Analyzing data and creating the resulting maps was slow and labor intensive. Digital maps, thanks to the ever-falling cost of processing power and storage, have opened up a whole new range of possibilities. With the click of a mouse or a few lines of code, your computer analyzes, draws, and color-themes your map data. From the global positioning system (GPS) in your car to the web site displaying local bus routes, digital mapping has gone mainstream.

Of course, learning to produce digital maps requires some effort. Map data can be used incorrectly, resulting in maps with errors or misleading content. Digital mapping doesn't guarantee quality or ethics, just like conventional mapping.

The Power of Digital Maps

When you contrast the methods of conventional and digital mapping, the power of digital mapping becomes evident. The process of conventional mapping includes hand-drawn observations of the real world, transposed onto paper. If a feature changes, moves, or is drawn incorrectly, a new map needs to be created to reflect that change. Likewise if a map shows the extent of a city and that city grows, the extent of the map will need to be changed and the map will need to be completely recreated.

These problems are reduced with digital mapping. Because features are stored as distinct layers in a computer file, you can modify a map without starting from scratch. Once a feature is modified, the computer-based map instantly reflects the change the next time the feature is viewed. Interactive maps allow the user to view the precise area they are interested in, rather than be confined by the dimensions of a printed page. The user can also choose to view only certain pieces of content. The mapmaker doesn't have to guess which information the viewer wants to see but can make it possible for the reader to choose.

Instead of focusing on the details of a particular area of the world to map, the digital mapmaker can focus on how to best present information. This is much like the difference between an author and a web page designer. When you move into the digital realm, the focus is more on helping others find information rather than presenting static representations of information, as on a printed page. Today's mapmaker is often a web site developer, programmer, or some sort of geographic information analyst. Her focus is on managing and presenting information to a specific audience, be it in finance, forestry, or national defense, for instance.

The Difficulties of Making Maps

If you've worked with maps, digital or conventional, you'll know that despite my enthusiasm, mapping isn't always easy. Why do we often find it so difficult to make maps of the world around us? How well could you map out the way you normally drive to the supermarket? Usually, it's easier to *describe* your trip than it is to draw a map. Perhaps we have a perception of what a map must look like and therefore are afraid to draw our own, thinking it might look silly in comparison. Yet some maps drawn by a friend on a napkin might be of more use than any professional city map could ever be.

Personal Maps

The element of *personal* knowledge, rather than *general* knowledge, is what can make a somewhat useful map into one that is very powerful. When words fail to describe the location of something that isn't general knowledge, a map can round out the picture for you. Maps can be used to supplement a verbal description, but because creating a map involves drawing a perspective from your head, it can be very intimidating. That intimidation and lack of ownership over maps has created an interesting dilemma. In our minds, maps are something that *professionals* create, not the average person. Yet a map like the one shown in Figure 1-1 can have much more meaning to someone than a professional map of the same area. So what are the professional maps lacking? They show mostly common information and often lack personal information that would make the map more useful or interesting to you.

Technology Barriers

Digital mapping isn't a new topic. Ever since computers could create graphic representations of the earth, people have been creating maps with them. In early computing, people used to draw with ASCII text-based maps. (I remember creating ASCII maps for role-playing games on a Tandy color computer.) However, designing graphics with ASCII symbols wasn't pretty. Thankfully, more sophisticated graphic techniques on personal computers allow you to create your own high-quality maps.

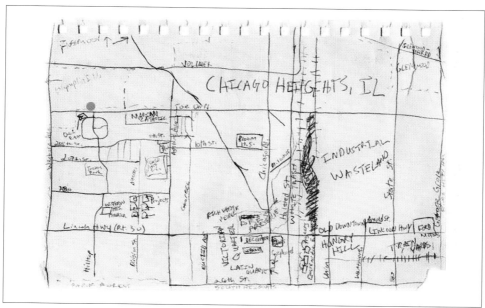

Figure 1-1. A personal map drawn by Ryan Mendenhall showing Chicago Heights, Illinois, U.S.A.; this map is courtesy of Lori Napoleon's maps project web site: http://www.subk.net/maps.html

You might already be creating your own maps but aren't satisfied with the tools. For some, the cost of commercial tools can be prohibitive, especially if you just want to play around for a while to get a feel for the craft. Open source software alleviates the need for immediate, monetary payback on investment.

For others, cost may not be an issue but capabilities are. Just like proprietary software, open source mapping products vary in their features. Improved features might include ease of use or quality of output. One major area of difference is in how products communicate with other products. This is called *interoperability* and refers to the ability of a program to share data or functions with another program. These often adhere to *open standards*—protocols for communication between applications. The basic idea is to define standards that aren't dependent on one particular software package; they would depend instead on the communication process a developer decided to implement. An example of these standards in action is the ability of your program to request maps from another mapping program over the Internet. The real power of open standards is evident when your program can communicate with a program developed by a different group/vendor. This is a crucial issue for many large organizations, especially government agencies, where sharing data across departments can make or break the efficiency in that organization. Products that implement open standards will help to ensure the long-term viability of applications you build. Be warned, however, that some products claim to be interoperable yet stop

Open Source Software

Open source software refers to a type of software product that has the programming source code available. This may not seem important for nonprogrammers, but it has very serious implications in today's software industry. Programmers who decide to release their work as open source choose an open source license to cover their program. In most cases, these licenses help make the program freely available.

There are thousands of programmers and supporters of open source projects. They come from government agencies, nonprofit groups, academia, and even private industry. Some businesses make all their source code openly available, and their clients simply pay for them to make improvements to the code.

Public and private groups have been working on mapping or geographic information system (GIS) projects and releasing them as open source. This means that the program itself is free and, if you have the ability and desire, you can modify it to suit your needs.

The key to open source software is *freedom*—freedom to use and change a program as required. This book focuses on open source mapping and GIS tools.

For more information on open source software see the following resources:

- Open Source Initiative web site: *http://opensource.org/*
- O'Reilly's *Open Sources*: *http://www.oreilly.com/catalog/opensources/*

short of implementing the full standards. Some companies modify the standards for their product, defeating the purpose of those standards. Interoperability standards are also relatively young and in a state of flux.

Costs and capabilities may not be the main barrier for you. Maybe you want to create your own maps but don't know how. Maybe you don't know what tools are available. This book describes some of the free tools available to you, to get you moving toward your end goal of map production.

Another barrier might be that you lack the technical know-how required for digital mapping. While conventional mapping techniques cut out most of the population, digital mapping techniques also prohibit people who aren't very tech-savvy. This is because installing and customizing software is beyond the scope of many computer users. The good news is that those who are comfortable with the customization side of computerized mapping can create easy-to-use tools for others. This provides great freedom for both parties. Those who have mastered the computer skills involved gain by helping fill other's needs. New users gain by being able to view mapping information with minimal effort through an existing mapping application.

Technological barriers exist, but for those who can use a computer and want to do mapping with that computer, the possibilities are endless. The mapping tools described here aren't necessarily easy to use: they require a degree of technical skill. Web mapping programs are more complicated than traditional desktop software. There are often no simple, automated installation procedures, and some custom configuration is required. But in general, once set up, the tools require minimal intervention.

Different Kinds of Web Mapping

One very effective way to make map information available to a group of nontechnical end users is to make it available through a web page. Web mapping sites are becoming increasingly popular. There are two broad kinds of web mapping applications: static and interactive.

Static maps displayed as an image on a web page are quite common. If you already have a digital map (e.g., from scanning a document), you can be up and running very quickly with a static map on your web page. Basic web design skills are all you need for this because it is only a single image on a page.

 This book doesn't teach web design skills. O'Reilly has other books that cover the topic of web design, from basic to advanced, including: *Learning Web Design*, *Web Design in a Nutshell*, *HTML and XHTML: The Definitive Guide*, and many more.

Interactive maps aren't as commonly seen because they require specialized skills to keep such sites up and running (not to mention the potential costs of buying off-the-shelf software). The term *interactive* implies that the viewer can somehow interact with the map. This can mean selecting different map data layers to view or zooming into a particular part of the map that you are interested in. All this is done while interacting with the web page and a map image that is repeatedly updated. For example, MapQuest is an interactive web mapping program for finding street addresses and driving directions. You can see it in action at *http://www.mapquest.com*.

Interactive maps that are accessed through web pages are referred to as *web-based maps* or simply *web maps*. These maps can be very powerful, but as mentioned, they can also be difficult to set up due to the technical skills required for maintaining a web server, a mapping server/program and management of the underlying map data. As you can see, these types of maps are fundamentally different from static maps because they are really a type of web-based program or application. Figure 1-2 shows a basic diagram of how an end user requests a map through a web mapping site and what happens behind the scenes. A user requests a map from the web server, and the server passes the request to the web mapping server, who then pulls together all the data. The map is passed all the way back to the end user's web browser.

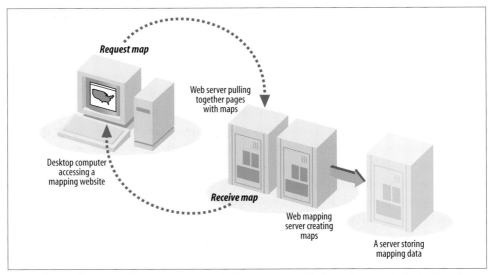

Figure 1-2. A diagram of how a mapping web site interacts with the end user and the back-end programs running on the servers

Web Map Users

Generally speaking, there are two types of people who use web maps: service providers and end users.

For instance, I am a service provider because I have put together a web site that has an interactive mapping component you can see it at: *http://spatialguru.com/maps/apps/global*. One of the maps available to my end users shows the locations of several hurricanes. I'm safely tucked away between the Rocky and Coastal mountain ranges in western Canada, so I wouldn't consider myself a user of the hurricane portion of the site. It is simply a service for others who are interested.

An end user might be someone who is curious about where the hurricanes are, or it may be a critical part of a person's business to know. For example, they may just wonder how close a hurricane is to a friend's house or they may need to get an idea of which clients were affected by a particular hurricane. This is a good example of how interactive mapping can be broadly applicable yet specifically useful.

End-user needs can vary greatly. You might seek out a web mapping site that provides driving directions to a particular address. Someone else might want to see an aerial photo and topographic map for an upcoming hiking trip. Some end users have a web mapping site created to meet their specific needs, while others just look on the Internet for a site that has some capabilities they are interested in.

Service providers can have completely different purposes in mind for providing a web map. A service provider might be interested in off-loading some of the repetitive tasks that come his way at the office. Implementing a web mapping site can be an excellent way of taking previously inaccessible data and making it more broadly available. If an organization isn't ready to introduce staff to more traditional GIS software (which can have a steep learning curve), having one technical expert maintain a web mapping site is a valuable service.

Another reason a service provider might make a web mapping site available is to more broadly disseminate data without having to transfer the raw data to clients. A good example of this is my provincial government, the Province of British Columbia, Canada. They currently have some great aerial photography data and detailed base maps, but if you want the digital data, you have to negotiate a data exchange agreement or purchase the data from them. The other option is to use one of their web mapping sites. They have a site available that basically turns mapping into a self-serve, customizable resource; check it out at: *http://maps.gov.bc.ca*.

Web Sites with a Web Mapping Component

There are many web mapping sites available for you to use and explore. Table 1-1 lists a few that use software or apply similar principles to the software described in this book.

Table 1-1. A few MapServer-based web sites that have interactive mapping

Web site	Description
http://www.dmsolutions.ca/solutions/tsunami.html	Tsunami disaster mapping site
http://topozone.com/	Portal to U.S. topographic, imagery, and street maps
http://www.dnr.state.mn.us/maps/	Various recreational and natural resource mapping applications for the state of Minnesota, U.S.A.
http://www.trailscanada.com	Portal for Canadian trails information and maps
http://www.mapitout.com/restaurants	Restaurant locating and viewing site for the city of Winnipeg, Canada
http://www.gommap.org/	Portal to Gulf of Maine (U.S.A.) mapping applications and web services
http://www.mapsherpa.com/hawaii2/	Comprehensive atlas of Hawaii, U.S.A.
http://mesonet.tamu.edu/	Real-time U.S.A. weather maps
http://spatialguru.com/maps/apps/global	View global imagery and places

Figures 1-3, 1-4, and 1-5 show the web pages of three such sites. They show how diverse some MapServer applications can be, from street-level mapping to statewide overviews.

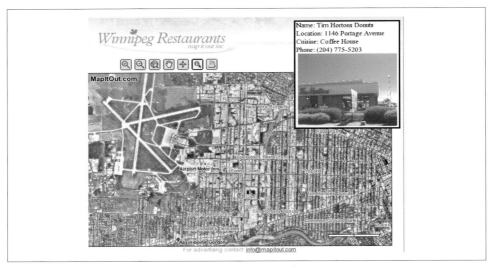

Figure 1-3. The MapServer-based restaurant mapping application from MapItOut

Figure 1-4. A MapServer-based tourism application for Hawaii from MapSherpa

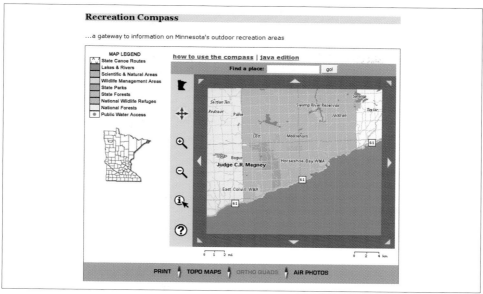

Figure 1-5. A web map for finding recreation sites in Minnesota, U.S.A.

Of course, not all maps out there are built with MapServer; Table 1-2 lists other mapping sites that you may want to look to for inspiration.

Table 1-2. Some popular web mapping sites or resources, not built with MapServer

Web site	Description
http://nationalatlas.gov	U.S. portal to maps and mapping data
http://www.multimap.com/	Locate hotels, tourism, and street maps
http://www.geographynetwork.com/	Portal to applications and data
http://mappoint.msn.com	Search for a place; find an address
http://www.mapquest.com/	Find an address; plan a route
http://www.moximedia.com:8080/ imf-ows/imf.jsp?site=ms_users	Maps showing the location of some MapServer users
http://davidrumsey.com/	Thousands of rare/antique maps
http://maps.yahoo.com/	Find an address; get driving directions, or check real-time traffic
http://maps.google.com/	Google maps that focus on North America and require Windows
http://toporama.cits.rncan.gc.ca/	Canadian topographic maps and aerial photos
http://geodiscover.cgdi.ca/ http://geogratis.gc.ca/ http://atlas.gc.ca/	Canadian portals to geographic information and services; include premade maps

Behind the web page

To some people, web mapping sites may appear quite simple, while to others, they look like magic. The inner workings of a web mapping site can vary depending on the software used, but there are some common general concepts:

- The web server takes care of web page requests and provides pages with images, etc. included, back to the requestor.
- The web mapping server accepts requests relayed from the web server. The request asks for a map with certain content and for a certain geographic area. It may also make requests for analysis or query results in a tabular form. The web mapping server program then creates the required map images (or tabular data) and sends them back to the web server for relay back to the end user.
- The web mapping server needs to have access to the data sources required for the mapping requests, as shown in Figure 1-2. This can include files located on the same server or across an internal network. If web mapping standards are used, data can also come from other web mapping servers through live requests.

More information on the process of web mapping services can be found in Chapters 4, 11, and 12: those chapters discuss MapServer in depth.

Making your own web mapping site

This book will teach about several of the components necessary to build your web mapping site, as well as general map data management. To give you an overview of the kinds of technology involved, here are some of the basic requirements of a web mapping site. Only the web mapping server and mapping data components from this list are discussed in this book.

A computer
> This should be a given, but it's worth noting that the more intensive the web mapping application you intend to host, the more powerful the computer you will want to have. Larger and more complex maps take longer to process; a faster processor completes requests faster. Internet hosting options are often too simplistic to handle web mapping sites, since you need more access to the underlying operating system and web server. Hosting services specifically for web mapping may also be available. The computer's operating system can be a barrier to running some applications. In general, Windows and Linux operating systems are best supported, whereas Mac OS X and other Unix-based systems are less so.

An Internet connection
> It is conceivable that you would have a web mapping site running just for you or for an internal (i.e., corporate) network, but if you want to share it with the public, you need a publicly accessible network connection. Some personal Internet accounts limit your ability to host these types of services, requiring additional

business class accounts that carry a heavier price tag. Performance of a web mapping site largely depends on the bandwidth of the Internet connection. If, for example, you produce large images (that have larger file sizes), though they run instantaneously on your computer, such images may take seconds to relay to an end user.

A web server

A web server is needed to handle the high-level communications between the end user (who is using a web browser to access your mapping site) and the underlying mapping services on your computer. It presents a web page containing maps and map-related tools to the end user. Two such servers are Apache HTTP Server (*http://httpd.apache.org/*) and Microsoft Internet Information Services (IIS) (*http://www.microsoft.com/WindowsServer2003/iis/default.mspx*). If you use an Internet service provider to host your web server, you may not be able to access the required underlying configuration settings for the software.

A web mapping server

The web mapping server is the engine behind the maps you see on a web page. The mapping server or web mapping program needs to be configured to communicate between the web server and assemble data layers into an appropriate image. This book focuses on MapServer, but there are many choices available.

Mapping data

A map isn't possible without some sort of mapping information for display. This can be satellite imagery, database connections, GIS software files, text files with lists of map coordinates, or other web mapping servers over the Internet. Mapping data is often referred to as spatial or geospatial data and can be used in an array of desktop mapping programs or web mapping servers.

Mapping metadata

This isn't a basic requirement, but I mentioned it here because it will emerge as a major requirement in the future. Metadata is data about data. It often describes where the mapping data came from, how it can be used, what it contains, and who to contact with questions. As more and more mapping data becomes available over the Internet, the need for cataloging the information is essential. Services already exist that search out and catalog online data sources so others can find them easily.

Over the course of this book, you'll learn to assemble these components into your own interactive mapping service.

CHAPTER 2
Digital Mapping Tasks and Tools

Maps can be beautiful. Some antique maps, found today in prints, writing paper, and even greeting cards, are appreciated more for their aesthetic value than their original cartographic use. The aspiring map maker can be intimidated by these masterpieces of science and art. Fortunately, the mapping process doesn't need to be intimidating or mystical.

Before you begin, you should know that all maps serve a specific purpose. If you understand that purpose, you've decoded the most important piece of a mapping project. This is true regardless of how the map is made. Traditional tools were pen and ink, not magic. Digital maps are just a drawing made up of points strung together into lines and shapes, or a mosaic of colored squares.

The purpose and fundamentals of digital mapping are no different and no more complex than traditional mapping. In the past, a cartographer would sit down, pull out some paper, and sketch a map. Of course, this took skill, knowledge, and a great deal of patience. Using digital tools, the computer is the canvas, and software tools do the drawing using geographic data as the knowledge base. Not only do digital tools make more mapping possible, in most cases digital solutions make the work ridiculously easy.

This chapter explores the common tasks, pitfalls, and issues involved in creating maps using computerized methods. This includes an overview of the types of tasks involved with digital mapping—the communication of information using a variety of powerful media including maps, images, and other sophisticated graphics. The goals of *digital mapping* are no different than that of traditional mapping: they present geographic or location-based information to a particular audience for a particular purpose. Perhaps your job requires you to map out a proposed subdivision. Maybe you want to show where the good fishing spots are in the lake by your summer cabin. Different reasons yield the same desired goal: a map.

For the most part, the terms *geographic information* and *maps* can be used interchangeably, but maps usually refer to the output (printed or digital) of the mapping process. Geographic information refers to digital data stored in files on a computer that's used for a variety of purposes.

When the end product of a field survey is a hardcopy map, the whole process results in a paper map and nothing more. The map might be altered and appended as more information becomes available, but the hardcopy map is the final product with a single purpose.

Digital mapping can do this and more. Computerized tools help collect and interact with the map data. This data is used to make maps, but it can also be analyzed to create new data or produce statistical summaries. The same geographic data can be applied to several different mapping projects. The ability to render the same information without compiling new field notes or tracing a paper copy makes digital mapping more efficient and more fun.

Digital mapping applies computer-assisted techniques to a wide range of tasks that traditionally required large amounts of manual labor. The tasks that were performed are no different than those of the modern map maker, though the approach and tools vary greatly. Figure 2-1 shows a conceptual diagram of the digital mapping process.

Map data source   Mapping program   Map product

Figure 2-1. Digital maps are made using a mapping program that accesses mapping data and gives the resulting map back to the user

Common Mapping Tasks

The process that produces a map requires three basic tasks: quantifying observations, locating the position of your observations, and visualizing the locations on a map. Digital tools have made these tasks more efficient and more accurate.

Quantifying observations

Measuring equipment such as laser range finders or imaging satellites provide discrete measurements that are less affected by personal interpretations. Traditional observations, such as manual photo interpretation or drawing features by hand, tend to introduce a biased view of the subject.

Locating positions of observations

Geographic referencing tools such as GPS receivers link on-the-earth locations to common mapping coordinate systems such as latitude and longitude. They calculate the receiver's location using satellite-based signals that help the GPS receiver calculate its location relative to satellites whose positions are well known. They act as a type of digital benchmark rather than using traditional survey or map referencing (best guess) methods. Traditional astronomical measurements or ground-based surveying techniques were useful but we now have common, consistent, and unbiased methods for calculating location.

Visualizing these locations on a map

Desktop mapping programs allow the user to compare location information with digital base map data. Traditional hand-drawn paper maps can't compete with the speed and flexibility of digital desktop mapping programs. Of course, digital mapping data is needed to do the job, but once data is available, infinite renditions of maps using the same base data is possible.

If a tool described here isn't effective, other tasks are affected. For example, poor recording of observations can still produce a map, but its accuracy is questionable.

The end goal of mapping is to present information about our observations of the world. The better that can be done, the better the goal has been met. When these tools are working together, the cartographic process can be very efficient.

Common Pitfalls, Deadends, and Irritations

Many maps can now be created in the safety of a home or office without the need to sail the seas to chart new territories. The traditional, nondigital methods of surveying to produce maps held certain dangers that are quite different from those of today. However, digital mapping has its own problems and irritations. The pitfalls today may not involve physical danger but instead involve poor quality, inappropriate data, or restricted access to the right kind of information.

Finding Good Source Data

A bad map isn't much better than a blank map. This book doesn't discuss good map design (the art of cartography), but an equally important factor plays into digital mapping: the quality of source data. Because maps are based on some sort of source data, it is imperative to have good quality information at the beginning. The maxim *garbage in, garbage out* definitely applies; bad data makes for bad maps and analysis. This is discussed in more detail in Chapter 5.

Dependency on Digital Tools

With the advent of digital mapping has come the loss of many traditional mapping skills. While digital tools can make maps, there are some traditional skills that are helpful. You might think that training in digital mapping would include the theory and techniques of traditional mapping processes, but it often doesn't. Today, many who do digital mapping are trained to use only a specific piece of software. Take away that software or introduce a large theoretical problem, and they may be lost. Map projection problems are a good example. If you don't understand how projections work, you can severely degrade the quality of your data when reprojecting and merging datasets as described in Chapter 8 and discussed in Appendix A.

Another example would be the ignorance of geometric computations. It was quite humiliating to realize that I didn't know how to calculate the area of an irregular polygon; nor was it even common knowledge to my most esteemed GIS colleagues. Figure 2-2 shows a range of common shapes and the formulae used to calculate their area.

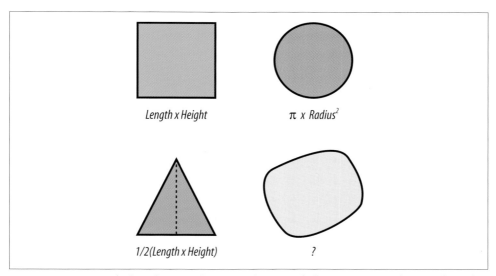

Figure 2-2. How to calculate the area of common shapes, including a square, circle, triangle, and the infamous irregular polygon

Many of the calculations were taught in elementary school but not for the irregular polygon. It doesn't use a simple formula, and there are multiple ways to calculate the area. One method is to triangulate all the vertices that make up the polygon boundary and then calculate and sum the area of all those triangles. You can see why we let the computer do this kind of task!

It was rather amusing to realize that we used digital tools to calculate areas of polygons all the time but had little or no idea of how it was done. On the other hand it was disconcerting to see how much of our thinking was relegated to the computer. Most of us could not even verify computed answers if we wanted to!

Digital mapping and GIS need to become more than just a tool for getting to the end goal. More theory and practice of manual skills would better enable the map maker and analyst to use digital tools in a wise manner. It goes without saying that our dependency on digital tools doesn't necessarily make us smarter. Because this book doesn't teach cartographic theory, I recommend you find other texts that do. There are many available, including:

- M.J. Kraak and F.J. Ormeling. *Cartography: Visualization of Spatial Data*. London: Longman. 1996.
- Alan M. MacEachren. *Some Truth with Maps*. Washington: Penn State. 1994.

Understanding Data Formats

There are many different mapping data formats in use today. In order to use map data effectively you must understand what format your data is in, and you must know what data format you need. If the current format isn't suitable, you must be able to convert it to an intermediate format or store it in a different manner.

The range of different software and data formats is confusing. Many different vendors have created their own proprietary data formats. This has left users tied to a format as long as they use that product. Vendors are starting to work together to develop some independent standards, which will help those using data with their products.

Make sure you understand what task you are going to need the source data for. Will you be printing a customized map and combining it with other pieces of data, or will you simply view it on the screen? Will you need to edit the data or merge it with other data for analysis? Your answers to these questions will help you choose the appropriate formats and storage methods for your tasks.

Using the Right Tools

There are numerous digital mapping tools available. This makes the choice of any given tool difficult. Some think that the biggest, most expensive tools are the only way to go. They may secretly believe that the product is more stable or better supported (when, in fact, it may just be slick marketing). Choosing the right tool for the job is very difficult when you have so many (seemingly) comparable choices. For example, sometimes GIS tools are used when a simple drawing program may have been more effective, but this was never considered because the users were thinking in terms of a GIS software package.

Examples of extreme oversimplification and extreme complexity are frequently found when using mapping and GIS software. You can see the best example of this problem when comparing computer-aided design (CAD) technicians and GIS analysts. GIS analysts often maintain very modular, relatively simple pieces of data requiring a fair bit of work to make a nice visual product. CAD users have a lot of options for graphical quality, but often lack easy-to-use analytical tools. The complexity of trying to understand how to style, move, or edit lines, etc., makes many CAD programs difficult to use. Likewise, the complexities of data management and analytical tools make some GIS software daunting.

Identifying the Types of Tasks for a Project

Just like carpenters, map makers know the value of using the right tool for the job. The digital map maker has a variety of tools to choose from, and each tool is designed for a certain task. Many tools can do one or two tasks well, and other tasks moderately well or not at all. There are five different types of tools used in digital mapping and its related disciplines. These are general categories which often overlap.

Viewing and Mapping

Viewing and mapping data aren't necessarily the same thing. Some applications are intended only for visualizing data, while others target map production. Map production is more focused on a high-quality visual product intended for print. In the case of this book, *viewing tools* are used for visually gathering information about the map data—how the data is laid out, where (geographically) the data covers, comparing it to other data, etc.

Mapping tools are used to publish data to the Internet through web mapping applications or web services. They can also be used to print a paper map. The concepts of viewing and mapping can be grouped together because they both involve a graphic output/product. They tend to be the final product after the activities in the following categories are completed.

Analysis

Just viewing maps or images isn't usually the final goal of a project. Certain types of analysis are often required to make data visualization more understandable or presentable. This includes data classification (where similar features are grouped together into categories), spatial proximity calculations (features within a certain distance of another), and statistical summary (grouping data using statistical functions such as average or sum). Analysis tends to summarize information temporarily, whereas manipulating data can change or create new data.

Creating and Manipulating

This category can include creating features, which uses a process often referred to as digitizing. These features may be created as a result of some sort of analysis. For example, you might keep features that are within a certain study area.

You can manipulate data with a variety of tools from command-line programs to drag and drop–style graphical manipulation. Many viewing applications can't edit features. Those that can edit often create new data only by drawing on screen (a.k.a. digitizing) or moving features. Some products have the ability to do more, such as performing buffering and overlap analysis or grouping features into fewer, larger pieces. Though these are common in many commercial products, open source desktop GIS products with these capabilities are just starting to appear.

Conversion

Certain applications require data to be in certain file or database formats. This is particularly the case in the commercial world where most vendors support their own proprietary formats with marginal support for others. This use of proprietary data formats has led to a historic dependency upon a vendor's product. Fortunately, recent advances in the geomatics software industry have led to cross-application support for more competitor formats. This, in turn, has led to interoperable vendor-neutral standards through cooperative organizations such as the Open Geospatial Consortium (OGC). The purpose of the OGC and their specifications are discussed in more detail in Chapter 12.

Source data isn't always in the format required by viewing or manipulating applications. If you receive data from someone who uses a different mapping system, it's more than likely that conversion will be necessary. Output data that may be created by manipulation processes isn't always in the format that an end user or client may require. Enter the role of data conversion tools that convert one format into another.

Data conversion programs help make data available in a variety of formats. There are some excellent tools available, and there are also support libraries for applications, making data conversion unnecessary. Data access libraries allow an application to access data directly instead of converting the data before using it with the application.

Some examples of these libraries are discussed later in this chapter. For an excellent commercial conversion tool, see Safe Software's Feature Manipulation Engine (FME) at *http://safe.com*.

Sharing

You are probably reading this book because you desire to share maps and mapping data. There is a certain pleasure in creating and publishing a map of your own. Because of the variety of free tools and data now available, this is no longer just a dream.

This book addresses two aspects of that sharing. First, sharing maps (static or interactive) through web applications and second, using web service specifications for sharing data between applications.

The term *web mapping* covers a wide range of applications and processes. It can mean a simple web page that shows a satellite image or a Flash-based application with high levels of interaction, animations, and even sound effects. But, for the most part, web mapping implies a web page that has some sort of interactive map component. The web page may present a list of layers to the user who can turn them on or off, changing the map as he sees fit. The page may also have viewing tools that allow a user to zoom in to the map and view more detail.

The use of Open Geospatial Consortium (OGC) web services (OWS) standards allow different web mapping applications to share data with each other or with other applications. In this case, an application can be web-enabled but have no graphical mapping interface component riding on top of it. Instead, using Internet communication standards other applications can make a request for data from the remote web service. This interoperability enables different pieces of software to talk to each other without needing to know what kind of server is providing the information. These abilities are still in their infancy, particularly with commercial vendors, but several organizations are already depending on them. Standardized web services allows organizations to avoid building massive central repositories, as well as access data from the source. They also have more freedom when purchasing software, with many more options to choose from. OWS is an open standard for sharing and accessing information; therefore organizations are no longer tied to a particular vendor's data format. The software needs only to support OWS. For example, Figure 2-3 shows a map created from multiple data sources. Several layers are from a copy of map data that the mapping program accesses directly. The other two layers are from OWS data sources: one from a company in The Netherlands (elevation shading), and the other (weather radar imagery) from a university in the United States.

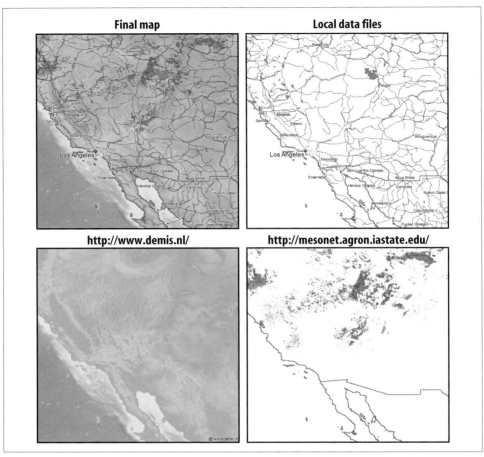

Figure 2-3. A map made from multiple remote servers using an OWS specification

## CHAPTER 3

Converting and Viewing Maps

While presenting maps on the Web is fantastic, the data for those maps has to come from somewhere. You'll also want to have a toolkit for creating or modifying maps to fit your needs, especially if you're developing in an environment that isn't already GIS-oriented. This chapter introduces end-user applications for viewing and sharing data as well as low-level tools for data access and conversion.

While many other open source GIS and mapping tools exist, this chapter covers the small selection used throughout the remainder of this book. While many other excellent options exist, the sample of tools described here are robust enough for professional use. These free and open source GIS/mapping products are successfully used throughout industry, government, and academia.

For more general information and links to other tools, see the following reference web sites:

http://freegis.org
http://opensourcegis.org
http://maptools.org

If you have the funds or already have the tools, you can, of course, use proprietary GIS software to create the data you'll be presenting with open source software. One of the best features of the open source tools is their ability to work with data created by proprietary applications and stored in proprietary formats.

Raster and Vector

The terms raster and vector are used throughout this chapter. They both refer to specific types of data. *Raster data* is organized as a matrix or grid that has rows and columns; each row/column intersection is a cell or pixel. Each cell has a value, for example, an elevation. Images and digital elevation models are rasters. They are a specific number of pixels high and wide, with each pixel representing a certain size on the ground; for example, Landsat satellite images are 185×185 km in size. Each pixel is 30×30 m in size.

Vector data is represented as coordinates that define points or points that are strung together to make lines and polygons. This data often has an associated table of information, one for every feature (point, line, or polygon) in the dataset. Keeping these distinctions in mind will help you better understand the remaining parts of this chapter.

OpenEV

OpenEV is a powerful open source desktop viewer. It allows users to explore data in any of the image and vector data formats supported by the Geospatial Data Abstraction Library (GDAL/OGR), which will be introduced later in the chapter. OpenEV can be used for custom image analysis as well as drawing simple maps and creating new data. OpenEV comes as part of the FWTools package, available at *http://fwtools. maptools.org*.

Many users overlook OpenEV's ability to view and navigate in real time through images draped over 3D landscapes. Figure 3-1 shows an example of an image being viewed with OpenEV, and Figure 3-2 shows the same image but modified with one of the OpenEV image enhancement tools.

OpenEV is a good example of how GDAL/OGR capabilities can be accessed through other programming languages. OpenEV is built using Python, which makes OpenEV extensible and powerful because it has the flexibility of that language running behind it. The most powerful feature of OpenEV may be its ability to use Python capabilities within OpenEV; this allows access to GDAL/OGR functions and to any other Python module you need.

MapServer

MapServer is the primary open source web mapping tool used in this book. The main MapServer site is at *http://mapserver.gis.umn.edu*.

There are numerous reasons people decide to use MapServer. One is the ability to make their mapping information broadly accessible to others, particularly over the Internet. Many GIS and mapping analysts need to create custom mapping products for those they support or work for; MapServer makes it possible for users to create maps without needing particular tools installed or assistance from mapping analysts. This in turn reduces the pressure on specialized staff.

Others come to MapServer because it is one of few solutions available for those with diverse data formats. MapServer, through the use of libraries such as GDAL/OGR, can access various data formats without data conversion.

Figure 3-1. A raw Landsat satellite image being viewed with OpenEV

Consider that you could have a collection of 10 different sets of mapping data, all of which need to appear on the same map simultaneously without any of the data being converted from its native format. The native formats can include those used by different commercial vendors. ESRI shapefiles, Intergraph Microstation design files (DGN), MapInfo TAB files, and Oracle spatial databases can all be mapped together without conversion. Other nonproprietary formats can be used as well, including the OGC standards for Geography Markup Language (GML), Web Map Server (WMS), Web Feature Server (WFS), and PostGIS and other databases. The ability to have simultaneous access to diverse data formats on the fly without conversion makes MapServer one of the only options for those who can't (or won't) do a wholesale conversion to a specific format.

Figure 3-2. A Landsat satellite image being viewed with OpenEV and an equalization enhancement

Data Access and Performance

MapServer supports a variety of formats. Some are native to the MapServer executable, while others are accessed through the GDAL/OGR libraries. The latter approach is necessary for formats not programmed directly into MapServer. Access through the libraries adds an extra level of communication between MapServer and the data source itself (which can cause poor performance in some cases).

In general, formats supported natively by MapServer should run faster than those using GDAL/OGR. For example, the most basic format MapServer uses is the ESRI shapefile or GeoTiff image. OGR supports the U.S. Census TIGER file format. The performance difference between loading TIGER or shapefiles can be considerable.

However, using GDAL/OGR may not be the problem. Further investigation shows that the data formats are often the bottleneck. If the data in a file is structured in a way that makes it difficult to access or requires numerous levels of interpretation, it affects map drawing speed.

The general rule of thumb for best performance is to use ESRI shapefile format or Geo-Tiff image format. Because `gdal_translate` and `ogr2ogr` can write into these formats, most source data can be translated using these tools. If you access data across a network, storing data in the PostGIS database may be the best option. Because PostGIS processes your queries for data directly on the server, only the desired results are sent back over the network. With file-based data, more data has to be passed around, even before MapServer decides which pieces it needs. Server-side processing in a PostGIS database can significantly improve the performance of MapServer applications.

Wholesale conversions aren't always possible, but when tweaking performance, these general rules may be helpful.

Portability

MapServer and its supporting tools are available for many hardware and operating systems. Furthermore, MapServer functionality can be accessed through a variety of programming language interfaces, making it possible to integrate MapServer functionality into custom programs. MapServer can be used in custom environments where other web mapping servers may not run.

Because MapServer is open source, developers can improve, fix, and customize the actual code behind MapServer and port it to new operating systems or platforms. In fact, if you require a new feature, a developer can be hired to add it, and everyone in the community can benefit from the work.

MapServer is primarily a viewing and mapping application; users access maps through a web browser or other Internet data sharing protocols. This allows for visual sharing of mapping information and real-time data sharing with other applications using the OGC specifications. MapServer can perform pseudo data conversion by reading in various formats and providing access to another server or application using common protocols. MapServer isn't an analysis tool, but it can present mapping information using different cartographic techniques to visualize the results.

Geospatial Data Abstraction Library (GDAL)

GDAL is part of the FWTools package available at *http://fwtools.maptools.org*. GDAL's home page (*http://www.gdal.org*) describes the project as:

> ...a translator library for raster geospatial data formats... As a library, it presents a single abstract data model to the calling application for all supported formats.

GDAL (often pronounced *goodle*) has three important features. First, it supports over 40 different raster formats. Second, it is available for other applications to use. Any application using the GDAL libraries can access all its supported formats, making custom programming for every desired format unnecessary. Third, prebuilt utilities help you use the functionality of the GDAL programming libraries without having to write your own program.

These three features offer a powerhouse of capability: imagine not worrying about what format an image is in. With GDAL supporting dozens of formats, the odds are that the formats you use are covered. Whether you need to do data conversion, display images in your custom program, or write a new driver for a custom image format, GDAL has programming interfaces or utilities available to help.

Raster Formats Supported by GDAL

GDAL supports dozens of raster formats. This list is taken from the GDAL web site formats list page found at *http://www.gdal.org/formats_list.html*.

Arc/Info Binary Grid (*.adf*)
Microsoft Windows Device Independent Bitmap (*.bmp*)
BSB Nautical Chart Format (*.kap*)
VTP Binary Terrain Format (*.bt*)
CEOS (Spot, for instance)
First Generation USGS DOQ (*.doq*)
New Labelled USGS DOQ (*.doq*)
Military Elevation Data (*.dt0*, *.dt1*)
ERMapper Compressed Wavelets (*.ecw*)
ESRI *.hdr* labeled
ENVI *.hdr* labeled Raster
Envisat Image Product (*.n1*)
EOSAT FAST Format
FITS (*.fits*)
Graphics Interchange Format (*.gif*)
Arc/Info Binary Grid (*.adf*)
GRASS Rasters
TIFF/GeoTIFF (*.tif*)
Hierarchical Data Format Release 4 (HDF4)
Erdas Imagine (*.img*)
Atlantis MFF2e
Japanese DEM (*.mem*)
JPEG, JFIF (*.jpg*)
JPEG2000 (*.jp2*, *.j2k*)
NOAA Polar Orbiter Level 1b Data Set (AVHRR)
Erdas 7.x .LAN and .GIS

In Memory Raster
Atlantis MFF
Multi-resolution Seamless Image database
NITF
NetCDF
OGDI Bridge
PCI *.aux* labeled
PCI Geomatics database file
Portable Network Graphics (*.png*)
Netpbm (*.ppm*, *.pgm*)
USGS SDTS DEM (**CATD.DDF*)
SAR CEOS
USGS ASCII DEM (*.dem*)
X11 Pixmap (*.xpm*)

This list is comprehensive but certainly not static. If a format you need isn't listed, you are encouraged to contact the developers. Sometimes only a small change is required to meet your needs. Other times it may mean your request is on a future enhancement waiting list. If you have a paying project or client with a particular need, hiring the developer can make your request a higher priority. Either way, this is one of the great features of open source software development—direct communication with the people in charge of development.

All these formats can be read, but GDAL can't write to or create new files in all these formats. The web page shown earlier lists which ones GDAL can create.

Programming Libraries

As mentioned earlier, an important feature of GDAL is its availability as a set of programming libraries. Developers using various languages can take advantage of GDAL's capabilities, giving them more time to focus on other tasks. Custom programming to support formats already available through GDAL isn't necessary: reusability is a key strength of GDAL.

GDAL's application programming interface (API) tutorial shows parallel examples of how to access raster data using C, C++, and Python. You can also use the Simplified Wrapper and Interface Generator (SWIG) to create interfaces for other programming languages such as Perl, Java, C#, and more. See *http://www.swig.org/* for more information on SWIG.

The ability to directly link to GDAL libraries has helped add features to an array of GIS and visualization programs both commercial and open source. The GDAL website lists several projects that use GDAL, including FME, MapServer, GRASS, Quantum GIS, Cadcorp SIS, and Virtual Terrain Project.

GDAL Utilities

GDAL also has some powerful utilities. Several command-line data access/manipulation utilities are available. All use the GDAL libraries for tasks such as the following:

gdalinfo

Interrogates a raster/image file and gives information about the file. This command, when given a raster file/data source name, provides a listing of various statistics about the data, as shown in the following code:

```
# gdalinfo vancouver.tif
Driver: GTiff/GeoTIFF
Size is 1236, 1028
Coordinate System is:
PROJCS["NAD83 / UTM zone 10N",
    GEOGCS["NAD83",
        DATUM["North_American_Datum_1983",
            SPHEROID["GRS 1980",6378137,298.2572221010042,
                AUTHORITY["EPSG","7019"]],
            AUTHORITY["EPSG","6269"]],
        PRIMEM["Greenwich",0],
        UNIT["degree (supplier to define representation)",0.01745329251994328],
        AUTHORITY["EPSG","4269"]],
    PROJECTION["Transverse_Mercator"],
    PARAMETER["latitude_of_origin",0],
    PARAMETER["central_meridian",-123],
    PARAMETER["scale_factor",0.9996],
    PARAMETER["false_easting",500000],
    PARAMETER["false_northing",0],
    UNIT["metre",1,
        AUTHORITY["EPSG","9001"]],
    AUTHORITY["EPSG","26910"]]
Origin = (480223.000000,5462627.000000)
Pixel Size = (15.00000000,-15.00000000)
Corner Coordinates:
Upper Left  (  480223.000, 5462627.000) (123d16'19.62"W, 49d18'57.81"N)
Lower Left  (  480223.000, 5447207.000) (123d16'16.88"W, 49d10'38.47"N)
Upper Right (  498763.000, 5462627.000) (123d 1'1.27"W, 49d18'58.96"N)
Lower Right (  498763.000, 5447207.000) (123d 1'1.10"W, 49d10'39.61"N)
Center      (  489493.000, 5454917.000) (123d 8'39.72"W, 49d14'48.97"N)
Band 1 Block=256x256 Type=Byte, ColorInterp=Red
Band 2 Block=256x256 Type=Byte, ColorInterp=Green
Band 3 Block=256x256 Type=Byte, ColorInterp=Blue
```

Various pieces of important information are shown here: image format, size, map projection used (if any), geographic extent, number of colors, and pixel size. All these pieces of information can be very useful when working with data, particularly data that is from an external source about which little is known.

gdal_translate

Translates a raster/image between formats. It has numerous powerful functions such as image resizing, adding ground control points for geo-referencing, and

---

taking subsets of data. This tool can also manipulate any supported format for other purposes, such as web or graphic design. This is particularly useful when images are very large and not easily handled by other software.

gdaladdo

Adds overview levels to a file. This feature improves application performance viewing a file. Applications that are able to read these overviews can then request appropriate resolutions for the display and map scale without loading the full resolution of the file into memory. Instead, portions of an image at reduced resolution are quickly provided.

gdalwarp

Takes a source image and reprojects it into a new image, warping the image to fit the output coordinate system. This is very useful when source data isn't in the required coordinate spatial reference system. For example, a geo-referenced satellite image may be projected into UTM projection with meter units, but the application requires it to be unprojected in geographic coordinates (latitude/longitude) measured in degrees.

gdal_merge.py

A very powerful tool that takes multiple input images and stitches them together into a single output image. It is a Python script that requires the Python interpreter software to be installed on your system and the GDAL Python module to be loaded. This is a good example of how powerful programs can be built on top of GDAL using higher-level languages such as Python. See *http://python.org/* for more information about the programming language. Recent download packages of FWTools include GDAL and Python as well. See *http://fwtools.maptools.org/*.

gdaltindex

Creates or appends the bounds of an image into an index shapefile. You run gdaltindex with image names as a parameter. GDAL checks the geographic extents of the image and creates a rectangular shape. The shape and the name of the image files are then saved to the output shapefile. This image index can be used by MapServer to define a single layer that is actually made up of more than one image. It works as a virtual image data source and helps MapServer find the right image efficiently.

In general, GDAL aids in accessing, converting, and manipulating rasters/images. When further programming is done using languages such as Python, GDAL can also serve as a powerful analysis tool. In one sense GDAL can also be used as a rough viewing tool because it allows conversion into commonly viewable formats (e.g., JPEG) for which many non-GIS users may have viewing software.

 If you use the GDAL utilities that come with FWTools for Windows, you will have a desktop icon called FWTools Shell. This launches a command window for running these utilities.

OGR Simple Features Library

OGR is part of the FWTools package that's available at *http://fwtools.maptools.org*. The OGR project home page (*http://www.gdal.org/ogr*) describes OGR as:

> ... a C++ open source library (and command line tools) providing read (and sometimes write) access to a variety of vector file formats including ESRI Shapefiles, S-57, SDTS, PostGIS, Oracle Spatial, and Mapinfo mid/mif and TAB formats.

 The historical definition of the acronym OGR is irrelevant today, but it's used throughout the code base, making it difficult to change.

OGR supports more than 16 different vector formats and has utilities similar to GDAL's raster utilities.

Vector Formats Supported by OGR

The following list of the vector data formats supported by OGR was taken from the OGR formats web page at *http://www.gdal.org/ogr/ogr_formats.html*. The web page also shows which formats can be written or only read by OGR.

Arc/Info Binary Coverage
ESRI shapefile
DODS/OPeNDAP
FMEObjects Gateway
GML
IHO S-57 (ENC)
Mapinfo file
Microstation DGN
OGDI vectors
ODBC
Oracle Spatial
PostgreSQL
SDTS
UK .NTF
U.S. Census TIGER/Line
VRT: Virtual Datasource

OGR is part of the GDAL/OGR project and is packaged with GDAL. GDAL deals with raster or image data, and OGR deals with vector data. GDAL is to painting as OGR is to connect-the-dot drawings. These data access and conversion libraries cover the breadth of mapping data.

OGR Utilities and Examples

Like GDAL, OGR consists of a set of libraries that can be used in applications. It also comes with some powerful utilities:

ogrinfo

> Interrogates a vector dataset and gives information about the features. This can be done with any format supported by OGR. The following code shows ogrinfo being used to show information about a shapefile:

```
# ogrinfo -summary placept.shp placept
Had to open data source read-only.
INFO: Open of `placept.shp'
using driver `ESRI Shapefile' successful.

Layer name: placept
Geometry: Point
Feature Count: 497
Extent: (-140.873489, 42.053455) - (-52.808067, 82.431976)
Layer SRS WKT:
(unknown)
AREA: Real (12.3)
PERIMETER: Real (12.3)
PACEL_: Integer (10.0)
PACEL_ID: Integer (10.0)
UNIQUE_KEY: String (5.0)
NAME: String (50.0)
NAME_E: String (50.0)
NAME_F: String (50.0)
UNIQUE_KEY: String (5.0)
UNIQUE_KEY: String (5.0)
REG_CODE: Integer (2.0)
NTS50: String (7.0)
POP91: Integer (7.0)
SGC_CODE: Integer (7.0)
CAPITAL: Integer (3.0)
POP_RANGE: Integer (3.0)
```

This example shows many vital pieces of information including geographic extent of features, a list of the attributes, their types, and how many features are in the file. Additional parameters can be added that help access desired information more specifically.

Running it in different modes (the example shows summary mode) will reveal more or less detail. A complete listing of all the values and geographic locations of the features is possible if you remove the -summary option. You can also specify criteria using standard database query statements (SQL), as shown in the following code. This is a very powerful feature that provides access to spatial data using a common database querying language. Even file-based OGR data sources can be queried using SQL statements. This function isn't limited to database data sources. For more information on OGR's SQL query capabilities, see *http://www.gdal.org/ogr/ogr_sql.html*.

```
# ogrinfo placept.shp -sql "select NAME, NTS50, LAT, LONG, POP91 from placept
where NAME = 'Williams Lake'"

OGRFeature(placept):389
  NAME (String) = Williams Lake
  NTS50 (String) = 093B01
  POP91 (Integer) = 10395
  POINT (-122.16555023 52.16541672)
```

ogr2ogr

Takes an input OGR-supported dataset, and converts it to another format. It can also be used to reproject the data while converting into the output format. Additional actions such as filtering remove certain features and retain only desired attributes. The following code shows a simple conversion of a shapefile into GML format.

```
# ogr2ogr -f "GML" places.gml placept.shp
```

This code takes an ESRI shapefile and easily converts it to GML format or from/into any of the other formats that OGR supports writing to. The power of these capabilities is surpassed by few commercially available packages, most notably SAFE Software's Feature Manipulation Engine (FME).

Note that the syntax for ogr2ogr puts the destination/output filename first, then the source/input filename. This order can be confusing when first using the tool. Many command-line tools specify input and then output.

OGR, like GDAL, aids in accessing, converting, and manipulating data, specifically vector data. OGR can also be used with scripting languages, allowing programmatic manipulation of data. GDAL/OGR packages typically come with OGR modules for Python. In addition to Python bindings, Java and C# support for GDAL/OGR are in development as of Spring 2005. Perl and PHP support may also be available in the future.

A PHP extension for OGR is available but isn't supported or actively developed. It was developed independent of the main GDAL/OGR project and is available at: *http://dl.maptools.org/dl/php_ogr/*. If you can't wait for official PHP support through the GDAL/OGR project, give this one a try.

PostGIS

PostgreSQL is a powerful enterprise-level relational database that is free and open source but also has commercial support options. It is the backbone of data

---

repositories for many applications and web sites. Refractions Research (*http://www. refractions.net*) has created a product called PostGIS that extends PostgreSQL, allowing it to store several types of geographic data. The result is a robust and feature-rich database for storing and managing tabular and geographic data together. Having this ability makes PostgreSQL a *spatial* database, one in which the shapes of features are stored just like other tabular data.

 PostgreSQL also has several native geometry data types, but according to Refractions, these aren't advanced enough for the kind of GIS data storage they needed. The PostGIS functions handle the PostGIS geometry types and not the native PostgreSQL geometry types.

This description is only part of the story. PostGIS isn't merely a geographic data storage extension. It has capabilities from other projects that allow it to manipulate geographic data directly in the database. The ability to manipulate data using simple SQL sets it ahead of many commercial alternatives that act only as proprietary data stores. Their geographic data is encoded so that only their proprietary tools can access and manipulate the data.

 The more advanced PostGIS functions rely on an underlying set of libraries. These come from a Refraction project called Geometry Engine Open Source (GEOS). GEOS is a C++ library that meets the OGC specification for Simple Features for SQL. GEOS libraries can be used in custom applications and were not designed solely for use with PostGIS. For more information on GEOS, see *http://geos.refractions.net/*.

GIS Analysis with SQL

PostGIS allows you to use SQL statements to manipulate and create geographic data—for example, to buffer points and create circles. This is just the tip of the iceberg. PostGIS can be a GIS in and of itself while at the same time, all the power of PostgreSQL as a tabular database is available. GIS overlays, projecting and reprojecting of features into other coordinate systems, and spatial proximity queries are all possible using PostGIS. It is possible to have all the standard GIS overlay and data manipulation processes available in a server-side database solution. Example 3-1 illustrates the marriage of SQL and GIS capabilities by selecting points contained by another shape. More examples are shown in Chapter 13.

Example 3-1. An SQL command that takes a polygon shape from one table and finds all the points that are within a feature in another table

```
> SELECT town_name
    FROM towns, ontario
    WHERE Contains(ontario_polygon,#first feature
                town_points);   #containing the others
```

```
       town_name
-------------------
 Port Hope Simpson
 Hopedale
 Makkovik
 Churchill Falls
 North West River
 Rigolet
 Cartwright
 Tignish
 Cheticamp
 Sheet Harbour
(10 rows)
```

PostGIS is increasingly used as a tool for map data storage and manipulation. It is ideal for situations in which multiple applications access information simultaneously. Regular processing tasks can be set up while also making the data available to a web mapping site.

Other GIS and mapping tools are able to interact with PostGIS data. OGR, for example, can read/write PostGIS data sources. MapServer can also access PostGIS data. Many people rely on this combination to serve up their maps. Some use custom MapServer applications to add or update information stored in PostGIS-enabled databases. A product called GeoServer (see *http://geoserver.sourceforge.net*) uses the OGC Transactional Web Feature Server (WFS-T) standard for read/write access to PostGIS and other formats. A PostGIS function exists for returning Scalable Vector Graphics (SVG) representations of geometries. The Quantum GIS (QGIS) desktop program (see *http://www.qgis.org*) can also read from PostGIS, and current development will extend that to also allow editing.

The internal programming capabilities of PostgreSQL (using related procedural languages such as Pl/Pgsql and Pl/Python) allow programmatic access to various PostGIS functions and PostGIS data. Many PostGIS functions allow for a range of manipulation as well as conversion into different data types (e.g., as simple text strings, binary, or even as SVG).

A PostGIS spatial has many of the functions of a normal database—one being that they both use SQL commands to access data. With PostGIS, the information can also include the PostGIS geometry data. PostGIS functions can then manipulate, summarize, or create new spatial data.

You may wonder what the differences are between the spatial component of MySQL databases and PostGIS. The main difference is that MySQL lacks many of the spatial functions found in PostGIS. Also, MySQL doesn't support transactional integrity for spatial features.

Summary of Applications

Table 3-1 summarizes the functions of each application discussed in this chapter: one checkmark shows peripheral use; two checks denotes common use.

Table 3-1. Summary of the types of functions each application generally plays

	GDAL	OGR	PostGIS	OpenEV	MapServer
Viewing and mapping	✓			✓✓	✓✓
Analysis	✓		✓✓	✓	✓
Manipulation	✓	✓	✓✓	✓	
Conversion	✓✓	✓✓			
Sharing			✓		✓✓

Though the applications may fit more than one category, this table is intended to show the most common ways they are used. For some tasks, there are several applications that can meet your needs. Ultimately, your end goal will help determine which is best to use.

CHAPTER 4
Installing MapServer

Whether you are preparing static map images for a web page or publishing an interactive web site, MapServer can do the job. Interactive maps allow users to zoom in to particular areas and turn map layers on or off. Applications can be made that let the user select a feature on the map and link it to other data. The possibilities are endless, but the final product is usually a point, click, and view process. The user identifies an area to view or a layer to look at, and the web page is updated with the requested content. If you need a static map, you can save the map for later use.

You can use MapServer from the command line or, for interested programmers, through an API. MapServer also can be used as a common gateway interface (CGI) application or scripted using common web programming languages such as PHP, Perl, Python, and Java. Whether using the CGI version or scripting your own, MapServer's runtime configuration files control what layers are shown and how they are drawn. Mapping data can easily be added to an existing application by editing the configuration file.

This chapter discusses what MapServer is, how it can be used, and how it works. It also covers how to set up the underlying programs that make up MapServer, so it can be used in custom applications. Examples of MapServer application development are given in Chapters 10 and 11.

How MapServer Applications Operate

MapServer usually works behind a web server application. The web server receives requests for maps and passes them to MapServer to create. MapServer generates the requested map image and hands it to the web server, which transmits it back to the user. Figure 4-1 shows how the user interacts with the web server which, in turn, makes requests to the MapServer program.

MapServer's primary function is reading data from various sources and pulling these layers together into a graphic file, also known as the *map image*. One layer may be a

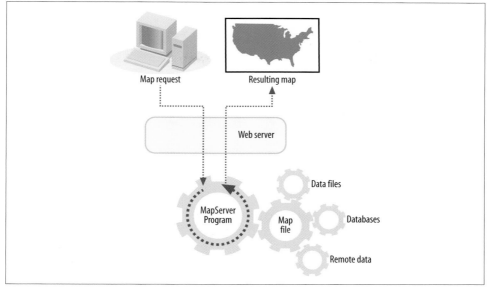

Figure 4-1. A diagram showing the basic operation of a MapServer application

satellite image, another the outline of your country or points showing a major city. Each layer is overlaid or drawn on top of the others and then printed into a web-friendly graphic for the user to see. A good example of the results of the overlapping and mapping process can be seen in Figure 4-2. You can see a satellite image (from a remote server), road lines, and city locations; the city labels are dynamically generated by MapServer.

This drawing process (a.k.a. *rendering*) occurs each time a request for a new map is made to MapServer, for instance, when a user zooms into the map for a closer look. This process also occurs when a user manually requests a redraw, such as when the content of one data layer changes, and the user wants to see the change.

Walkthrough of the Main Components

MapServer produces output graphic files based on the input requests from the user and how the map is defined. Key components include the MapServer executable or CGI program, a map file, data sources and output images. Figure 4-3 shows how all these components work together: after a user request, the MapServer CGI program accesses a map file, draws information from the data sources, and returns an image of the map.

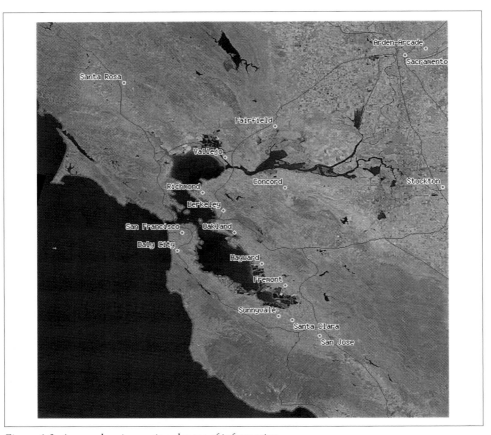

Figure 4-2. A map showing various layers of information

MapServer Executable

The simplest form of MapServer runs as an executable CGI application on a web server. Technically, MapServer is considered an HTTP-based stateless process. Stateless means that it processes a request and then stops running. A CGI application receives requests from a web server, processes them, and then returns a response or data to the web server. CGI is by far the most popular due to its simplicity: no programming is required to get it working. You edit the text-based, runtime configuration file, create a web page, and then set them up to be served by a web server.

> If you are a programmer, you don't need to use MapServer in CGI mode. Instead, you can create custom applications that use the MapServer API. However, this is considered an advanced topic, and an overview is discussed in Chapter 14.

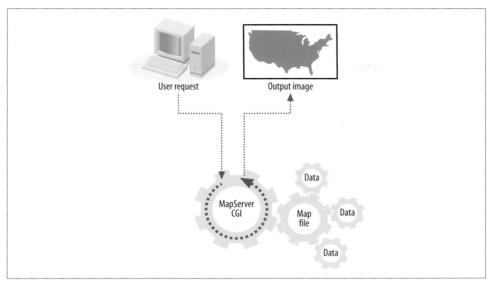

Figure 4-3. Main MapServer application components

The MapServer CGI executable acts as a middle man between the mapping data files and the web server program requesting the map. The requests are passed in the form of CGI parameters from the web server to MapServer. The images that are created by MapServer are then fed back to the web server and, ultimately, to the user's web browser. More on the MapServer executable and how to install it is discussed later in this chapter.

Web Server Considerations

MapServer depends on the web server; because of this, you need to remember how important the web server is. MapServer application developers need to be aware of changes in web server development that might affect their applications. This book doesn't describe how to install or manage a web server, but other books are available. O'Reilly has web server management and web development titles available at *http://web.oreilly.com/*. Two of the hottest web server topics are managing large volumes of requests and properly handling security; both are equally important for MapServer applications. O'Reilly books such as *Web Security, Privacy, and Commerce* or *Apache: The Definitive Guide* may be helpful.

In general, MapServer application developers should rely on web server managers to help make sure the applications are secure and can handle the load.

The focus of this chapter is on using MapServer to create a map image. MapServer can also create scale bars, legends, and reference/key maps for your application, as discussed in Chapters 10 and 11.

MapServer's Map File

MapServer is like an engine that requires fuel to run and a fuel delivery system to get the fuel to the engine. The MapServer program needs to know what map layers to draw, how to draw them, and where the source data is located. The data is the fuel, and the map file—also known as the *mapping file* or *.map* file—serves as the delivery system. The map file is a text configuration file that lists the settings for drawing and interacting with the map. It includes information about what data layers to draw, where the geographic focus of the map is, what projection system is being used, and which output image format to use, and it sets the way the legends and scale bars are drawn. An extremely simple version of a map file is shown in Example 4-1.

Example 4-1. A basic mapping file with one layer

```
MAP
  SIZE 600 300
  EXTENT -180 -90 180 90
  LAYER
    NAME countries
    TYPE POLYGON
    STATUS DEFAULT
    DATA countries.shp
    CLASS
      OUTLINECOLOR 100 100 100
    END
  END
END
```

When a request comes to a MapServer application, the request must specify what map file to use. Then MapServer creates the map based on the settings in the map file. This makes the map file the central piece of any MapServer application. Map files are covered in greater detail in Chapter 10, where the process of creating a MapServer application is discussed.

Data Sources

If the map file is the fuel delivery system, the data sources are the fuel. MapServer can use a vast array of data sources to create maps. Out-of-the-box support covers the most common formats. Optional data access add-ons open up access to dozens of vector and raster formats (formats supported by the GDAL and OGR libraries). These may be GIS data files, database connections, or even flat comma-separated text files using the Virtual Spatial Data format capabilities of OGR.

MapServer can also use the OGC web specifications to access and share data across the Internet. Map layers can be requested from remote servers that also use OGC specifications. More on data sources is discussed in Chapter 5. For more about the purpose and goals of the OGC and OGC web services, see Chapter 12.

Output Map Image

While the map file is the central part of any MapServer application, the map image that is generated is usually what the end user is after. After all the layers are processed and written to a web-friendly graphics file, the user's web browser is then directed to load the image into the web page for viewing. Many first-time users experience problems with MapServer not returning the output map image. Chapter 11 covers in more detail how to set up MapServer to handle the map image.

The map isn't the only image that can be created. Scale bars, graphic legends and reference maps can also be part of a MapServer application. These are handled in a similar manner as the map image. Chapters 10 and 11 show examples that use these.

Installing MapServer

MapServer runs on a variety of platforms, and the details for installing it vary depending on where you want to run it and how you want to integrate it with the rest of your system.

Platforms

Many operating systems and processors can run MapServer successfully. A recent survey of MapServer application developers showed dozens of different implementations running on many processor speed and type combinations. Included in the survey results were the following operating systems:

- Windows 2000, XP, 95
- RedHat/SuSE/Debian/Mandrake Linux, Versions 6 through 9
- Solaris
- Mac OS X Panther
- Vmware running Windows and Linux
- FreeBSD
- SCO Open Server
- SGI IRIX

Reported processor speeds were as low as 120 MHz and as little as 64 MB of memory. Others use the latest processing and memory resources available. With the diversity and flexibility required to meet these cross-platform requirements many developers have found MapServer to be the only option for serving web-based maps.

Acquiring MapServer Binaries

Many documents or how-tos include information on compiling MapServer, which can lead you to assume that compiling MapServer from source code is required. For most users it isn't required. *Acquiring binaries* refers to the process of downloading executables and libraries that are ready to run on your operating system of choice, without compiling from source code.

Windows versions

MapServer application designers wanting to use Microsoft Windows to run MapServer can download standard Windows packages that include everything you need to get started. The packages include all the required MapServer programs zipped into a single file for download. Packages are available from a few locations, including the main MapServer web site (*http://mapserver.gis.umn.edu/win32binaries. html*), the *MapTools.org* site (*http://dl.maptools.org/dl/*), or from other users via mailing list discussions.

The MapTools.org web site has the easiest-to-use package and is highly recommended for inexperienced MapServer application developers using Windows. The package is called MapServer For Windows (MS4W for short) and is located at *http:// maptools.org/ms4w/*.

MS4W was put together by DM Solutions Group (Ottawa, Canada). This company is involved in the development, implementation, and support of MapServer and related technologies. They provide this Windows package to help their users get up and running quickly.

The package is a single ZIP file containing everything needed to get started with MapServer—including an Apache web server. This requires no configuration! If you have shied away from toying with web servers, this is the package for you. To install MS4W, simply unzip the package file into the root of a drive (e.g. *C:*). It should automatically create a set of subfolders under *C:\MS4W*, including a folder called *Apache* within which the web server program resides.

 The package can be moved to other locations on your filesystem, but this requires changing various web server settings.

To start the web server, run the Apache executable from *C:\ms4w\apache\bin\apache. exe*. This can be done from within Explorer and doesn't have to be run from the command line. If you open your browser and go to *http://localhost*, you should see an

MS4W welcome screen. This means that Apache is up and running. At this point you are ready to develop a MapServer application. The MS4W package contains all the libraries, programs, and configuration files you require. A summary of what MS4W contains is shown in Table 4-1. Using these files to create an application is discussed further in Chapter 10.

Table 4-1. Summary of components included in MapServer for Windows (MS4W)

Component	Description
Apache	Web server
PHP	Scripting language
mapserv.exe	MapServer CGI program
php-mapscript.dll	PHP/MapScript scripting libraries; see Chapter 14 for more on MapScript
proj.exe/cs2cs.exe, etc.	PROJ.4 projection utilities and libraries
shp2img.exe/shptree.exe/scalebar.exe	MapServer command-line utilities
ogr2ogr.exe/ogrinfo.exe/ogrtindex.exe	OGR command-line utilities

Linux binaries

An emerging project called Free Open Source Software GIS Suite (FGS) is available at *http://maptools.org/fgs/*. This project provides a packaging mechanism for all the required binaries, libraries, and other support files needed to run FGS applications. The initial version installs a minimal environment for Apache, PHP, and MapServer.

Linux GIS distributions

There are at least four Linux distributions that include MapServer and related applications.

DebianGIS

This Debian-based distribution includes various GIS applications. See *http://pkg-grass.alioth.debian.org/cgi-bin/wiki.pl*.

HostGIS

This distribution includes MapServer, PostGIS, PHP, Python, Perl, and many other standard GNU/Linux applications. It's based on Slackware Linux. See *http://hostgis.com/linux.html*.

STARCD

This live CD distribution runs off a bootable CD-ROM. Includes MapServer, QGIS, and other GIS applications, including GRASS GIS. It's based on Mandrake Linux. See *http://rslultra.star.ait.ac.th/~yann/starcd/*.

GIS-Knoppix

This bootable CD distribution includes a large number of major packages, including MapServer, PostGIS, Terraview, JUMP, QGIS, Thuban, Maplab, etc. See *http://www.sourcepole.com/sources/software/gis-knoppix/*.

Linux RPM versions

Linux RedHat Package Manager (RPM) files are available from several sites. While some of these have a comprehensive set of files, you may still need to get some support to help iron out dependencies. If you take all the packages from one site, you still might not have everything you need.

LinGIS
>   The LinGIS distribution of RPM files is packaged specifically for SuSE but will work on other Linux distributions as well. CD-ROM ISO images containing these RPM files are provided at *http://lingis.org/*.

Mapping Hacks GIS RPMs for Fedora Core
>   Locative Technologies (*http://locative.us*) has packages specifically for Fedora Core. They are available at *http://mappinghacks.com/rpm/*.

Debian Linux versions

There are several Debian Linux package repositories with MapServer available. They vary in features and dependencies. One repository is at *http://agrogeomatic.educagri. fr/debian/*.

Mac OS X

A somewhat outdated MapServer installation package is available at *http://www. serverlogistics.com/mapserver.php*. Most OS X users appear to compile MapServer and other packages from source code. A detailed explanation of that process is at *http://webpages.charter.net/kyngchaos/macosx/mapservinstall.html*.

Compiling MapServer Source Code

Any project claiming to be open source must provide access to the source code. In MapServer's case, this allows you to modify the MapServer code to meet your specific needs. Even if you don't plan to modify the source code, you may still want to compile directly from the source code. Some MapServer users find they need to compile their own version to include (or exclude) certain features. For example, there are a variety of data formats usually included in the binary distributions of MapServer. Quite often there are more formats than you require for a given application and you can remove support for those formats. If a certain format isn't available by default, it can usually be added during the compilation process.

The compilation examples in this chapter are shown using Linux and open source compiling tools from the GNU project (see *http://gnu.org*). Tools and commands are run from the command line or shell console. Compiling for other operating systems varies depending on what tools are available. This section assumes that you are comfortable compiling code and have the appropriate tools available, including a C compiler such as gcc and configuration/building tools such as autoconf and automake.

Downloading sources

Current packages of source code are available from the MapServer web site download page *http://mapserver.gis.umn.edu/dload.html*. Those interested in the latest, greatest features may consider downloading one of the interim builds, which is a copy of the latest code from the developer code repository.

> Source code download using Concurrent Versioning System (CVS) tools is available for those who want the absolute latest code. Access instructions are available at *http://cvs.gis.umn.edu/cvs.html*. CVS tracks changes to programming code and is used for managing the development of many software projects. For more information on CVS see *http://www.gnu.org/software/cvs/*.

Once the sources are downloaded, you need to unzip and untar them. This can be done in one step, as in the following command, which uses the GNU tar command:

```
# tar -xzvf mapserver-4.4.0.tar.gz
```

This unzips the files into a new folder and creates a subfolder structure containing all the code. Once this is done, move into that directory and get ready to configure the build.

Configuring sources

You need to configure your options for compiling the MapServer program. This required step prepares the source code for compilation. The program file *configure* exists in the top level of the source tree, which you moved into after unzipping the sources. If you run the `configure` program without specifying any options, it uses a set of defaults. This may be all you need to do to get MapServer running. Several status messages, observations, and dependency checks are listed on the screen when configure is running. Running `configure`, as in Example 4-2, shows the results of the configuration process configure launches.

Example 4-2. Running configure and the resulting output from the configuration process

```
# ./configure
loading cache ./config.cache
checking for gcc... (cached) gcc
checking whether the C compiler (gcc  ) works... yes
checking whether the C compiler (gcc  ) is a cross-compiler... no
checking whether we are using GNU C... (cached) yes
checking whether gcc accepts -g... (cached) yes
checking for c++... (cached) c++
checking whether the C++ compiler (c++  ) works... yes
checking whether the C++ compiler (c++  ) is a cross-compiler... no
....
checking where PNG is installed...
checking for png_init_io in -lpng... no
        PNG (libpng) library cannot be found, possibly needed for GD
```

Example 4-2. Running configure and the resulting output from the configuration process (continued)

```
checking where libXpm is installed...
checking for XpmFreeXpmImage in -lXpm... no
        XPM (libXpm) library cannot be found, possibly needed for GD
checking where libiconv is installed...
checking for libiconv_open in -liconv... no
        libiconv library cannot be found, possibly needed for GD
checking for GD 2.0.12 or higher...
checking for gdImageSetAntiAliased in -lgd... yes
        using libgd 2.0.12 (or higher) from system libs
            (-L/usr/lib -lgd -ljpeg -lfreetype  -lz  ).
....
checking whether we should include PROJ.4 support...
        PROJ.4 support not requested.
checking whether we should include thread safe support...
        thread safe support disabled.
checking whether we should include ESRI SDE support...
        ESRI SDE support not requested.
checking whether we should compile in MPATROL support...
        MPATROL support not requested.
checking whether we should include OGR support...
        OGR support not requested.
checking if GDAL support requested... no
checking if PostGIS support requested... no
checking if MyGIS support requested... no
checking if OracleSpatial support requested... no
checking if MING/Flash support requested... no
checking whether we should include WMS Server support...
        OGC WMS Compatibility not enabled (PROJ.4 is required for WMS).
checking whether we should include WFS Server support...
        OGC WFS Server support not requested.
checking whether we shou install/erase scriptlets from  package(s)
ld include WMS Client Connections support...
        OGC WMS Client Connections not enabled (PROJ.4 and libcurl required).
checking whether we should include WFS Client Connections support...
        OGC WFS Client Connections not enabled (PROJ.4, libcurl and OGR required).
....
updating cache ./config.cache
creating ./config.status
creating Makefile
```

There are several things to note in the Example 4-2 output from the configure command. First, it checks to see if you have all the tools required to compile the source code. If you don't, for example, have a C compiler, it will bail out on you and complain, as in Example 4-3.

Example 4-3. Configure fails when a C compiler can't be found

```
loading cache ./config.cache
checking for gcc... (cached) gcc
checking whether the C compiler (gcc  ) works... no
configure: error: installation or configuration problem:
                C compiler cannot create executables.
```

That's good to know. After all, there is no sense continuing to prepare if you'll get stuck later on.

configure checks on your system for various graphics libraries such PNG and GD and tests them out. If they are available, configure requests to use them during the compilation process.

Here's the typical error message you receive when a set of libraries can't be found:

```
PNG (libpng) library cannot be found, possibly needed for GD
```

This is important to know, especially if you plan to use PNG image formats instead of GIF files in your maps. What you don't see in the example is that it also checks for GIF and JPEG files. These can be used in place of PNG.

Next, configure checks for requests to build in support for various data formats and supporting applications. It helps to know what each format is. If configure can't find them, they won't be supported by your final MapServer program. Some may appear unimportant, unless you know what they are. The following example shows one such notice:

```
PROJ.4 support not requested.
```

This notice isn't good if you plan to use data that is projected into different coordinate systems. MapServer can take data in different coordinate systems and reproject them into a common system for the final map. You likely want to request PROJ.4 support, which means you also need to have the PROJ.4 files installed on your system. Enabling support for optional libraries, such as PROJ.4, is discussed later in this chapter.

Other format support statements are a bit more obvious, as seen in Example 4-4.

Example 4-4. Configure results from checking for requests to include various database formats

```
ESRI SDE support not requested.
checking if PostGIS support requested... no
checking if MyGIS support requested... no
checking if OracleSpatial support requested... no
```

These are all the checks for whether database support has been requested. None are selected by default, and are used only if the options are chosen. You'll see more on configuration options in the next section.

Other important options not included by default include GDAL, OGR, and OGC specifications. The average user will appreciate having GDAL and OGR support. The utility of the OGC WMS/WFS client and server support options are for more advanced applications and have more advanced dependencies.

The configure process ends successfully by saying something like Example 4-5.

Example 4-5. A successful completion of the configuration process

```
updating cache ./config.cache
creating ./config.status
creating Makefile
```

You will notice that the last step is creating the Makefile. This file contains all the information for the make command to compile the sources (and link in the appropriate libraries, etc). This process is discussed in more detail later. If you are compiling from source code, I assume you aren't afraid to run configure. The output appears somewhat cryptic to the average user. If you have a problem that is critical, the process usually quits and leaves its last observation for you to read. Understanding the output is necessary only when you have a problem.

In Example 4-3, configure couldn't find the C compiler; it stopped right there and said there was a problem testing gcc (the GNU Compiler Collection typically used on Linux operating systems for compiling program code). If the message you see doesn't make sense to you, don't despair. The last few lines of the output are often all you need to get help from the mailing list (support references are at end of this chapter). The output from configure, however cryptic it may appear, will probably mean something to somebody.

configure options

Now that you've seen some examples of deciphering the output from configure, it is time to consider some of the options you can use with the configure command. Options are specified by adding parameters to the end of the configure command. This is done by using two dashes and a parameter name and value such as --with-sde after the configure command. To determine what options are available, you run configure with the --help parameter, as shown in the following code:

```
# ./configure --help | more
```

There are four sections to the configure help listing:

- Configuration
- Directory and filenames
- Host type
- Features and packages

The average user is interested only in the options under "Features and packages," as shown in Example 4-6. The first few lines under this section show the syntax to use, then list the available MapServer-specific options.

Example 4-6. Listing of configuration options for features and packages

```
--with-jpeg[=DIR]      Include JPEG support (DIR is LibJPEG's install dir).
--with-freetype=DIR    GD: Specify where FreeType 2.x is installed
                          (DIR is path to freetype-config program or install dir).
```

Example 4-6. Listing of configuration options for features and packages (continued)

```
--with-zlib=DIR GD: Specify where zlib is installed (DIR is path to zlib install dir).
--with-png=DIR GD: Specify where PNG is installed (DIR is path to PNG install dir).
--with-xpm=DIR   GD: Specify where libXpm is installed (DIR it the libXpm install prefix).
--with-libiconv=DIR      GD: Specify where libiconv is installed
                            (DIR is path to libiconv install dir).
--with-gd[=[static,]DIR] Specify which version of GD to use (DIR is GD's install dir).
--with-pdf[=DIR]         Include PDF support (DIR is PDFlib's install dir).
--with-tiff[=DIR]        Include TIFF support (DIR is LibTIFF's install dir).
--with-eppl              Include EPPL7 support.
--with-proj[=DIR]        Include PROJ.4 support (DIR is PROJ.4's install dir).
--with-threads[=linkopt]Include thread safe support
--with-sde[=DIR]         Include ESRI SDE support (DIR is SDE's install dir).
--with-sde-version[=VERSION NUMBER]  Set ESRI SDE version number (Default is 80).
--with-mpatrol[=DIR]     Include MPATROL support (DIR is MPATROL's install dir).
--with-ogr[=PATH]        Include OGR support (PATH is path to gdal-config).
--with-gdal[=PATH]       Include GDAL support (PATH is path to gdal-config)
--with-postgis[=ARG]     Include PostGIS Support (ARG=yes/path to pg_config)
--with-mygis[=ARG]       Include MyGIS Support (ARG=yes/path to my_config)
--with-oraclespatial[=ARG] Include OracleSpatial Support (ARG=yes/path to Oracle home)
--with-ming[=DIR]        Include MING/Flash Support (DIR=path to Ming
                            directory)
--with-wfs               Enable OGC WFS Server Support (OGR+PROJ4 required).
--with-wmsclient         Enable OGC WMS Client Connections (PROJ4 and libcurl
                            required).
--with-wfsclient         Enable OGC WFS Client Connections (PROJ4, libcurl and
                            OGR required).
--with-curl-config=PATH Specify path to curl-config.
--with-httpd             Specify path to 'httpd' executable.
--enable-ignore-missing-data   Ignore missing data file errors at runtime
                            (enabled by default).
--enable-debug           Include -g in CFLAGS for debugging and enable
                            msDebug() output to stderr (i.e. server log file).
--with-php=DIR           Specify directory where PHP4 source tree is
                            installed. Required in order to compile the
                            PHP/MapScript module.
```

That's a lot of options! If they look confusing, don't fret. The ones that concern you most will most likely be apparent; you can probably ignore or disable the rest. Each option can't be discussed here, so it will take some guesswork on your part. Each item is for enabling data format support or output formats you want to use. If you know what formats you need to use, you should make note of them. Likewise, if you know what formats you want to output the data, find them on this list. If you don't care what image format the output is in, the default will probably suffice.

Many parameters can be specified with either an --enable or --disable option, which is equivalent to --with and --without, respectively. In order to simplify the above list, I haven't shown all the disable options.

Most parameters will seem straightforward after a simple introduction. There are books that specialize in teaching source code compiling techniques, so only the bare minimum required to configure and compile MapServer is presented here. For much more depth on the configuration and compilation process, consider reading:

- *GNU Autoconf, Automake and Libtool* (New Riders); online at *http://sources. redhat.com/autobook/*
- *Programming with GNU Tools* (O'Reilly)
- *Managing Projects with GNU make* (O'Reilly)
- *GNU Make: A Program for Directing Compilation* (GNU Press); online at: *http:// www.gnupress.org/book8.html*

There are essentially two different ways to specify parameters:

- specifying `--enable-x` or `--with-x`
- adding a value to the end, such as `--enable-x=y`

The first usage is quite simple: if you want to enable a feature, add a parameter that specifies to enable it with x being the name of the feature, as shown in the help listing.

The following example shows how to direct `configure` to find the library or programs needed to add in JPEG image support; `configure` will complain if it doesn't find what it needs.

```
./configure --with-jpeg
```

If the required libraries aren't found, in this case the JPEG libraries, you may need to use the second method of specifying the parameter. Notice that the help listing (Example 4-6) said:

```
--with-jpeg[=DIR]
```

The `[=DIR]` is an optional part of the parameter. Any parameters enclosed in the square brackets aren't always required. What `configure` wants is some help finding the JPEG library-related files. You have to tell it where they are installed. When in doubt as to what `configure` wants to know, look back at the help listing (Example 4-6). Beside the JPEG option it says:

```
Include JPEG support (DIR is LibJPEG's install dir)
```

So if you know where the `LibJPEG` files are located, you can explicitly tell `configure` to go look there.

 Finding dependency locations is discussed in the next section.

Sometimes `configure` needs the *include* and *lib* files associated with the library. This is the case with the `LibJPEG` configuration. You must point to the root folder in which the libraries have been installed; it has the *include* and *lib* folders, including `LibJPEG` files. This can also be the source directory in which you compiled `LibJPEG` before installing it. For example, I compile all my source code in */home/tyler/src/*. If I compile LibJPEG from source in */home/tyler/src/jpeg*, I can point configure to that location instead.

In my case, libJPEG was installed into */usr/lib* and therefore I'd run configure as in the following example:

```
./configure --with-jpeg=/usr
```

Because this is a fairly common location for these libraries, I probably didn't need to specify the location; configure probably would have searched there anyway. However, if you've installed the libraries in an uncommon location (e.g., in a personal folder for testing MapServer), this option is important to understand.

Not all parameter options want a folder. Some require a [=PATH] or [=ARG] value to be specified. For example with the GDAL option as seen earlier (Example 4-6):

```
--with-gdal[=PATH] Include GDAL support (PATH is path to gdal-config)
```

Reading the description on the right is critical to specifying this parameter properly. It doesn't just want the folder that gdal-config is located in, it wants the full path to the gdal-config file. Because this path argument is optional, it looks for the file in a few obvious places. If you have it tucked away somewhere strange, you will need to be more specific and put the entire path into the parameter, as in the following code. After deciding what options you want to include, you string them into one long command and let configure do its work.

```
./configure --with-jpeg --with-png --with-ogr --with-gdal=/usr/local/bin/gdal-config
--with-postgis
```

You need to be explicit with DIR and PATH arguments only when necessary. When running configure after selecting the options, review the output text configure prints to your screen and find the lines that pertain specifically to the options you chose. If you see that an item doesn't check out properly, as in the following example, you've done something wrong.

```
checking whether we should include OGR support...
./configure: line 1: /usr/local/bin/gdal-config: No such file or directory
```

In this case, a location for gdal-config was specified, but the file didn't exist because GDAL wasn't installed (this is a separate, optional process described further in Chapter 4). Sometimes it keeps looking around and finds the file, despite the wrong PATH argument, but don't bet on it. If you get a bunch of errors, you can reenter your configure command and change the parameters until they work.

Dependencies

Perhaps one of MapServer's greatest strengths is its ability to draw upon already existing libraries. The developers have focused on supporting a small central core of requirements while allowing increased functionality by relying on external libraries rather than building more dependencies into the basic project. The result is a powerful product that can be extended to include other functionality without major changes to the core program.

For those who need just the bare-bone basics for their application, there are very few external dependencies. On many systems, the required libraries or external programs may already be installed.

Potential dependencies include:

- Image format libraries: JPEG, PNG, XPM, LIBICONV
- Graphic formatting/add-on libraries: GD, FREETYPE, PDF, MING
- Data format/application support libraries: TIFF, EPPL, SDE, MPATROL, OGR, GDAL, POSTGIS, MYGIS, ORACLESPATIAL
- Coordinate Projection library: PROJ.4
- Web services options: WMS, WFS, CURL, HTTPD, PHP

How do you know which external libraries you need? Usually the configure and make programs will notify you of any missing libraries.

Understanding the role that key supporting libraries play can help make the messages (from configure and make) less cryptic. It can also help you plan ahead to prepare the libraries you might need but don't already have.

For the most basic MapServer, the only documented requirement is access to the GD image creation library (from *http://www.boutell.com/gd/*). This library is used to create the map images.

 When I saw my first MapServer application, I was blown away by its ability to create an image so quickly from fairly complex vector and raster data. This was thanks to the GD library. GD is an image processing and creation environment, and a core requirement of MapServer.

The GD library is so critical to MapServer that if you try to disable GD or don't have it available, configure won't let you continue, as shown in Example 4-7.

Example 4-7. Trying to disable GD support during configuration

```
# ./configure --without-gd
...
checking for GD 2.0.12 or higher...
configure: error: GD library cannot be disabled
```

Aside from GD, there are no other basic requirements for MapServer. However, for GD to produce usable images for MapServer, it requires some sort of image library support. In order for GD to be properly installed, you need a PNG or JPEG library. You may already have one or more of these on your system.

MapServer can produce output images in a variety of formats. Perhaps the best known are JPEG, GIF, and PNG formats. Support libraries for the formats you want to use must be available to GD.

Most modern Linux platforms have Version 2 of GD installed; it's called GD2. MapServer 4.4 requires GD2 libraries. You will also need to have development files for GD2, which include supporting files for other programs compiling in GD2 support. If installing from RPMs, the `gd2-devel` package will give you the development files. To check if a package is already installed, run:

```
rpm -qa | grep <name of package>
```

For example, to see if `gd` is installed, you can run:

```
rpm -qa | grep gd
```

Installed packages are listed. No response means no RPM packages are installed. Older versions of Linux, and other operating systems, won't have GD2. In this case, you still need development libraries for the version of GD you are running. In some cases, this may limit you to using pre-4.4 versions of MapServer.

 If PNG support is desired, ZLIB libraries are also required. In order to install GD, you will most likely need to have PNG/ZLIB, JPEG, and FreeType libraries available.

The most basic version you can compile will likely find PNG, JPEG, WBMP (Windows bitmap) and FREETYPE (TrueType font) supporting libraries already on your system and automatically build them in.

If you run `configure` and explicitly use `--without` for every option, `configure` still finds a few libraries and incorporates them (despite the request not to). What you are left with is a setup that will read only two types of files: JPEG images and ESRI shapefile-format vector data files. This minimalistic setup can output into image types PNG, JPEG, and WBMP and, optionally, render TrueType Fonts (TTF) as labels on the map image.

What this leaves you with is very basic, but it will get you started testing the basics of MapServer. Many people just run `./configure` without any options and see if there are any obvious problems. In some cases, this is enough for a simple MapServer setup.

Making a compile

When the configuration process is complete, you are ready to start compiling the application. Depending on the options to be included, this process can take quite a while to complete. The compilation process begins by running the `make` command as shown in Example 4-8.

After running make, you will see numerous commands and information scrolling up the screen. When the compilation process is complete, there won't be a message; you are just returned to the command prompt. Example 4-8 shows some sample output from the beginning and end of the make process.

Example 4-8. Results of running the make command to start compiling

```
# make
gcc -c -O2 -Wall -DIGNORE_MISSING_DATA -DUSE_TIFF -DUSE_JPEG -DUSE_GD_PNG
   -DUSE_GD_JPEG -DUSE_GD_WBMP -DUSE_GD_FT -I/usr/include maptemplate.c -o maptemplate.o
gcc -c -O2 -Wall -DIGNORE_MISSING_DATA -DUSE_TIFF -DUSE_JPEG -DUSE_GD_PNG
   -DUSE_GD_JPEG -DUSE_GD_WBMP -DUSE_GD_FT -I/usr/include mapbits.c -o mapbits.o

[ *.........80+ lines removed...........* ]

gcc -O2 -Wall -DIGNORE_MISSING_DATA -DUSE_TIFF -DUSE_JPEG -DUSE_GD_PNG
   -DUSE_GD_JPEG -DUSE_GD_WBMP -DUSE_GD_FT -I/usr/include sortshp.o
   -L. -lmap -lgd -L/usr/lib -lgd -ljpeg -lfreetype -lz -ltiff -ljpeg
   -lfreetype -lz -ljpeg -lm -lstdc++ -o sortshp
touch mapscriptvars
pwd > mapscriptvars
echo -DIGNORE_MISSING_DATA -DUSE_TIFF -DUSE_JPEG -DUSE_GD_PNG
   -DUSE_GD_JPEG -DUSE_GD_WBMP -DUSE_GD_FT >> mapscriptvars
echo -I.  -I/usr/include >> mapscriptvars
echo  -L. -lmap -lgd -L/usr/lib -lgd -ljpeg -lfreetype -lz -ltiff -ljpeg
   -lfreetype -lz -ljpeg -lm -lstdc++ >> mapscriptvars
echo   >> mapscriptvars
gcc -c -O2 -Wall -DIGNORE_MISSING_DATA -DUSE_TIFF -DUSE_JPEG -DUSE_GD_PNG
   -DUSE_GD_JPEG -DUSE_GD_WBMP -DUSE_GD_FT -I/usr/include tile4ms.c -o tile4ms.o
gcc -O2 -Wall -DIGNORE_MISSING_DATA -DUSE_TIFF -DUSE_JPEG -DUSE_GD_PNG
   -DUSE_GD_JPEG -DUSE_GD_WBMP -DUSE_GD_FT -I/usr/include tile4ms.o
   -L. -lmap -lgd -L/usr/lib -lgd -ljpeg -lfreetype -lz -ltiff -ljpeg
   -lfreetype -lz -ljpeg -lm -lstdc++ -o tile4ms
#
```

You may see various warning messages in the output listing. They can be ignored, as long as you don't get an error that kicks you out of the process.

If you have compiled programs before, you will be tempted to run make install next. That's fine, but ineffective. There is no install process for MapServer; you simply copy the mapserv executable into your web server's *cgi-bin* directory. If you run make install, you get further instructions as a reminder of what to do, as in Example 4-9.

Example 4-9. The results of running make install

```
# make install
***** MapServer Installation *****
To install MapServer, copy the 'mapserv' file to your web server's cgi-bin
directory.
If you use MapScript then see the documentation for your specific MapScript
version for installation instructions.
```

The make command has produced the *mapserv* executable file this message is referring to. If you don't have a file called *mapserv* after the make command is run, it did not complete properly. The message also refers to MapScript. MapScript is an advanced scripting option for MapServer that's discussed further in Chapter 14.

You can test the mapserv executable by running it with the -v parameter, as in Example 4-10. This lists the version and optional parameters that are compiled into MapServer.

Example 4-10. Requesting the version and formats supported by the MapServer CGI program

```
# ./mapserv -v
MapServer version 4.4.0 OUTPUT=PNG OUTPUT=JPEG OUTPUT=WBMP
   SUPPORTS=FREETYPE INPUT=TIFF INPUT=JPEG INPUT=SHAPEFILE
```

This example shows the various input and output data format options selected during the configuration process. You can run mapserv without the -v parameter, but it will remind you, as in Example 4-11, that it isn't meant to be run as a standalone program.

Example 4-11. Running mapserv from the command line without any options

```
# ./mapserv
This script can only be used to decode form results and
should be initiated as a CGI process via a httpd server.
```

If you call the mapserv program without any parameters from a web page, you get a slightly different message:

```
http://localhost/cgi-bin/mapserv
No query information to decode. QUERY_STRING is set, but empty.
```

This can become a useful way to make sure mapserv is installed properly; it's discussed in more detail in Chapter 11.

Other programs are created at the same time as mapserv. These include scalebar, shp2img, shptree, tile4ms, and more; they are discussed further in Chapter 10.

 How-to documents for compiling MapServer are available on its web site *http://mapserver.gis.umn.edu/doc/*.

Installation

Another strength of MapServer is its ability to run multiple versions that include different abilities, all on the same computer. One application could be set up to use a more stable version while another may use a recent test version. This flexibility is possible because the mapserv program runs as a CGI application through a web server. Any MapServer web application can call a specific version of the mapserv executable. You will learn more about this in Chapter 11.

The typical method of installation is to copy the *mapserv* file into a web server's *cgi-bin* folder. If the file is in a folder that the web server can execute the file from (for example, the *cgi-bin* folder), that's all that is required to install the CGI version of MapServer. More advanced configurations will have more dependencies, but ultimately the main installation step is to copy the *mapserv* file into the *cgi-bin* folder, or one with equivalent properties.

RPM packages do some of this work for you, but you need to make sure you know where the *mapserv* file is put. For example, the RPM may try to put the *mapserv* file in */var/www/cgi-bin* by default, but you may need it somewhere else. On SuSE Linux running Apache, it should go in */srv/www/cgi-bin*.

If you plan to install MapServer from an RPM package, it is wise to get a listing of the files and locations the RPM creates. This can be done using the RPM package query and list functions as shown in Example 4-12.

Example 4-12. Listing the contents of the MapServer RPM package

```
# rpm -qpl mapserver-4.0.1-1.i386.rpm
/usr/bin/shp2img
/usr/bin/shptree
/usr/bin/sortshp
/usr/bin/tile4ms
/var/www/cgi-bin/mapserv
```

Once installation is complete, mapserv can process CGI requests and return maps. This requires other parts of the overall MapServer framework to be set up, as discussed in Chapter 11.

A quick test of the install

You can run a basic test on MapServer by running the mapserv or mapserv.exe program. The simplest test you can do is from the command line. First, you open a command prompt, and change into, or at least find, the folder that contains mapserv, mapserv.exe, or mapserv_*xx* where *xx* can be a version number such as 44 for mapserv Version 4.4. For MS4W, mapserv.exe is located in the *c:\ms4w\apache\cgi-bin* folder.

If you compile from source, mapserv is in the source code folder it was compiled in. If you install from an RPM binary, mapserv is in the default Apache web server folder. For example, on SuSE, it's in */srv/www/cgi-bin*, and on Fedora, it's in */var/www/cgi-bin*.

From the command prompt, execute the mapserv program. For example, on SuSE Linux, use the command:

```
/srv/www/cgi-bin/mapserv
```

With MS4W, use:

```
c:\ms4w\apache\cgi-bin\mapserv.exe
```

Either way, the output you get should look like:

```
This script can only be used to decode form results and
should be initiated as a CGI process via a httpd server.
```

Yes, this is an error message, but it confirms that you at least have a working version of the MapServer program. Congratulations—you are ready to start working with MapServer in Chapters 10 and 11.

If all the dependencies for MapServer aren't available, you may get a different error message. Figure 4-4 shows an example of a Windows error message when a supporting library, GDAL for instance, can't be found.

Figure 4-4. Dependency error message from MapServer on Windows

Getting Help

During setup and installation of MapServer, there are different ways to get some help. These include commercial support, mailing lists, and an Internet relay chat (IRC) channel.

MapServer web site

- The main web site with documentation is at *http://mapserver.gis.umn.edu.*
- An FAQ is available at *http://mapserver.gis.umn.edu/doc/mapserver-FAQ.html.*
- Bug tracking/reporting can be found at *http://mapserver.gis.umn.edu/bugs/index.cgi.*

MapServer mailing lists

- Look for MapServer users at *http://lists.umn.edu/archives/mapserver-users.html.*
- Find older archives at *http://mapserver.gis.umn.edu/cgi-bin/wilma/mapserver-users.*
- Check out a searchable GMANE archive at *http://dir.gmane.org/gmane.comp.gis.mapserver.user.*
- Find MapServer-dev at *http://lists.gis.umn.edu/mailman/listinfo/mapserver-dev.*

MapServer IRC channel

- Look for *#mapserver* at *irc.freenode.net.*

Other references

- A map of other users/consultants is at *http://moximedia.com/imf-ows/imf. jsp?site=ms_users*.
- A support site that includes MapServer category is at *http://www. findopensourcesupport.com*.
- Check out the *Mapping Hacks* book (O'Reilly) at *http://mappinghacks.com*.

Table 4-2 lists commercial options for support or development of MapServer applications.

Table 4-2. Organizations that provide commercial services for MapServer

Organization	Country	Web site
Laboratório de Computação Aplicada - G10	Brazil	*http://g10.cttmar.univali.br*
WebMapIt	Brazil	*http://www.webmapit.com.br*
BGC Engineering Inc.	Canada	*http://www.bgcengineering.ca*
DM Solutions Group	Canada	*http://www.dmsolutions.ca*
Handyside Web Programming	Canada	*http://www.hwps.ca*
Refractions Research	Canada	*http://refractions.net*
T-MAPY	Czech Republic	*http://www.tmapserver.com*
CCGIS	Germany	*http://www.ccgis.de*
Geo-Consortium	Germany	*http://www.geo-consortium.de*
Intevation	Germany	*http://www.intevation.de*
Orkney, Inc.	Japan	*http://www.orkney.co.jp*
Camptocamp SA	Switzerland	*http://www.camptocamp.com*
TYDAC	Switzerland	*http://www.mapserver.ch*
Geodan	The Netherlands	*http://www.geodan.com*
Syncera IT Solutions	The Netherlands	*http://www.syncera-itsolutions.nl*
HostGIS	USA	*http://www.hostgis.com*
PeopleGIS	USA	*http://peoplegis.com*
Sean Gillies	USA	*http://www.zcologia.com*
Steve Lime	USA	*sdlime@comcast.net*
Locative Technologies	USA/UK	*http://locative.us*

## CHAPTER 5

Acquiring Map Data

You are probably eager to start on a project and try out all of these great tools. However, before you can jump in, you have some homework to do. The first step in any mapping project is identifying your data needs. Finding the information you require is your next step.

Appraising Your Data Needs

What you need will vary greatly depending on your goal, so you should first determine the goal or final product of your work. Along with this comes the need to assess what kind of map information you want to portray and at what level of detail. The following sections are a guide to thinking through all your requirements before starting a project.

Vector Maps or Raster Maps?

If you want to make a custom map, you need to determine what kind of map data you require. There are two kinds of maps, each requiring different kinds of map data.

A *vector map* shows features made up of points, lines, or polygon areas, as in Figure 5-1. For instance, this can be a local road map or a global map showing locations of power stations and their respective countries.

An image or *raster map* is made from data sources such as aerial photography, satellite imagery, or computer-generated images of Earth's surface. Figure 5-2 shows an example of a raster map made from weather satellite data.

One variant of the raster map is the scanned map. When a paper map is scanned, it is converted into a digital raster map and can then be used as a layer on other maps. This is one way to make mapping data more readily available without having to recreate the maps using digital sources.

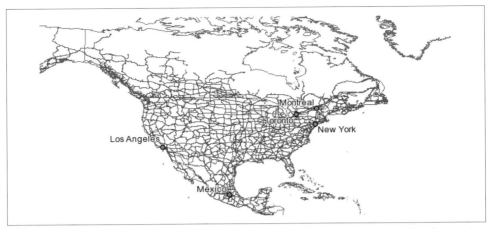

Figure 5-1. A vector map showing roads, country borders, and some major cities in North America

Figure 5-2. A raster map showing cloud cover over North America

A map often combines vector and raster data to create a more effective map than either could produce in isolation, as in Figure 5-3. Pure vector maps and pure raster maps are at opposite ends of a continuum of map types; many maps include both kinds of data.

What Kind of Vector Data Do You Require?

Each of the three types of vector data (point, line, and polygon) can be used to show certain types of information on a map. Points can show the location of towns or the position of a radio tower. Lines can show travel routes or boundaries. Polygons can be shaded to show a lake or highlight a country on a world map. Each piece of vector

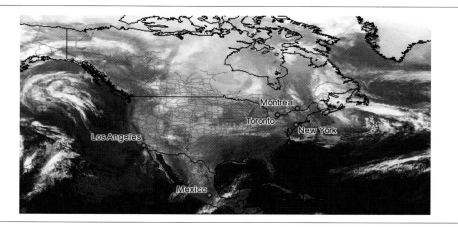

Figure 5-3. A combined vector and raster map over North America

data can have other information associated with it that could, for example, be used to label a feature on the map.

When determining what kind of vector data you require, consider what you want to draw on your map. Will you need to draw text labels on top of line features? Are you planning to use a simple list of coordinates (e.g., in a spreadsheet) to show the point location of features, or do you need more complex boundary data to outline an area?

What Kind of Raster Data Do You Require?

Digital images, such as aerial photographs or satellite images, are part of the raster family of mapping data. A raster represents a continuous grid of data. The grid is made up of small squares, also known as cells or pixels. Each square can have one or more values associated with it. Values used in color images, like photographs, represent the levels of red, green, and blue in a cell. Values can also represent elevations when used in a digital elevation model (DEM) raster.

Decide what kind of raster data you need. Then, when you've found some data, you need to decide whether it is useful as is or if you need to modify or enhance it.

What Scale of Map Do You Require?

If you've ever looked for a small lake near your home on a map of the world, you'll understand that maps can't show every tiny feature. If you took a 12-inch map of the world and stretched it to fit the side of a house, you might be able to see some smaller features; they would be larger than they were before. This kind of map would be called large-scale because it makes features larger for the viewer. A smaller-scale map shrinks these features but can cover a greater area.

Geographers use map scales in a way that seems counter-intuitive, but really does make sense. The average map reader may assume that a scale of 1:1,000 is larger scale than 1:500, because 1,000 is a larger number than 500. This way of writing scales is called a representative fraction (RF). An RF is a fraction: 1:500 means 1/500 or 0.002. 1:1,000 means 1/1,000 or 0.001. Because 1/500 represents a larger value, we say it is a larger scale map.

The scale 1:500 also shows more detail because features are drawn larger than at 1:1,000. This is the second reason for calling 1:500 a larger scale than 1:1,000.

For further reading on map scales, see Sonoma University's web page dedicated to this topic at *http://www.sonoma.edu/geography/resources/mapscale.htm*.

Understanding the size and scale of the map you want to create is very important because it will dictate the precision of data you require. For example, if you want to make a map of your neighborhood, basic world map data may not be detailed enough to even show your street. Likewise, if you want to create a global map that shows the distribution of weather patterns, highly detailed road line data is probably going to be irrelevant.

Most data is created to be viewed at a specific scale. If you try to use the data at a different scale than it was intended for, it may not look right and might not align with other features properly. Decide on the size of map you want to create, especially if you plan to print the map onto paper. Then decide what you want to fit onto that map—something showing your country or your city? How big do you really want it to end up being drawn? If it is only going to be a digital map, how much of the map do you want to see on the screen? This will help you know what scale of information to hunt down. Of course, if it is a digital map, you will have a lot more flexibility than if you are looking to print the final product.

Do You Need Three Dimensions?

Sometimes you want to create a map that can give a three dimensional (3D) perspective to your data. This type of analysis can be complex.

Three-dimensional perspectives simulate what an area of land looks like from above looking down or from the ground looking up. These maps are used in areas where a good view of the physical relief is required, such as when planning a hike up a mountain range or planning a hydroelectric dam project. A traditional 2D map is still quite useful, but there is nothing like creating a map that makes information look more like the real world.

If you want to try 3D mapping, you need to keep a few things in mind. First, you need to decide how you are going to represent the elevation data. An elevation model is often represented by a 2D raster that shows the changes in elevation. In general, the raster is shaded from dark to light to represent these elevation changes, and each square on the raster is shaded to show a certain elevation. Figure 5-4 shows an elevation shaded raster where black is the lowest level, and white is the highest. In some programs, this type of raster is called a height field map or *hillshade*.

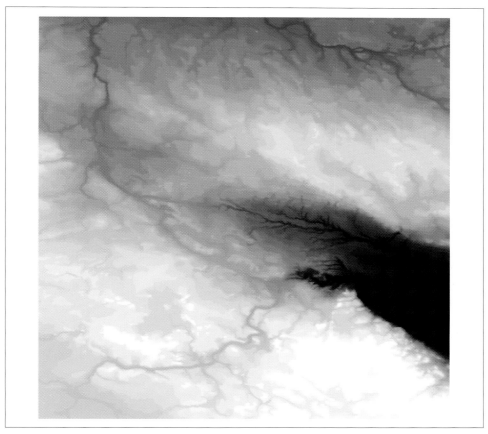

Figure 5-4. Example hillshade image in northern Minnesota, U.S.A.

The other element to 3D mapping is the type of information you want to lay on top of the elevation model. Other images or vectors can be overlaid on top of the elevation model through a process known as draping. *Draping* is named after the concept of laying a piece of light fabric on a bumpy surface, like a bed sheet over a basketball. The draped layer takes the form of the underlying elevation model to give a unique perspective to the draped information. Figure 5-5 shows the same image as in Figure 5-4 but represented in 3D using OpenEV.

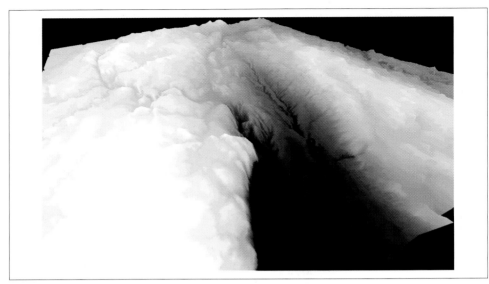

Figure 5-5. Example hillshade image draped over a 3D surface

If you can't find elevation model data or decide what types of information to drape over it, you will probably not be able to do 3D mapping. Specific examples of 3D mapping are given in Chapter 8.

Acquiring the Data You Need

Once you have determined your mapping and data needs, you have to find the appropriate data. To find such data, you can, for example, search the Internet, trade with friends, or download from a government site. This chapter takes you through several examples from searching for premade maps to finding data to do your own mapping and conversion.

Finding Premade Maps

Sometimes all you want is a premade, basic map of the world or a specific country. The Internet can be a good place to find these. One excellent site is the CIA World Factbook at *http://www.cia.gov/cia/publications/factbook/geos/ag.html*. Here you will find a basic political map for every country and also a detailed demographic, cultural, and political summaries. Large-size, print-quality reference maps are also available in Portable Document Format (PDF).

Another good resource is the University of Texas Online Map Library at *http://www.lib.utexas.edu/maps/*. With a brief walk through some of the links, you can find diverse maps that show, for example, a street map of Baghdad or a shaded relief map of the United Kingdom, nicely showing the Scottish Highlands. The library has scanned many of these maps and made them available to the public domain.

Finding Satellite Images or Shaded Surface Maps

Premade maps from images or shaded elevation models are also available. The CIA Factbook (*http://www.cia.gov/ciapublications/factbook*) has small political maps for each country. Other reference maps that show more physical data (e.g., bathymetry and elevation) or even photographic examples of the earth can be found. The U.S. National Geophysical Data Center (NGDC) includes some beautiful premade gallery images of their more detailed source data; look for them at *http://www.ngdc. noaa.gov/seg/topo/globegal.shtml*.

Finding Map Data

The Internet contains a wealth of geographic information for your projects. It is a natural place to begin your quest for mapping data. Some government agencies make their mapping data freely available on the Internet. Certain organizations have even made it their mission to make mapping data available for others for free. Other groups have created catalogs of mapping data you can search.

Plenty of Internet map data sources are available for the United States. North American data is also widely accessible, with Canada having some excellent products. Global data is more of a challenge. International organizations such as the United Nations or even American-based organizations that observe global events, such as the National Oceanic and Atmospheric Administration (NOAA), are some of the better sources for global data.

There are a variety of data repositories on the Internet to choose from, and they each have a certain target scale of application that can't be ignored. For example, a satellite image can show pictures of where you live. Figure 5-6, for example, shows the different colors of surfaces such as roads, fields, and waterways, but only to a certain level of detail. If you hope to use it for planning a walk to the corner store, you will be sorely disappointed. However, if you want to see how your city is laid out, you will probably be satisfied. Figure 5-7 shows a closer look at the same image as Figure 5-6. The maximum amount of detail has been reached, and the image looks bad. This is an attempt to use the image beyond its intended scale of application.

There are multiple ways to hunt for good data. You can announce your search to email mailing lists or review web sites that summarize free data sources. Local mapping companies and government agencies are also a good place to start. Many states, provinces, and municipalities have their own GIS and mapping offices. Your search can also include local consulting companies, industries, or nonprofit organizations related to environmental or natural resource management and use. Just ask to speak to someone in the mapping or GIS department. Most people in these organizations

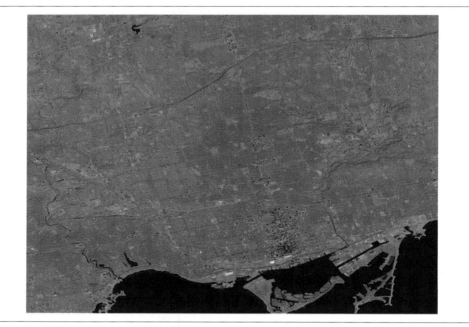

Figure 5-6. A Landsat satellite image showing the region around Toronto

Figure 5-7. A closer (though fuzzy) look at the Landsat image used in Figure 5-6

are willing to discuss what data they can share. If they can't share the data, they can at least point you to the original source for you to seek out on your own. Table 5-1 lists a few web sites and email lists that include free map data or people who can help you find data.

Table 5-1. A few web sites and mailing lists offering free map data resources and discussions

Web site	Description
Canada GeoBase Portal	*http://www.geobase.ca/*
Canadian Government	*http://geogratis.cgdi.gc.ca/download/*
Earth Observation Portal	*http://maps.eoportal.org/*
FreeGIS.org data/mailing list	*http://freegis.org*
GeoConnections Discovery Portal	*http://geodiscover.cgdi.ca/*
GIS Data Depot	*http://data.geocomm.com/catalog/*
Global Change Master Directory	*http://gcmd.nasa.gov/*
Global Land Cover	*http://glcf.umiacs.umd.edu/data/*
GTOPO Elevation Data	*http://edcdaac.usgs.gov/gtopo30/gtopo30.asp*
MapServer list	*http://lists.gis.umn.edu/mailman/listinfo/mapserver-users*
NASA Topography	*http://www2.jpl.nasa.gov/srtm/dataprod.htm*
U.S. Geologic Survey	*http://edcsns17.cr.usgs.gov/EarthExplorer/*
U.S. Maps and Data	*http://geodata.gov*
U.S. National Atlas	*http://www.nationalatlas.gov/atlasftp.htm*
U.S. National Geospatial Data Clearinghouse	*http://clearinghouse1.fgdc.gov/*

Best Data Not Always Available

Organizations and individuals who maintain data repositories are called *custodians*. Some custodians aren't interested in sharing their data with the public. This is a well debated topic, especially for regional and federal governments who have, traditionally, been the custodians of massive government map data repositories. Sometimes they are the only ones who use the data and are often responsible for keeping the data unavailable.

As digital mapping capabilities have infiltrated various domains, the pressure on governments to give data away (to companies, the public, nongovernment organizations and even other government departments) has increased dramatically. The arguments are usually somewhere between *"Taxpayers paid for it, I have a right to use it!"* and *"Our department budget has gone down, and we need to recover costs, therefore you must pay for it."* On the one hand, public agencies are funded by public tax dollars to collect the data. On the other, the same agencies may have tight budgets and will try to make money selling the data. So beware, the company or organization that has the best mapping data available may not be willing or able to share it with you.

There are some proactive ways to get access to data. If your project needs a certain type of data and you can help meet the objectives of the custodian as well, it might be a good idea to enter into a project together. One group puts time and effort into the project, and the other contributes data. A long-term data exchange agreement may also play a mutually beneficial role. The idea is that one party provides mapping data, and the other gets open access to it. In return, the user provides their updates of the data back to the custodian. Of course, each agreement should be negotiated to include only certain kinds of updates or sharing of only certain pieces of data (such as nonconfidential information).

This data sharing/update model is increasingly common, but at the same time many groups are making their information freely available for open use. It is important to get a broad feel for others who are also interested in, or may already have, the data you are looking for. Data can be shared without having to copy source data by using OGC web specifications. For example, the satellite image in Figure 5-6 is from a free web service and requested by a mapping application. See Chapter 12 for more about the OGC and web services.

Finding and getting access to data aren't the only problems. Some data may be unusable or inappropriate for the task at hand. This goes beyond matters of scale and resolution, referring more to accuracy and supplementary attributes. One example is a forestry initiative of the government of British Columbia (Canada) to map certain types of pest-infected trees. Traditionally this has been mapped using a fixed-wing aircraft carrying a reconnaissance mapper who spots the trees and then draws their location on a paper map. At the office, the paper maps are digitized onto a base map in the computer. While these maps are useful for general landscape-level analysis, you would not want to depend on the map to lead you to a particular tree in the middle of a dense forest. Wise use and understanding of the appropriate application of your data will help you have realistic expectations when starting your mapping project.

The Internet isn't the only source of mapping data. Chapter 9 discusses how to create some of your own data with map-editing tools or using coordinates taken from a GPS receiver.

## CHAPTER 6

Analyzing Map Data

Finding data is helpful, but sometimes you need to explore it or do basic manipulation before you're ready to use it in your own maps. This chapter will lead you through acquiring the tools and data for some sample projects. Some of this sample data will be used in examples in other chapters as well. The techniques shown here don't produce lovely maps by themselves, but they can save you immense frustration when you go to use data to create maps.

Downloading the Demonstration Data

This section will walk you through the process of acquiring some fairly simple data for the U.S. state of Minnesota. In order to keep things simple, you will use a well-known MapServer demonstration dataset. The MapServer web site always has copies of the latest versions of MapServer software available as well as demonstration datasets and applications.

First, go to *http://mapserver.gis.umn.edu/dload.html*. Beside the latest download version file, you will see a link to *demo*. This links to a ZIP file called *workshop.zip*.

The full path is *http://maps.dnr.state.mn.us/mapserver_demos/workshop.zip*. Now, download, and unzip the contents of this file. All you really need is the *workshop/ data* folder.

 Where you unzip doesn't matter, but you need to ensure that the folders contained in the archive are recreated when unzipped. This is usually the default for your archive software. In Winzip, this option is called Use Folder Names.

Installing Data Management Tools: GDAL and FWTools

If you examine the contents of the *data* folder you will find 49 files. These are map data files in ESRI shapefile format and GeoTIFF images. To learn more about them, you will use a tool from the GDAL project. GDAL comes bundled with the FWTools package, as does the OpenEV viewer and other utilities used in this book.

You can acquire the latest version of FWTools for your operating system or distribution from *http://fwtools.maptools.org/*. Examples used in this book are for the Linux operating system, but for Windows users, I have included notes where steps or usage varies.

Windows users

FWTools comes as an installation/setup file. First, download and execute the file. It should walk you through the setup steps. The setup program should place an FWTools Shell icon on your desktop. Launching this icon gives you a command prompt window for running FWTools commands.

Linux users

First, download the most recent tarball version of FWTools (e.g., *FWTools-linux-0.9.8.tar.gz*), and unzip/untar it into any folder you have handy. Linux users will be working from the command prompt/shell console to enter commands.

Now, open a console, and move into the folder that the file was saved in. This can be done using the cd command followed by the path to the folder. You can unzip the file by running:

```
> tar -xzvf FWTools-linux-0.9.8.tar.gz.
```

Run the installer by typing ./install.sh. This prepares the installation and creates a folder called *bin_safe*. Now, run the command:

```
> . /fwtools_env.sh
```

(Note the space after the period.) This command loads all the environment variables and settings, even though it might appear to not do anything. You are now ready to use FWTools commands.

You will be running some of programs to manipulate, examine, and convert the MapServer demo data. In the examples, commands that you type are prefixed by the greater than symbol, >. This isn't part of the command and isn't typed, but it indicates that everything after it is. The > symbol is how the command prompt tells you it is ready for another command. The command prompt symbol varies depending on operating system.

Examining Data Content

Examining data content is an important part of any project. Understanding information specific to your dataset will help you use it more effectively. Each piece of spatial data will have some geographic component to it (coordinates describing the location of real features), but it will also have what are called *attributes*. These are non-geographic data about the geographic feature, such as the size of population, the name of a building, the color of a lake, etc. You will often hear the geographic coordinate data described as spatial data and the attribute information referred to as tabular, attribute, or nonspatial data. It is equally valid to call any dataset spatial if it has some geographic component to it.

Viewing Summary Information About Airports

The MapServer demo data includes a variety of vector spatial files; therefore you will use the ogrinfo tool to gather information about the files. At the command prompt, change into the workshop folder, and run the ogrinfo command to have it list the datasets that are in the data folder. The output from the command will look like Example 6-1.

Example 6-1. Showing a list of the layer names available in a folder containing shapefiles

```
> ogrinfo data
INFO: Open of 'data'
using driver 'ESRI Shapefile' successful.
1: twprgpy3 (Polygon)
2: rmprdln3 (Line String)
3: lakespy2 (Polygon)
4: stprkpy3 (Polygon)
5: ctyrdln3 (Line String)
6: dlgstln2 (Line String)
7: mcd90py2 (Polygon)
8: twprdln3 (Line String)
9: plsscpy3 (Polygon)
10: mcdrdln3 (Line String)
11: majrdln3 (Line String)
12: drgidx (Polygon)
13: airports (Point)
14: ctybdpy2 (Polygon)
```

This shows that there are 14 layers in the data folder (the order of the listing may vary on other systems). You can also see that the folder contains ESRI shapefile format files. Each shapefile is a layer in this listing. If you look at the files located in the data folder, you will see that there are way more than 14 files. This is because a shapefile consists of more than one file: one holds spatial data, another holds tabular data, etc.

A summary of more information for each layer can be seen by adding the name of the layer to the ogrinfo command and a -summary parameter, as shown in Example 6-2.

Example 6-2. Showing the attributes, extent, and other information about a particular layer

```
> ogrinfo -summary data airports
INFO: Open of 'data'
using driver 'ESRI Shapefile' successful.

Layer name: airports
Geometry: Point
Feature Count: 12
Extent: (434634.000000, 5228719.000000) - (496393.000000, 5291930.000000)
Layer SRS WKT:
(unknown)
NAME: String (64.0)
LAT: Real (12.4)
LON: Real (12.4)
ELEVATION: Real (12.4)
QUADNAME: String (32.0)
```

This example shows information about the airports layer.

```
Geometry: Point
```

The geographic features in this file are points. In the next example, you will see that each airport feature has one pair of location coordinates.

```
Feature Count: 12
Extent: (434634.000000, 5228719.000000) - (496393.000000, 5291930.000000)
```

There are 12 airport features in this layer, and they fall within the range of coordinates shown in the Extent line. The coordinates are measured in meters and are projected into the Universal Transverse Mercator (UTM) projection.

```
Layer SRS WKT:
(unknown)
```

This explains what map projection the data is in. SRS stands for spatial reference system and WKT for well-known text format. Without getting into too much detail, these are terms popularized or created by the OGC. The SRS gives information about projections, datums, units of measure in the data, etc. WKT is a method for describing those statistics in a text-based, human-readable format (as opposed to a binary format). Refer to Appendix A for more information about map projections, SRS, and the EPSG numbering system. See Chapter 12 for more information on the OGC and its role in setting standards.

The previous example also says unknown because the creator of the data didn't explicitly include projection information within the file. This isn't very helpful if you don't know where the data is from. However, those familiar with the data might guess that it is in UTM coordinates.

```
NAME: String (64.0)
LAT: Real (12.4)
LON: Real (12.4)
ELEVATION: Real (12.4)
QUADNAME: String (32.0)
```

These five lines tell you about the other types of nonspatial information that accompany each geographic feature. A feature, in this case, is a coordinate for an airport. These different pieces of information are often referred to as attributes, properties, columns, or fields. Each attribute has a name identifier and can hold a certain type of information. In the previous example, the text before the colon is the name of the attribute. Don't be confused by the fact that there is also an attribute called NAME in this file. The first line describes an attribute called NAME. The word after the colon tells you what kind of data can be held in that attribute—either String (text characters) or Real (numbers). The numbers in the parentheses tell more specifically how much of each kind of data can be stored in the attribute. For example NAME: String (64.0) means that the attribute called NAME can hold up to 64 letters or numbers. Likewise ELEVATION: Real (12.4) means that the ELEVATION attribute can hold up to only 12-digit numbers with a maximum of 4 decimal places.

You may be wondering why this is important to review. Some of the most common errors in using map data can be traced back to a poor understanding of the data. This is why reviewing data with tools such as ogrinfo can be very helpful before launching into mapmaking. If you don't understand what kind of attributes you have at your disposal, you may not use the data to its fullest potential or you may push its use beyond appropriate bounds. Understanding your data in this depth will prevent future mistakes during the mapping process or during any analysis you may undertake. If your analysis relies on a certain kind of numbers with a level of precision or expected length of text, you need to make sure that the data you are analyzing actually holds these kinds of values, or you will get misleading results. Having this knowledge early in the process will help you have a more enjoyable experience along the way.

Viewing Detailed Airport Location Information

Summary information tells only part of the story. The same tools can be used to provide detailed information about the geographic data and its attributes. To get details, instead of summary information, you can use ogrinfo with a dataset and layer name like that in Example 6-3, but don't include the -summary parameter.

Example 6-3. Showing all the details about a shapefile layer

```
> ogrinfo data airports
INFO: Open of 'data'
using driver 'ESRI Shapefile' successful.
```

Example 6-3. Showing all the details about a shapefile layer (continued)

```
Layer name: airports
Geometry: Point
Feature Count: 12
Extent: (434634.000000, 5228719.000000) - (496393.000000, 5291930.000000)
Layer SRS WKT:
(unknown)
NAME: String (64.0)
LAT: Real (12.4)
LON: Real (12.4)
ELEVATION: Real (12.4)
QUADNAME: String (32.0)
OGRFeature(airports):0
  NAME (String) = Bigfork Municipal Airport
  LAT (Real) =      47.7789
  LON (Real) =     -93.6500
  ELEVATION (Real) =     1343.0000
  QUADNAME (String) = Effie
  POINT (451306 5291930)

OGRFeature(airports):1
  NAME (String) = Bolduc Seaplane Base
  LAT (Real) =      47.5975
  LON (Real) =     -93.4106
  ELEVATION (Real) =     1325.0000
  QUADNAME (String) = Balsam Lake
  POINT (469137 5271647)
```

This view of the airport details tells you what value each airport has for each attribute. As you can see, the summary information is still included at the top of the listing, but then there are small sections for each feature. In this case there are seven lines, or attributes, for each airport. For example, you can see the name of the airport, but you can also see the UTM coordinate shown beside the POINT attribute.

> This dataset also has a set of LAT and LON fields that are just numeric attributes and have nothing to do with using this data in a map. Not all types of point data have these two attributes. They just happened to be part of the attributes the creator wanted to keep. The actual UTM coordinates are encoded in the last attribute, POINT.

Only two features are shown in this example, the first starting with OGRFeature(airports):0. The full example goes all the way to OGRFeature(airports): 11, including all 12 airports. The rest of the points aren't shown in this example, just to keep it simple.

ogrinfo is a great tool for digging even deeper into your data. There are more options that can be used, including a database query–like ability to select features and the ability to list only features that fall within a certain area. Running man ogrinfo (if your operating system supports manpages) shows the full usage for each parameter.

Otherwise, the details are available on the OGR web site at *http://www.gdal.org/ogr/ogr_utilities.html*. You can also run the ogrinfo command with the --help parameter (ogrinfo --help) to get a summary of options. Example 6-4 shows some examples of how they can be used with your airport data.

Example 6-4. Listing the features that meet a specific attribute query

```
> ogrinfo data airports -where "name='Bolduc Seaplane Base'"
INFO: Open of 'data'
using driver 'ESRI Shapefile' successful.

Layer name: airports
Geometry: Point
Feature Count: 1
Extent: (434634.000000, 5228719.000000) - (496393.000000, 5291930.000000)
Layer SRS WKT:
(unknown)
NAME: String (64.0)
LAT: Real (12.4)
LON: Real (12.4)
ELEVATION: Real (12.4)
QUADNAME: String (32.0)
OGRFeature(airports):1
  NAME (String) = Bolduc Seaplane Base
  LAT (Real) =     47.5975
  LON (Real) =    -93.4106
  ELEVATION (Real) =    1325.0000
  QUADNAME (String) = Balsam Lake
  POINT (469137 5271647)
```

This example lists only those airports that have the name Bolduc Seaplane Base. As you can imagine, there is only one. Therefore, the summary information about this layer and one set of attribute values are listed for the single airport that meets this criteria in Example 6-5. The -sql option can also specify what attributes to list in the ogrinfo output.

> If you are familiar with SQL, you will understand that the -sql option accepts an SQL statement. If SQL is something new to you, please refer to other database query language documentation, such as:
>
> - *SQL in a Nutshell* (O'Reilly)
> - SQL tutorial at *http://www.w3schools.com/sql/*
>
> Many database manuals include a comprehensive reference section on SQL. The implementation of SQL in ogrinfo isn't complete and supports only SELECT statements.

Example 6-5. Selecting certain features and showing specific attributes in the results

```
> ogrinfo data airports -sql "select name from airports where quadname='Side Lake'"
INFO: Open of 'data'
using driver 'ESRI Shapefile' successful.
```

layer names ignored in combination with -sql.

```
Layer name: airports
Geometry: Point
Feature Count: 2
Extent: (434634.000000, 5228719.000000) - (496393.000000, 5291930.000000)
Layer SRS WKT:
(unknown)
name: String (64.0)
OGRFeature(airports):4
  name (String) = Christenson Point Seaplane Base
  POINT (495913 5279532)

OGRFeature(airports):10
  name (String) = Sixberrys Landing Seaplane Base
  POINT (496393 5280458)
```

The SQL parameter is set to show only one attribute, NAME, rather than all seven attributes for each feature. It still shows the coordinates by default, but none of the other information is displayed. This is combined with a query to show only those features that meet a certain QUADNAME requirement.

Example 6-6 shows how ogrinfo can use some spatial logic to find features that are within a certain area.

Example 6-6. Listing features that are located within a range of coordinates

```
> ogrinfo data airports -spat 451869 5225734 465726 5242150
Layer name: airports
Geometry: Point
Feature Count: 2
Extent: (434634.000000, 5228719.000000) - (496393.000000, 5291930.000000)
Layer SRS WKT:
(unknown)
NAME: String (64.0)
LAT: Real (12.4)
LON: Real (12.4)
ELEVATION: Real (12.4)
QUADNAME: String (32.0)
OGRFeature(airports):7
  NAME (String) = Grand Rapids-Itasca County/Gordon Newstrom Field
  LAT (Real) =      47.2108
  LON (Real) =     -93.5097
  ELEVATION (Real) =     1355.0000
  QUADNAME (String) = Grand Rapids
  POINT (461401 5228719)

OGRFeature(airports):8
  NAME (String) = Richter Ranch Airport
  LAT (Real) =      47.3161
  LON (Real) =     -93.5914
```

```
ELEVATION (Real) =    1340.0000
QUADNAME (String) = Cohasset East
POINT (455305 5240463)
```

The ability to show only features based on where they are located is quite powerful. You do so using the -spat parameter followed by two pairs of coordinates. The first pair of coordinates 451869 5225734 represent the southwest corner of the area you are interested in querying. The second pair of coordinates 465726 5242150 represents the northeast corner of the area you are interested in, creating a rectangular area.

> This is typically referred to as a *bounding box*, where one pair of coordinates represents the lower-left corner of the box and the other pair represents the upper right. A bounding box gives a program, such as ogrinfo, a quick way to find features you need.

ogrinfo then shows only those features that are located within the area you define. In this case, because the data is projected into the UTM coordinate system, the coordinates must be specified in UTM format in the -spat parameter. Because the data is stored in UTM coordinates, you can't specify the coordinates using decimal degrees (°) for instance. The coordinates must always be specified using the same units and projection as the source data, or you will get inaccurate results.

Example 6-7 is similar to a previous example showing complex query syntax using the -sql parameter, but it differs in one respect.

Example 6-7. Summary information about the results of a complex SQL query

```
> ogrinfo data airports -sql "select * from airports where elevation > 1350 and quadname
like '%Lake'" -summary
INFO: Open of 'data'
using driver 'ESRI Shapefile' successful.
layer names ignored in combination with -sql.

Layer name: airports
Geometry: Point
Feature Count: 5
Extent: (434634.000000, 5228719.000000) - (496393.000000, 5291930.000000)
```

If you add the -summary option, it doesn't list all the attributes of the features, but shows only a summary of the information. In this case, it summarizes only information that met the criteria of the -sql parameter. This is very handy if you just want to know how many features meet certain criteria or fall within a certain area but don't care to see all the details.

Viewing Statistics About a Satellite Image

You can download a sample satellite image from *http://geogratis.cgdi.gc.ca/download/ RADARSAT/mosaic/canada_mosaic_lcc_1000m.zip*. If you unzip the file, you create a file called *canada_mosaic_lcc_1000m.tif*. This is a file containing an image from the RADARSAT satellite. For more information about RADARSAT, see *http://www.ccrs. nrcan.gc.ca/ccrs/data/satsens/radarsat/rsatndx_e.html*.

To better understand what kind of data this is, use the gdalinfo command. Like the ogrinfo command, this tool lists certain pieces of information about a file, but the GDAL tools can interact with raster/image data. The output from gdalinfo is also very similar to ogrinfo as you can see in Example 6-8. You should change to the same folder as the image before running the gdalinfo command.

Example 6-8. Listing information about the downloaded image

```
> gdalinfo canada_mosaic_lcc_1000m.tif
Driver: GTiff/GeoTIFF
Size is 5700, 4800
Coordinate System is:
PROJCS["LCC         E008",
    GEOGCS["NAD83",
        DATUM["North_American_Datum_1983",
            SPHEROID["GRS 1980",6378137,298.2572221010042,
                AUTHORITY["EPSG","7019"]],
            AUTHORITY["EPSG","6269"]],
        PRIMEM["Greenwich",0],
        UNIT["degree",0.0174532925199433],
        AUTHORITY["EPSG","4269"]],
    PROJECTION["Lambert_Conformal_Conic_2SP"],
    PARAMETER["standard_parallel_1",49],
    PARAMETER["standard_parallel_2",77],
    PARAMETER["latitude_of_origin",0],
    PARAMETER["central_meridian",-95],
    PARAMETER["false_easting",0],
    PARAMETER["false_northing",0],
    UNIT["metre",1,
        AUTHORITY["EPSG","9001"]]]
Origin = (-2600000.000000,10500000.000000)
Pixel Size = (1000.00000000,-1000.00000000)
Corner Coordinates:
Upper Left  (-2600000.000,10500000.000) (177d17'32.31"W, 66d54'22.82"N)
Lower Left  (-2600000.000, 5700000.000) (122d54'49.00"W, 36d12'53.87"N)
Upper Right ( 3100000.000,10500000.000) (  9d58'39.57"W, 62d25'50.45"N)
Lower Right ( 3100000.000, 5700000.000) ( 62d32'49.65"W, 34d18'5.61"N)
Center      (  250000.000, 8100000.000) ( 89d56'43.00"W, 62d46'47.18"N)
Band 1 Block=5700x1 Type=Byte, ColorInterp=Gray
```

There are five main sections in this report. Unlike ogrinfo, there aren't a lot of different options, and attributes are very simplistic. The first line tells you what image format the file is.

```
Driver: GTiff/GeoTIFF
```

In this case, it tells you the file is a GeoTIFF image. TIFF images are used in general computerized photographic applications such as digital photography and printing. However, GeoTIFF implies that the image has some geographic information encoded into it. gdalinfo can be run with a --formats option, which lists all the raster formats it can read and possibly write. The version of GDAL included with FWTools has support for more than three dozen formats! These include several proprietary software vendor formats and many related to specific types of satellite data.

The next line shows the size of the image:

```
Size is 5700, 4800.
```

An image size is characterized by the number of data rows and columns. An image is a type of raster data. A raster is made up of numerous rows of adjoining squares called cells or pixels. Rows usually consist of cells that are laid out east to west, whereas columns of cells are north to south. This isn't always the case but is a general rule of thumb. This image has 5,700 columns and 4,800 rows. The first value in the size statement is usually the width, therefore the number of columns of cells. Row and column numbering usually begins at the upper-left corner of the image and increases toward the lower-right corner. Therefore, cell 0,0 is the upper left, and cell 5700, 4800 is the lower right.

Images can be projected into various coordinate reference systems (see Appendix A for more about map projections):

```
Coordinate System is:
PROJCS["LCC            E008",
    GEOGCS["NAD83",
        DATUM["North_American_Datum_1983",
            SPHEROID["GRS 1980",6378137,298.2572221010042,
                AUTHORITY["EPSG","7019"]],
            AUTHORITY["EPSG","6269"]],
        PRIMEM["Greenwich",0],
        UNIT["degree",0.0174532925199433],
        AUTHORITY["EPSG","4269"]],
    PROJECTION["Lambert_Conformal_Conic_2SP"],
    PARAMETER["standard_parallel_1",49],
    PARAMETER["standard_parallel_2",77],
    PARAMETER["latitude_of_origin",0],
    PARAMETER["central_meridian",-95],
    PARAMETER["false_easting",0],
    PARAMETER["false_northing",0],
    UNIT["metre",1,
        AUTHORITY["EPSG","9001"]]]
```

These assign a cell to a global geographic coordinate. Often these coordinates need to be adjusted to improve the appearance of particular applications or to line up with other pieces of data. This image is in a projection called Lambert Conformal Conic (LCC). You will need to know what projection data is in if you want to use it with other data. If the projections between data don't match, you may need to reproject them into a common projection.

 MapServer can reproject files/layers on the fly. This means you don't have to change your source data unless you want higher performance.

The latitude of origin and central meridian settings are given in geographic coordinates using degree (°) units. They describe where the coordinate 0,0 starts. Latitude 0° represents the equator. In map projections central meridians are represented by a longitude value. Longitude -95°, or 95° West, runs through central Canada.

```
PARAMETER["latitude_of_origin",0],
PARAMETER["central_meridian",-95],
```

Note that in the earlier projection, the unit setting is metre. When you look at Pixel Size in a moment, you will see a number but no unit. It is in this unit (meters) that the pixel sizes are measured.

Cells are given row and column numbers, but are also given geographic coordinate values. The origin setting tells what the geographic coordinate is of the cell at row 0, column 0. Here, the value of origin is in the same projection and units as the projection for the whole image. The east/west coordinate –2,600,000 is 2,600,000 meters west of the central meridian. The north/south coordinate is 10,500,000 meters north of the equator.

```
Origin = (-2600000.000000,10500000.000000)
Pixel Size = (1000.00000000,-1000.00000000)
```

Cells are also called pixels and each of them has a defined size. In this example the pixels have a size of 1000×1000: the -1000 is just a notation; the negative aspect of it can be ignored for now. In most cases, your pixels will be square, though it is possible to have rasters with nonsquare pixels. The unit of these pixel sizes is in meters, as defined earlier in the projection for the image. That means each pixel is 1,000 meters wide and 1,000 meters high.

 Each pixel has a coordinate value as well. This coordinate locates the upper-left corner of the pixel. Depending on the size of a pixel, it can be difficult to accurately locate it: a pixel is a square, not a discrete point location. Therefore, the upper-left corner of the pixel covers a different place on the ground than the center, but both have the same location coordinate. The accuracy of raster-based data is limited by the size of the pixel.

Much like the previous origin settings, corner coordinates tell you the geographic coordinate the corner pixels and center of the image have:

```
Corner Coordinates:
Upper Left   (-2600000.000,10500000.000) (177d17'32.31"W, 66d54'22.82"N)
Lower Left   (-2600000.000, 5700000.000) (122d54'49.00"W, 36d12'53.87"N)
Upper Right  ( 3100000.000,10500000.000) (  9d58'39.57"W, 62d25'50.45"N)
Lower Right  ( 3100000.000, 5700000.000) ( 62d32'49.65"W, 34d18'5.61"N)
Center       (  250000.000, 8100000.000) ( 89d56'43.00"W, 62d46'47.18"N)
```

Notice that the coordinates are first given in their projected values, but also given in their unprojected geographic coordinates, longitude, and latitude. Knowing this will help you determine where on the earth your image falls. If you thought this image was in Greece, you'd be wrong. The geographic coordinates clearly put it in the western hemisphere: 177d17'32.31"W is 177 degrees, 17 minutes, 32.31 seconds west of the prime meridian.

Images are made up of different bands of data. In some cases, you can have a dozen different bands, where each band stores values about a specific wavelength of light that a sensor photographed. In this case, there is only one band Band 1. The ColorInterp=Gray setting tells you that it is a grayscale image, and Type=Byte tells you that it is an 8-bit (8 bits=1 byte) image. Because 8 bits of data can hold 256 different values, this image could have 256 different shades of gray.

```
Band 1 Block=5700x1 Type=Byte, ColorInterp=Gray
```

> If you have more than one band in an image, you can start to have color images that combine values from, for example, red, green, and blue (RGB) bands. Most normal digital photographs you see are set up this way, with each band having 256 values of its specific color. When combined, they can be assigned to specific RGB values on, for example, your computer monitor. That type of image would be considered a 24-bit image (8 bits per band × 3 bands).

If you add the -mm parameter to the gdalinfo command, as shown in Example 6-9, you get a summary of the minimum and maximum color values for the bands in the image.

Example 6-9. Using the min/max summary option

```
> gdalinfo canada_mosaic_lcc_1000m.tif -mm
...
Band 1 Block=5700x1 Type=Byte, ColorInterp=Gray
    Computed Min/Max=0.000,255.000
```

This shows that there are 256 different values used in this image (with 0 being the minimum value).

Summarizing Information Using Other Tools

While ogrinfo and other ogr utilities are powerful tools, basic text-processing tools such as sort, uniq, wc, and sed can give them an extra bit of flexibility. The tools here are readily available for Unix-type operating systems (like Linux) by default. They are also available for other operating systems but you may need to download a package (e.g., from *http://gnu.org*) to get them for your system.

Each command can receive text streams. In this case, the text stream will be the lines of information coming from ogrinfo and listed on the screen. These commands take in those lines and allow you to, for example, show only certain portions of them, to throw away certain lines, reformat them, do a search/replace function or count items. Many types of functions can be done using the ogrinfo -sql parameter, but the ultimate formatting of the results isn't always what is desired. These examples show some common patterns for extracting specific information and generating more custom stats.

Setting Up Processing Tools for Non-GNU Platforms

These text-processing tools are sometimes packaged together, but are usually separate projects in and of themselves. Most of them were formed as part of the GNU/Free Software Foundation and are registered with the GNU free software directory at *http://www.gnu.org/directory/*. The targets of GNU software are free operating systems, which can cause some problems if you are dependent on an operating system such as Microsoft Windows. Some operating system don't normally include these tools, but they can often be acquired from Internet sources or even purchased.

A very comprehensive set of these tools for Windows is available at *http://unxutils.sourceforge.net/*. You can download a ZIP file that contains all the programs. If you unzip the file and store the files in a common Windows folder, such as *C:\Windows\System32* or *C:\winnt\System32*, they will be available to run from the command prompt.

If the tool or command you want isn't included, the next place to look is the GNU directory (*http://gnu.org*). This is where to start if you are looking for a particular program. A home page for the program and more information about it are available. Look for the download page for the program first to see if there is a binary version of the tool available for your operating system. If not, you may need to download the source code and compile the utility yourself.

Another resource to search is the Freshmeat web site at *http://freshmeat.net*. This site helps users find programs or projects and also provides daily news reports of what is being updated. Many projects reported in Freshmeat are hosted on the Sourceforge web site at *http://sourceforge.net*.

One source that is commonly used on Windows is the Cygwin environment, which can be found at *http://www.cygwin.com*. The web site describes Cygwin as "a Linux-like environment for Windows." Cygwin can be downloaded and installed on most modern Windows platforms and provides many of the text-processing tools mentioned previously. Furthermore, it also provides access to source-code compilers such as GCC.

Mac OS X includes many of the same kinds of text-processing tools. They may not be exactly the same as the GNU programs mentioned here, but similar alternatives are available in the Darwin core underlying OS X. For ones that aren't available natively in OS X, they can be compiled from the GNU source code or acquired through your favorite package manager such as Fink.

Using ogrinfo to List Data in a Shapefile

The standard output of `ogrinfo` reports are a set of lines displaying information about each feature. As earlier, this output is quite verbose, showing some summary information first, then sections for each feature. In the case of the airport data, each airport has its own section of seven lines. Example 6-10 shows a couple of these sections covering 2 of the 12 features (the rest were removed to reduce unnecessary length).

Example 6-10. Basic output listing about the airports shapefile

```
> ogrinfo data airports
INFO: Open of 'data'
using driver 'ESRI Shapefile' successful.

Layer name: airports
Geometry: Point
Feature Count: 12
Extent: (434634.000000, 5228719.000000) - (496393.000000, 5291930.000000)
Layer SRS WKT:
(unknown)
NAME: String (64.0)
LAT: Real (12.4)
LON: Real (12.4)
ELEVATION: Real (12.4)
QUADNAME: String (32.0)
OGRFeature(airports):0
  NAME (String) = Bigfork Municipal Airport
  LAT (Real) =      47.7789
  LON (Real) =      -93.6500
  ELEVATION (Real) =    1343.0000
  QUADNAME (String) = Effie
  POINT (451306 5291930)

OGRFeature(airports):1
  NAME (String) = Bolduc Seaplane Base
  LAT (Real) =      47.5975
```

```
LON (Real) =     -93.4106
ELEVATION (Real) =    1325.0000
QUADNAME (String) = Balsam Lake
POINT (469137 5271647)
```

But what if you don't really care about a lot of the information that is displayed? You can use the ogrinfo options -sql and -where, but they still show you summary information and don't necessarily format it the way you want. Various other operating system programs can help you reformat the output of ogrinfo. Examples of these commands follow, starting with the grep command.

Using grep to Show Only the Names of the Airports

The grep commands can be used to show only certain lines being printed to your screen; for example, to find a certain line in a text file. In this case, we are piping the text stream that ogrinfo prints into the grep command and analyzing it. The results are that any line starting with two spaces and the word NAME are printed; the rest of the lines won't show. Note that the pipe symbol | is the vertical bar, usually the uppercase of the key \ on your keyboard. This tells the command-line interpreter to send all the results of the ogrinfo command to the grep command for further processing. You then add an option at the end of the command telling it which lines you want to see in your results, as shown in Example 6-11.

Example 6-11. Chaining together multiple commands to filter results from ogrinfo

```
> ogrinfo data airports | grep '  NAME'
  NAME (String) = Bigfork Municipal Airport
  NAME (String) = Bolduc Seaplane Base
  NAME (String) = Bowstring Municipal Airport
  NAME (String) = Burns Lake Seaplane Base
  NAME (String) = Christenson Point Seaplane Base
  NAME (String) = Deer River Municipal Airport
  NAME (String) = Gospel Ranch Airport
  NAME (String) = Grand Rapids-Itasca County/Gordon Newstrom Field
  NAME (String) = Richter Ranch Airport
  NAME (String) = Shaughnessy Seaplane Base
  NAME (String) = Sixberrys Landing Seaplane Base
  NAME (String) = Snells Seaplane Base
```

If you want some other piece of information to show instead, simply change 'NAME' (including two preceding spaces) to 'abc', which is the text or numbers you are interested in. For example, grep 'LAT' shows only the LAT lines. Notice that using 'NAME' without the preceding spaces as in NAME lists the QUADNAME attributes as well.

Using wc to Count the Number of Airport Names

Now that you have a list of attribute values in your *airports* file, you can start to use other commands. The wc command can perform a variety of analysis functions against a list of text. The name wc stands for word count. It can count the number of characters, words, or lines in a list of text (or a file) and report them back to you. Output from grep or ogrinfo can be redirected to wc to be further analyzed.

In this case we use wc to count the number of lines (using the -1 line count option). Combined with the grep command, as shown in the following example, this shows the number of airports that grep would have printed to your screen.

```
> ogrinfo data airports | grep ' NAME' | wc -l
12
```

Using sed to Find Specific Patterns in Airport Names

Another very powerful tool is the text stream-editing tool called sed. sed allows a user to filter a list of text (in this case the listing from ogrinfo) and perform text substitutions (search and replace), find or delete certain text, etc. If you are already familiar with regular expression syntax, you will find yourself right at home using sed, because it uses regex syntax to define its filters.

In this example, you take the full output of the ogrinfo command again and search entries that contain the words Seaplane Base. What makes this different than the grep example is the inclusion of the trailing dollar $ sign at the end of the phrase. This symbol represents the end of the line. This example, therefore, prints only airport names that have Seaplane Base at the end of the name; it doesn't print any airport without Seaplane Base in its name and also excludes airports that have the phrase in anything but the last part of the name. As in Example 6-12, the airport named Joes Seaplane Base and Cafe wouldn't be returned.

Example 6-12. Using sed to do basic filtering of results

```
> ogrinfo data airports | sed -n '/Seaplane Base$/p'
  NAME (String) = Bolduc Seaplane Base
  NAME (String) = Burns Lake Seaplane Base
  NAME (String) = Christenson Point Seaplane Base
  NAME (String) = Shaughnessy Seaplane Base
  NAME (String) = Sixberrys Landing Seaplane Base
  NAME (String) = Snells Seaplane Base
```

Further text-processing can be done with the awk command. For example, to remove the NAME (String) text, pipe the results through awk:

```
| awk -F= '{print $2}'.
```

Use sed to Reformat Print Results

The display of the previous example may be fine only for purposes of quick data review. When some type of report or cut/paste function needs to take place, it is often best to reformat the results. Example 6-13 uses grep to filter out all the lines that aren't airport names, as in the previous example. It then uses two sed filters to remove the attribute name information, and then to remove any airports that start with B. As you can see, the example runs ogrinfo results through three filters and produces an easy-to-read list of all the airports meeting your criteria.

Example 6-13. Using sed to remove results with a certain starting letter

```
> ogrinfo data airports | grep '  NAME' | sed 's/  NAME (String) = //' | sed '/^B/d'
Christenson Point Seaplane Base
Deer River Municipal Airport
Gospel Ranch Airport
Grand Rapids-Itasca County/Gordon Newstrom Field
Richter Ranch Airport
Shaughnessy Seaplane Base
Sixberrys Landing Seaplane Base
Snells Seaplane Base
```

The usage of the last sed filter looks somewhat obscure, because it uses the caret ^ symbol. This denotes the start of a line, so, in this case, it looks for any line that starts with B. It doesn't concern itself with the rest of the line at all. The final /d means "delete lines that meet the ^B criteria."

Example 6-14 uses a similar approach but doesn't require the text to be at the beginning of the line. Any airport with the word Municipal in the name is deleted from the final list.

Example 6-14. Using sed to remove results containing a keyword

```
> ogrinfo data airports | grep '  NAME' | sed 's/  NAME (String) = //' | sed '/Municipal/d'
Bolduc Seaplane Base
Burns Lake Seaplane Base
Christenson Point Seaplane Base
Gospel Ranch Airport
Grand Rapids-Itasca County/Gordon Newstrom Field
Richter Ranch Airport
Shaughnessy Seaplane Base
Sixberrys Landing Seaplane Base
Snells Seaplane Base
```

Using sed to Remove Lines and Trim the Front End of Lines

sed has many different options and can be very sophisticated, especially when combining sed filters. Example 6-15 shows how you can string numerous commands together and do a few filters all at once.

Example 6-15. Multiple sed commands to provide groups of lines meeting certain criteria

```
> ogrinfo data airports | sed -n '/^  NAME/,/^  ELEVATION/p' | sed '/LAT/d' | sed '/LON/d'
| sed 's/..................//'
Bigfork Municipal Airport
=     1343.0000
Bolduc Seaplane Base
=     1325.0000
Bowstring Municipal Airport
=     1372.0000
Burns Lake Seaplane Base
=     1357.0000
Christenson Point Seaplane Base
=     1372.0000
Deer River Municipal Airport
=     1311.0000
Gospel Ranch Airport
=     1394.0000
Grand Rapids-Itasca County/Gordon Newstrom Field
=     1355.0000
Richter Ranch Airport
=     1340.0000
Shaughnessy Seaplane Base
=     1300.0000
Sixberrys Landing Seaplane Base
=     1372.0000
Snells Seaplane Base
=     1351.0000
```

This example uses sed to do only four filters on the list. The first is perhaps the most complex. It has two options separated by a comma:

    `'/^  NAME/,/^  ELEVATION/p'`

You can see the use of the caret again, which always denotes that the filter is looking at the beginning of the line(s). In this case it looks for the lines starting with NAME (including a couple spaces that ogrinfo throws in by default), but then there is also ELEVATION specified. The comma tells sed to include a range of lines—those that fall between the line starting with NAME and the next line starting with ELEVATION. NAME is called the start; ELEVATION is called the end. This way you can see a few lines together rather than selecting one line at a time. This is helpful because it shows the lines in the context of surrounding information and is important for text streams that are listed like ogrinfo output, which groups together attributes of features onto multiple lines.

    `sed '/LAT/d' | sed '/LON/d'`

The second and third filters are simple delete filters that remove any LAT and LON lines. Notice that these lines originally fell between NAME and ELEVATION in the list, so the filter is simply removing more and more lines building on the previous filter.

    `sed 's/..................//'`

The fourth filter isn't a joke, nor did I fall asleep on the keyboard. It is a substitute or search/replace filter, which is signified by the preceding s/. Each period represents a character that sed will delete from the beginning of each line.

The end result of these four filters is a much more readable list of all the airports in the shape file and their respective elevations.

Using sort to Create a List of Ordered Elevations

Another very handy command-line tool is sort. sort does just what the name promises: it puts text or numbers in a certain order. It sorts in ascending order by default, from smallest to highest or from lowest letter (closest to "a") to highest letter (closest to "z").

In Example 6-16 all the lines are filtered out except those including ELEVATION. Unwanted letters are then stripped from the beginning of each line. The output is then filtered through sort which reorders the output in ascending order.

Example 6-16. Using sort to reorder results

```
> ogrinfo data airports | grep 'ELEVATION' | sed -n 's/  ELEVATION (Real) =   //p' | sort
  1300.0000
  1311.0000
  1325.0000
  1340.0000
  1343.0000
  1351.0000
  1355.0000
  1357.0000
  1372.0000
  1372.0000
  1372.0000
  1394.0000
```

Using uniq to Summarize Results of Duplicate Lines

The output from sort includes some duplicate or repeated values. Obviously some airports rest at the same elevation: 1,372 feet. If this output is going to be used in a report, it may not make sense to include repeated values, especially when it is just a list of numbers.

The uniq command can help make the results more presentable. In Example 6-17, the results of grep, sed, and sort were passed to the uniq command. uniq processes the list and removes duplicate lines from the list. You'll notice only one occurrence of 1372 now.

Example 6-17. Using uniq to remove duplicates from the results

```
> ogrinfo data airports | grep 'ELEVATION' | sed -n 's/  ELEVATION (Real) =    //p' | sort
| uniq
 1300.0000
 1311.0000
 1325.0000
 1340.0000
 1343.0000
 1351.0000
 1355.0000
 1357.0000
 1372.0000
 1394.0000
```

uniq has some other options. As seen in Example 6-18, -c tells uniq to also print the number of times each line occurs. Notice that only elevation 1372 occurred more than once.

Example 6-18. Counting the number of unique occurrences in results using uniq

```
> ogrinfo data airports | grep 'ELEVATION' | sed -n 's/  ELEVATION (Real) =    //p' | sort
| uniq -c
       1  1300.0000
       1  1311.0000
       1  1325.0000
       1  1340.0000
       1  1343.0000
       1  1351.0000
       1  1355.0000
       1  1357.0000
       3  1372.0000
       1  1394.0000
```

The -d option for uniq shows only duplicate records. You can combine multiple options to help give you exactly what you are looking for. As shown in Example 6-19, if you are only interested in airports with the same elevation, and you want to know how many there are, you would only have to add d to the options for uniq.

Example 6-19. Using uniq to only show results that are duplicated

```
> ogrinfo data airports | grep 'ELEVATION' | sed -n 's/  ELEVATION (Real) =    //p' | sort
| uniq -cd
```

To add line numbers to you output, pass your text stream through the nl command. Example 6-20 shows what this looks like.

Example 6-20. Adding line numbers to text stream output using nl

```
> ogrinfo data airports | grep 'ELEVATION' | sed -n 's/  ELEVATION (Real) =   //p' | sort
| uniq -c | nl
     1       1  1300.0000
     2       1  1311.0000
     3       1  1325.0000
     4       1  1340.0000
     5       1  1343.0000
     6       1  1351.0000
     7       1  1355.0000
     8       1  1357.0000
     9       3  1372.0000
    10       1  1394.0000
```

Keep in mind that uniq checks each line only against surrounding lines, therefore the sort beforehand helps make sure that all duplicates are side by side. If they aren't, there is no guarantee that uniq will produce the expected results. Other text-processing commands may better suit you if you are unable to use sort. For example, tsort, referenced in the next section may do what you want.

Other Powerful Text-Processing Tools

Most Unix implementations, including Linux, have many more processing commands available. The list below shows a summary of the text-processing commands you may find useful. If you are wondering how to use some of them, you can usually add --help after the command name to get a list of options. Or you may also be able to read the manual for the command by typing man *<command name>*.

sort
> Sorts lines of text

paste
> Merges lines of files

sed
> Performs basic text transformations on an input stream

tsort
> Performs topological sort

join
> Joins lines of two files on a common field

awk
> Is a pattern scanning and processing language

uniq
> Removes duplicate lines from a sort file

head/tail
> Outputs the first/last part of files

wc   Prints the number of newlines, words, and bytes in files

expand/unexpand
    Converts to/from tabs and spaces

grep
    Prints lines matching a pattern

column
    Columnates lists

cut
    Removes sections from each line of files

look
    Displays lines beginning with a given string

colrm
    Removes columns from a file

nl   Numbers lines in text stream

I highly recommend the Linux Documentation Project site to get a comprehensive list and examples of these text-processing commands. This is helpful for those other platforms as well because these tools often exist for other platforms. The site address is *http://www.tldp.org/*—search for the "Text Processing" HOWTO document. Other HOWTO documents and tutorials go into more depth for specific text processing programs. Check out the O'Reilly book *Unix Power Tools* for more Unix help.

CHAPTER 7
Converting Map Data

Chapter 2 outlined the various tasks of digital mapping; one of those tasks involved converting data between different formats. In a perfect world there might only be one or two formats, but in reality there are dozens of different ways to store spatial information. Add to that both raster and vector data formats, and you've got quite an array of options. Like Chapter 6, this chapter by itself won't likely create beautiful maps, but the steps presented here are even more important because they are a key part of the path to producing useful maps.

The examples in this chapter use the GDAL/OGR utilities that are introduced in Chapter 6. They are part of the FWTools package.

Converting Map Data

Different data formats have sprung up because of the need for various capabilities and the desire for proprietary software control. Creating a better data format may be necessary to handle more complex information or improve performance, but having various data formats just because each vendor creates one for its own product is hardly productive. Fortunately, there are some excellent tools available for both raster and vector data conversion and for coordinate reprojection. By their natures, raster and vector data need to be handled differently, though the general concept is similar: take data in one format, and convert it to another format.

Data conversion can be necessary for a number of reasons:

- The source data may be in a format you aren't familiar with.
- Your mapping program may not know how to handle a particular format.
- You may just want to get a quick image snapshot in a common, non-GIS format.

Converting Vector Data

Quite often data isn't in a format that makes it readily available for both mapping software and people to read. Many data formats store the geographic data in a binary format. This format is normally readable only by computers and is designed for software to use. Some spatial data formats are in a simple text format, which is easier to explore.

Geography Markup Language (GML)

One example of a text-based format is Geography Markup Language (GML). It uses a text syntax to encode coordinates into a text file. GML can then be read or manually edited without needing a special piece of software or at least nothing more than a common text editor. Creating GML from scratch isn't very pleasant. Fortunately, another OGR utility exists that can convert OGR-supported data formats into and out of other formats, including GML.

GML has three different versions: GML1, GML2, and GML3. There are many subversions as well. The differences between versions can be a problem because certain features may not be directly transferable to another. The tools introduced in this chapter use ogr2ogr, which outputs to GML2 format.

GML was designed to be suitable for data interoperability, allowing the exchange of spatial data using a common format. This has opened up the possibilities for various web services that operate using different software yet can communicate using this standard format. See Chapter 12 to learn more about this example.

GML's downside is its size. Text files can't hold as much raw computer data as a binary file, so GML files tend to be much larger than other data formats. It isn't ideal to store all your data as GML, but it's perfect for sending data to someone who may not be able to support other formats. Because GML is text, it compresses very well using tools such as gzip and WinZip.

Extensible Markup Language (XML) is a popular standard for general data exchange, especially through the Internet. XML-based datafiles (such as GML) typically have an associated schema document. Schema documents aren't discussed, but you should know that they do exist. They describe how the data is structured in the XML data file—what attributes they have, what version of XML is being used, what type of information is in an attribute, etc. Schema documents have a filename suffix of *.xsd*. Therefore, a GML file called *airports.gml* also has an associated *airports.xsd* file describing the contents of *airports.gml*.

Converting a Shapefile to GML

Example 7-1 shows how to convert the airports data from shapefile format to GML using the ogr2ogr conversion utility.

Example 7-1. Using ogr2ogr to convert a shapefile into GML format

```
> ogr2ogr -f "GML" airports.gml data/airports.shp airports
> more airports.gml
<?xml version="1.0" encoding="utf-8" ?>
<ogr:FeatureCollection
     xmlns:xsi="http://www.w3c.org/2001/XMLSchema-instance"
     xsi:schemaLocation=". airports.xsd"
     xmlns:ogr="http://ogr.maptools.org/"
     xmlns:gml="http://www.opengis.net/gml">
  <gml:boundedBy>
    <gml:Box>
      <gml:coord><gml:X>434634</gml:X><gml:Y>5228719</gml:Y></gml:coord>
      <gml:coord><gml:X>496393</gml:X><gml:Y>5291930</gml:Y></gml:coord>
    </gml:Box>
  </gml:boundedBy>
  <gml:featureMember>
    <airports fid="0">
      <NAME>Bigfork Municipal Airport</NAME>
      <LAT>     47.7789</LAT>
      <LON>    -93.6500</LON>
      <ELEVATION>    1343.0000</ELEVATION>
      <QUADNAME>Effie</QUADNAME>
      <ogr:geometryProperty><gml:Point><gml:coordinates>451306,5291930</gml:coordinates>
              </gml:Point></ogr:geometryProperty>
    </airports>
  </gml:featureMember>
  <gml:featureMember>
    <airports fid="1">
      <NAME>Bolduc Seaplane Base</NAME>
      <LAT>     47.5975</LAT>
      <LON>    -93.4106</LON>
      <ELEVATION>    1325.0000</ELEVATION>
      <QUADNAME>Balsam Lake</QUADNAME>
      <ogr:geometryProperty><gml:Point><gml:coordinates>469137,5271647</gml:coordinates>
              </gml:Point></ogr:geometryProperty>
```

This converts the airports shapefile into GML format and can be read (by either humans or programs) with little effort. GML data can be changed or appended to and then reconverted or used as is if your application supports the GML format. For example if you want to change the location of an airport, simply edit the text file using a text editor such as Notepad (on Windows) or vim (on Unix). Programs such as Word or Wordpad can also be used as text editors, but you must specify to save the files as plain text, or the data is saved as a binary format made for a word processor.

In Example 7-1, I demonstrate the more command, which lists the contents of the file to your screen, one page at a time. This prevents the output from scrolling off the top of the screen so quickly that it can't be read. You should be aware that more can be found on various versions of Windows, but on other operating systems, it may have been replaced by the less program. Both programs can be used interchangeably here. You request another page of output by pressing the space bar. To view only the next line, press the Enter key.

When editing the *airports.gml* file, you can see there are hierarchical sections in the file. Each airport feature has a section starting with `<gml:featureMember>` and ending with `</gml:featureMember>`. The last attribute listed in each section is `<ogr:geometryProperty>`. This is the section containing all the geometry information. To edit an airport file, simply change the coordinates that are entered between the `<gml:coordinates>` tags. For example:

```
<gml:coordinates>444049,5277360</gml:coordinates>
```

can be changed to:

```
<gml:coordinates>450000,5260000</gml:coordinates>
```

ogrinfo can be used again to view information about the GML file, or ogr2ogr can be used to convert the data back into the shapefile format someone else may be expecting. This is shown in the following example:

```
> ogr2ogr -f "ESRI Shapefile" airport_gml.shp airports.gml airports
```

This takes the GML file and converts it back to shapefile format. Now ogrinfo can be run on it to compare the results with the earlier tests.

Creating a New File with Only a Subset of Point Features

You will find that sometimes you get a set of data for a project but are interested in only a small portion of it. For example, if I'm making a map of my local municipality, I might want only the location of the nearest airport and not all 12 that are available from my government data source. Reducing the set of features is possible using ogr2ogr, and the syntax that selects the feature(s) of interest is almost identical to ogrinfo.

Putting One Airport to a New Shapefile

It is possible to use ogr2ogr as a feature extraction tool. For example, if you want to make a map of the Bigfork airport, you can use ogr2ogr and the -where option to create a new shapefile that only includes the Bigfork Municipal Airport, as shown in the following example:

```
> ogr2ogr -f "ESRI Shapefile" bigfork data/airports.shp -where "name='Bigfork
Municipal Airport'"
```

The first parameter tells ogr2ogr to create a shapefile. The command then creates a folder called bigfork and creates the *airports* shapefile within it. As seen in Example 7-2, when you run ogrinfo against this dataset, you can see there is now only one feature, Bigfork Municipal Airport.

Example 7-2. Using ogrinfo to show only the filtered results from ogr2ogr command

```
> ogrinfo bigfork airports
INFO: Open of 'bigfork'
using driver 'ESRI Shapefile' successful.

Layer name: airports
Geometry: Point
Feature Count: 1
Extent: (451306.000000, 5291930.000000) - (451306.000000, 5291930.000000)
Layer SRS WKT:
(unknown)
NAME: String (64.0)
LAT: Real (12.4)
LON: Real (12.4)
ELEVATION: Real (12.4)
QUADNAME: String (32.0)
OGRFeature(airports):0
  NAME (String) = Bigfork Municipal Airport
  LAT (Real) =      47.7789
  LON (Real) =     -93.6500
  ELEVATION (Real) =    1343.0000
  QUADNAME (String) = Effie
  POINT (451306 5291930)
```

Converting Shapefiles to Other File Formats

The power of ogr2ogr is its ability to handle several vector data formats. To get a list of possible formats, run ogr2ogr without any parameters, as shown in Example 7-3. You will see the help information displayed as well as the -f format name options.

Example 7-3. Listing output file formats supported by ogr2ogr

```
 -f format_name: output file format name, possible values are:
     -f "ESRI Shapefile"
     -f "TIGER"
     -f "S57"
     -f "MapInfo File"
     -f "DGN"
     -f "Memory"
     -f "GML"
     -f "PostgreSQL"
```

Creating other formats is as easy as changing the -f option to the needed format, then entering in an appropriate output dataset name. The -where clause can remain as is.

The formats supported by ogr2ogr depend on which were built into ogr2ogr when it was compiled. If a format you need isn't shown in the list, you may need to find another version of ogr2ogr from somewhere else: try the mailing list, for example. There are also some formats ogr2ogr can't write to because the OGR library allows reading only of some formats. See this page for formats including those which OGR can read and write/create—*http://www.gdal.org/ogr/ogr_formats.html.*

Converting to other file-based formats is particularly easy. The following example shows how to create a GML file:

```
> ogr2ogr -f "GML" bigfork_airport.gml data/airports.shp -where "name='Bigfork
Municipal Airport'"
```

This example shows how to convert to DGN format:

```
> ogr2ogr -f "DGN" -select "" bigfork_airport.dgn data/airports.shp -where
"name='Bigfork Municipal Airport'"
```

DGN format can't support attribute fields. When converting to DGN, you'll see an error message:

```
ERROR 6: CreateField( ) not supported by this layer.
```

The file is created, but it doesn't include any attributes. One workaround to this problem is to use the -select option. With other formats, the -select option allows you to specify what attributes you want to convert into the destination layer. Because ogr2ogr can't convert any attributes to the DGN file, you select no fields by providing an empty value, such as two double quotes as shown in the DGN example.

Converting to a PostgreSQL Database

ogr2ogr can also convert data to database formats, such as PostgreSQL (using the PostGIS spatial extension if it is available). The syntax for the command is more complicated than simple file-based formats because there are certain parameters that must be used to connect to the destination database. These options aren't discussed in detail here but are covered in Chapter 13.

This example shows how to convert from a shapefile to a PostgreSQL database:

```
> ogr2ogr -f "PostgreSQL" "PG:dbname=myairports host=myhost.com user=pgusername"
data/airports.shp -where "name='Bigfork Municipal Airport'"
```

The command in this example connects to the myairports database on a server called myhost.com using the PostgreSQL database user pgusername. It then creates a table called airports. This is the same name as the input shapefile, which is the default.

Querying the database using the PostgreSQL query tool `psql` shows that the conversion was successful, as in Example 7-4.

Example 7-4. Checking results in PostgreSQL

```
psql> select * from airports;
-[ RECORD 1 ]+--------------------------------------------------
ogc_fid      | 1
wkb_geometry | SRID=-1;POINT(451306 5291930)
name         | Bigfork Municipal Airport
lat          | 47.7789
lon          | -93.6500
elevation    | 1343.0000
quadname     | Effie
```

 Other tools can convert shapefiles to PostgreSQL/PostGIS databases. `shp2pgsql` is a command-line program that exports a shapefile into SQL commands. These commands can be saved into a text file or sent directly to the database for execution. This utility comes with PostGIS.

The Quantum GIS (QGIS) desktop GIS also has a shapefile to the PostgreSQL/PostGIS conversion tool, and it has a plug-in for QGIS called SPIT. See *http://www.qgis.org* for more information about QGIS.

More detailed PostgreSQL usage is covered in Chapter 13, where an example problem shows how to load data into a spatial database and also extracts data from the database.

Converting Raster Data to Other Formats

Raster data, like vector data, can be stored in numerous formats. Some formats come from certain software requirements or from certain satellite image sources. Some are more general while others are better suited for more complex tasks. In this section, you will see how to use the `gdal_translate` raster translation utility and its various parameters to help you draw the most value out of an image.

Translating an Image to Another Format

Just as `ogr2ogr` has several conversion options, so does `gdal_translate`. The syntax for the command is slightly different but similar in concept. Here is the usage:

```
gdal_translate <options> <input_image> <output_image>
```

The options available can be listed by running the command without any parameters, as in Example 7-5.

Example 7-5. Checking the options for gdal_translate

```
> gdal_translate
Usage: gdal_translate [--help-general]
       [-ot {Byte/Int16/UInt16/UInt32/Int32/Float32/Float64/
             CInt16/CInt32/CFloat32/CFloat64}] [-not_strict]
       [-of format] [-b band] [-outsize xsize[%] ysize[%]]
       [-scale [src_min src_max [dst_min dst_max]]]
       [-srcwin xoff yoff xsize ysize] [-a_srs srs_def]
       [-projwin ulx uly lrx lry] [-co "NAME=VALUE"]*
       [-gcp pixel line easting northing]*
       [-mo "META-TAG=VALUE"]* [-quiet]
       src_dataset dst_dataset

GDAL 1.2.1.0, released 2004/06/23
```

This first part of the output of Example 7-5 shows the various options. Each item enclosed with brackets [] is optional. Without them, the program simply converts one image to another, creating the output in GeoTIFF format by default. Some options are used in the examples of the following sections and in more depth in other chapters of this book. Example 7-5 also shows the software version number and the official release date of the GDAL project.

Example 7-6 shows a list of all available image formats. This list will vary depending on the operating system and (only if you compiled it yourself) the options you specified during the configuration process. This lists many formats, though it may actually be able to read more image types. The list shows only potential output formats that can be used with the -of option. You supply this option with the abbreviated name for that format as shown in Example 7-6. For the latest capabilities, be sure to see the GDAL support formats page *http://www.gdal.org/formats_list.html*.

Example 7-6. Listing supported raster output formats

```
The following format drivers are configured and support output:
  VRT: Virtual Raster
  GTiff: GeoTIFF
  NITF: National Imagery Transmission Format
  HFA: Erdas Imagine Images (.img)
  ELAS: ELAS
  AAIGrid: Arc/Info ASCII Grid
  DTED: DTED Elevation Raster
  PNG: Portable Network Graphics
  JPEG: JPEG JFIF
  MEM: In Memory Raster
  GIF: Graphics Interchange Format (.gif)
  XPM: X11 PixMap Format
  BMP: MS Windows Device Independent Bitmap
  PCIDSK: PCIDSK Database File
  PNM: Portable Pixmap Format (netpbm)
  ENVI: ENVI .hdr Labelled
  EHdr: ESRI .hdr Labelled
  PAux: PCI .aux Labelled
```

Example 7-6. Listing supported raster output formats (continued)

```
MFF: Atlantis MFF Raster
MFF2: Atlantis MFF2 (HKV) Raster
BT: VTP .bt (Binary Terrain) 1.3 Format
JPEG2000: JPEG-2000 part 1 (ISO/IEC 15444-1)
FIT: FIT Image
USGSDEM: USGS Optional ASCII DEM (and CDED)
```

Keep in mind that any type of image format supported by GDAL can be translated, including digital camera photos or images from a web site. The most basic example of conversion, such as the following example, takes an image in one format and outputs it to another format.

```
> gdal_translate image1.png image1.tif
> gdal_translate -of "PNG" image1.tif image1.png
```

 Even though you specify the output file format, `gdal_translate` doesn't automatically create a filename suffix/extension for you. Remember to add your own to the end of the filename.

An image can be translated back to the same format too, if creation of that format is supported by GDAL.

Using gdal_translate to Create a JPEG Preview of a Satellite Image

In Chapter 6, gdalinfo was used to show the details of a RADARSAT image of Canada. The image was a whopping $5,700 \times 4,800$-pixel image and more than 25 MB in size. Only special image-handling programs like gdal-related tools can handle files that large. This isn't an image you would want to send to a friend as an email attachment! Not only would the file size be a problem but your friend probably could not use basic image viewers because it is a very large GeoTIFF file.

The gdal_translate utility is a handy tool for many things, one of which is reducing the size of an image and outputting it to a more usable format for the project at hand. In Example 7-7, gdal_translate reduces the size of the image to 5% and creates a small JPEG format file as output. Running gdalinfo against this new file shows that the resulting file is now a mere 285×240 pixels and is a JPEG format image. The file size is now less than 20 KB. This is easily viewable by the simplest image viewer on most personal computers.

Example 7-7. Converting a GeoTIFF and resizing it using gdal_translate

```
> gdal_translate -of "JPEG" -outsize 5% 5% canada_mosaic_lcc_1000m.tif can_radar.jpg
> gdalinfo can_radar.jpg
Driver: JPEG/JPEG JFIF
Size is 285, 240
```

Figure 7-1 shows what the `can_radar.jpg` image looks like after Example 7-13.

Figure 7-1. The original radar satellite image before clipping

Clipping an Area of Interest and Creating a Small JPEG of a Satellite Image

`gdal_translate` can also be used to specify only a portion of an image to be translated. The result is a clipped portion of the image being put into a new file. This is done using the `-projwin` option to specify geographic coordinates of the area to clip out, or `-srcwin` if you know which pixels you want to include. You can use OpenEV to preview the image and get an idea of what the upper-left and lower-right coordinates are around your area of interest. Then do the same type of translation as before, but provide coordinates in the `-projwin` parameter. Example 7-8 shows this kind of clipping as well as a conversion, all in one command.

Example 7-8. Converting and clipping out a portion of a satellite image using gdal_translate

```
> gdal_translate -of "JPEG" -projwin -2281300 7464800 -1812300 7001800 canada_mosaic_lcc_
1000m.tif can_radar_clip.jpg
Input file size is 5700, 4800
Computed -srcwin 318 3035 469 463 from projected window.
```

Depending on the image program you use and the image source, specifying coordinates for parameters like -projwin can be confusing. For some applications you specify a rectangle using the lower-left coordinate first and upper-right coordinates last. But in the previous example, because the origin pixel is in the upper-left corner, upper-left and lower-right coordinates must be used. If you mix them up, you will get strange errors.

Figure 7-2 shows the resulting clipped satellite image.

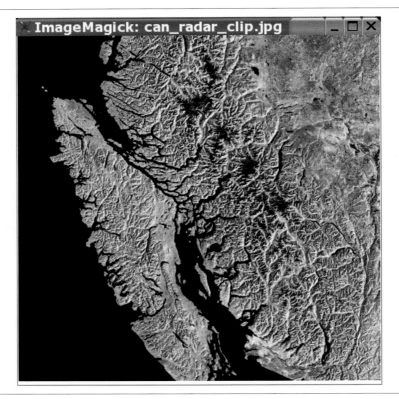

Figure 7-2. A satellite image clipped using the gdal_translate -projwin option

## CHAPTER 8

Visualizing Mapping Data in a Desktop Program

For many people, the prospect of creating a map is very exciting. Viewing a graphical representation of the world, especially a familiar part of the world, can kick-start your imagination and resolve unanswered questions. Where would we be if we couldn't view a map while planning a vacation and reserving the hotel? What would gardeners do if they couldn't look up the planting zone index for their area? How would trade prosper without a clear picture of other countries and trade routes? The questions can go on and on. So can the maps!

This chapter will show you how to use the open source spatial data viewer OpenEV to look at the data we used in the previous chapter. If you follow along, you will be able to create a customized view of Itasca County in Minnesota, U.S.A. By the end of the chapter, you should be comfortable using the tool for basic viewing, color-theming a map, and creating a simple 3D view.

Visualization and Mapping Programs

This chapter focuses on OpenEV, but there are many other GIS and mapping programs available. Some are open source and some are commercial.

Other Open Source Mapping Programs

Here is a list of some of the free and open source desktop GIS and mapping programs available today:

Quantum GIS (QGIS)
   http://www.qgis.org

Java Unified Mapping Platform (JUMP)
   http://jump-project.org

User-friendly Desktop GIS (UDIG)
   http://udig.refractions.net

Thuban
   http://thuban.intevation.org

OpenMap
   http://openmap.bbn.com

OpenEV
   http://fwtools.maptools.org

For more comprehensive lists of open source GIS and mapping tools, see:

   http://FreeGIS.org
   http://OpenSourceGIS.org

Other Free-to-Use Programs

Many of the major vendors distribute their own free viewers. These aren't considered freeware because you may not be able to freely distribute the programs. However, they are freely available to use:

ArcExplorer
   http://www.esri.com/software/arcexplorer/

GeoMedia Viewer
   http://imgs.intergraph.com/gviewer/

Geomatica FreeView
   http://www.pcigeomatics.com/product_ind/freeview.html

Freeware applications include:

Gaia
   http://www.thecarbonproject.com/products/gaia.html

Spring
   http://www.dpi.inpe.br/spring/

Map Maker
   http://www.mapmaker.com/products.htm

TatukGIS Viewer
   http://www.tatukgis.com/Products/viewer/viewer.aspx

Other Commercial Programs

There are also several commercial GIS and mapping programs available. This is a short list with an approximate single-user license cost (U.S. dollars) based on Internet price lists.

ArcGIS ArcView
   http://www.esri.com/software/arcgis/arcview/ ($1,500)

Manifold
   http://www.manifold.net/ ($245)

MapInfo
   http://www.mapinfo.com/ ($1,490)

If you use ArcView 3 and would like to start moving to an open source product, the Gix Exporter (*http://gix.sourceforge.net/*) may come in handy. It is an extension for ArcView 3 that can export to MapServer map files and JUMP, QGIS, Thuban, and OpenEV project formats. It can also export to a few vector graphics formats.

Using OpenEV

OpenEV was designed as an example of the kinds of tools that can be built on top of various open source GIS libraries. It has a variety of powerful features, is open to complete customization, and includes the ability to add in custom tools written in Python. For the purposes of this chapter, only some of the basic functions (not including Python scripting) will be demonstrated. These include the ability to view various formats of raster and vector data layers, change their colors, create labels, etc. It is also possible to create your own data; check for that in Chapter 9.

Follow along with the examples, and try them yourself to build up your familiarity and comfort with this tool. You will first test your installation of OpenEV, then create some custom maps using the demonstration datasets. Once the basic viewing capabilities are explored, you will learn to create some more sophisticated color classifications, and ultimately produce a 3D model to navigate through.

Installing OpenEV

Chapters 5 and 6 walked you through how to acquire sample data and review it using some simple tools. If you don't already have the MapServer demonstration data and the FWTools downloaded and installed, please refer back to these sections in Chapter 6.

You should have two things: a sample MapServer application known as *Workshop* and a copy of OpenEV that comes with FWTools. To test that you have OpenEV installed, launch the program. Windows users will launch the OpenEV_FW desktop shortcut. This will open a command window and create some windows.

Don't close the command window that appears. OpenEV needs this to stay open. It is safe to minimize the window while using OpenEV.

Linux users will launch the openev executable from the FWTools *bin_safe* folder.

Linux users: if you don't have a *bin_safe* folder, run the installer by typing:

> ./install.sh

This prepares the installation and creates a folder called *bin_safe*. Now, run the command:

> . /fwtools_env.sh

(Note the space after the period.) This loads all the environment variables. Now you should be able to run openev from anywhere.

When starting, the main window titled "OpenEV: View 1" should appear with a black background. The Layers windows will also appear.

Loading Sample Map Data into OpenEV

Starting from the default View 1 screen, you can add in sample data by selecting Open from the File menu, or by clicking on the folder icon on the left side of the main tool bar. The File Open window allows you to find a dataset on your filesystem and load it as a layer in OpenEV. All files are listed in the File Open window, whether or not they are spatial datafiles. OpenEV doesn't attempt to guess what they are until you actually try to open one.

Windows users may get confused when trying to find data on a drive with a different drive letter. The drive letters are listed below all the folders in the File Open window. You must scroll down to find them.

Open the Airports Shapefile

Navigate using the File Open window to the location where the workshop/data folder has been unzipped. In the data folder, you will see dozens of files listed. Select *airports.shp* to load the airports shapefile. As shown in Figure 8-1, 12 small green crosses should appear in the view. Each point represents the location of an airport from the demonstration dataset.

Using the Layers Window

OpenEV has other windows for different tasks. One of these is the Layers window. If it isn't already showing, select Layers from the Edit menu, as shown in Figure 8-2. This window lists the layers that are currently loaded into OpenEV. A layer can be an image or, as in our case, vector data. Only the airports layer should be loaded at this point. You will see the full path to the *airports.shp* file. Beside this layer name is an eye icon. This says that the layer is currently set to be visible in the view. Try clicking it on and off.

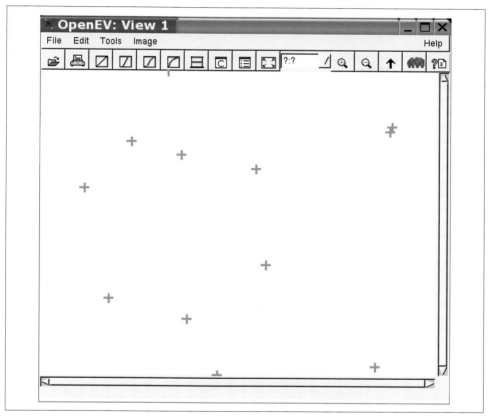

Figure 8-1. Initial loading of airport shape file

The layers window allows you to change certain graphical display settings for your layers. Access these settings by right-clicking on the layer name. The airport layer name may be somewhat obscured if you have the file deep in subfolders, because the default name for the layer is the whole path to the file. The layer window can be resized to show the full name more clearly if necessary.

Changing General Layer Settings

Right-click on the airports layer in the Layers window, you'll see the Properties window for the airports layer, as shown in Figure 8-3.

There are three options on the General tab of the Properties window:

Layer

This is the layer name. It can be changed to whatever you want it shown as in the Layers window. Changing this value won't affect the datafile itself. Because the default puts the whole path in as the layer name, change this to something

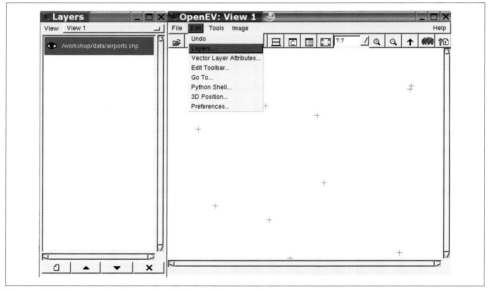

Figure 8-2. Viewing the layers loaded into the view

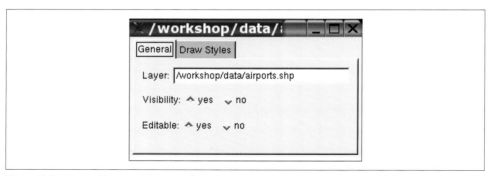

Figure 8-3. General layer settings window

more meaningful, such as "Airports". It will be updated in the Layers window the next time the layer is turned off and back on.

Visibility

This setting is changed when clicking on the eye icon in the layers window. When set to Yes, the layer shows in the view. Otherwise, it is turned off and won't be drawn.

Editable

Vector data files can be edited within OpenEV. This is a powerful feature that is often hard to find in free programs. Setting a layer to be editable allows you to move features around, create new ones, delete them, or reshape lines. The default setting is Yes. It is a good habit to change it to No so that you don't accidentally modify features.

Changing Draw Styles for Layers

The other tab at the top of the airports Properties window is called Draw Styles. Switch to this tab to see the various draw settings, as shown in Figure 8-4. There are five different groups of settings on this tab.

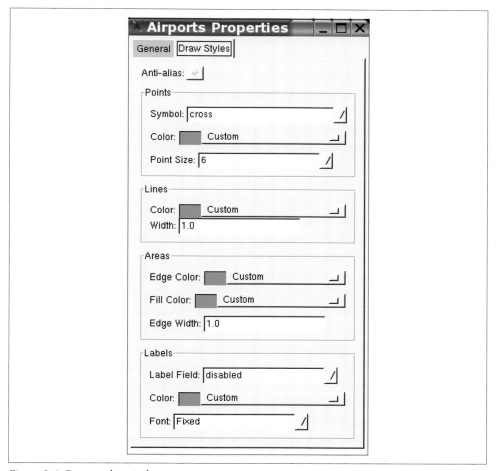

Figure 8-4. Draw styles window

Anti-alias

> The anti-alias setting is a checkbox; it is either on or off (it is off by default). This option allows your map features to be drawn more smoothly. It can often make your text and shapes look softer and less stark. The graphics of the airport layer

points are pretty simple. Using anti-aliasing won't make much difference. It is most noticeable with curved lines or text.

Points

Every airport point is given a specific symbol on the map. In this case, the airports are shown with the default symbol, a cross. There are several other options, and all are very simple. By default they are colored green; you can change the color by clicking on the word Custom or on the drop-down box square beside Custom. This provides a list of colors to choose from. Try some out, or select Custom from the list, and you are shown a color wheel. Note that the color wheel has an opacity setting that allows you to set the amount of transparency for your layer. Point size sets the size of the symbol on the map; this can be chosen from the drop-down list or typed in.

Lines

The settings for lines are fairly simple. You can set only the width and color.

Areas

Polygon features are also known as areas. Area features are made up of an edge line that draws the perimeter of the feature. It is possible to give that edge line a color and a width. You can also choose what color will fill the inside of the feature.

Labels

In many datasets, point features and label features look and act the same: they have a specific (point-like) location and some text associated with them. The text is shown for a layer when the Label Field is set. By default, it is disabled, and no labels are drawn. If the point dataset you are working with has attributes or fields of data for each point, you can select one from this list. With the airports layer, try setting the Label Field to NAME. This shows the name of each airport beside the point. Note that labels can't be drawn for line or area layers at this time.

When all the settings are complete, simply close the properties window by clicking on the X symbol in the top-right corner of the window. As you change settings, they are updated automatically in the view. Close the properties window, and return to the View 1 window.

Adding More Data to the View

One of the benefits of software like OpenEV is the ability to add many layers of data and compare them with each other. With some work setting draw styles, a simple map can be produced. The workshop dataset includes more than just an airports layer.

Click on the folder icon in View 1 to add another layer of features. The data is located in the same folder as the airports. This time add the file called *ctyrdln3.shp*. This is a layer containing road line data for the same county as the airports.

From the Layers window, right-click on the ctyrdln3 layer to open the layer properties window. Change the name to something obvious, such as Roads. You should also change the road line colors so they aren't the same as the airports. Notice that the road lines are being drawn on top of the airport symbols. The order of the layers is always important when creating a map, and, depending on your project, you may want to reorder the layers. This is done in the Layers window. Left-click on the layer name you want to change. The layer name will now be highlighted. Then select one of the up or down arrow buttons at the bottom of the Layers window. This moves the layer up or down in the draw order. The final product looks like Figure 8-5.

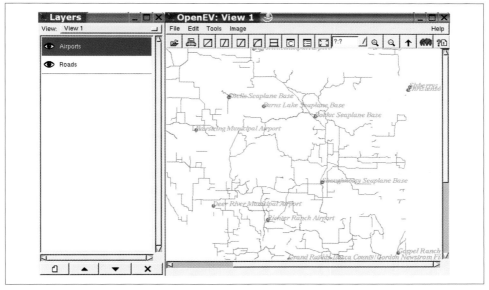

Figure 8-5. Road lines and airports loaded

OpenEV Basics

OpenEV has a variety of simple and complex tools. Many of the advanced tools have been designed with raster data in mind, but the basic toolsets and controls include many of the features needed to do quick visualization of both raster and vector data.

Zooming

One the first things you will want to do is zoom in to certain portions of your map. There are a couple ways to do this. The first is to use the plus and minus buttons on the toolbar of the view. The icons are a magnifying glass with a + and - symbol inside them. Clicking + zooms into the center of the screen, and clicking - zooms out from the center of the screen.

The more efficient way is to use the Zoom tool, which allows you to drag a rectangle on the screen and zoom in to that portion of the map. To enable the zoom tool, select the Edit Toolbar from the Edit menu, then choose Zoom from the list, as shown in Figure 8-6.

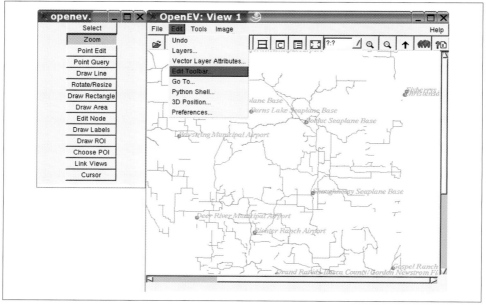

Figure 8-6. Activating the zoom tool

Now you can return to the view and click and hold the left mouse button to zoom in. You can also drag a rectangle around a portion of the screen and have it zoom in directly to that location. To do this, click and hold the left mouse button, then drag the mouse to another location. Watch as the rectangular zoom box appears, as in Figure 8-7. When the box covers the area you want, let go of the mouse button.

Zooming out can be done a few ways as well. As mentioned earlier, you can use the zoom-out magnifying glass button, but you can also hold the right mouse button down and slowly zoom out. Another method to use, if appropriate, is the Fit All Layers button on the main view tool bar. This button is a rectangle with four internal arrows pointing toward the corners of the rectangle, as shown in Figure 8-8. Clicking this button zooms out so far that all the data in all the layers can be seen.

 If you use this tool and find that you can no longer see your data, it is probably because one or more layers are in a different map projection. If you know the layer, remove it from the Layers window, and try Fit All Layers again. There is no tool to return you to the previous viewing extent.

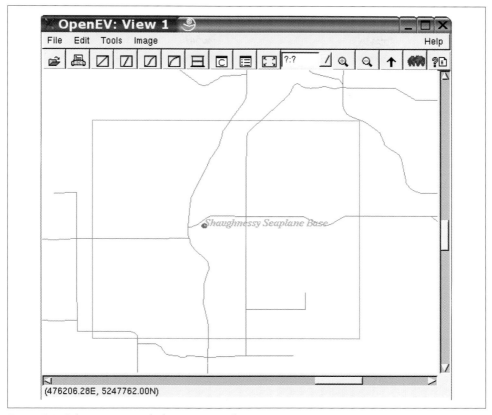

Figure 8-7. Select an area with the zoom in tool

Figure 8-8. The OpenEV toolbar, pointing out the Fit All Layers button

Panning

Many desktop mapping programs have a feature called *panning*. This is a way of sliding or moving the map around so you can look at different portions without having to zoom out and then back in again. The scrollbars in the view play this role. If there is map data beyond the sides of a view, you can slide the scrollbar or click on either arrow at the ends of the scrollbars. This moves you to the area you are looking for without changing the scale or size of the map features.

Color Theming

You probably don't always want to show all the features of a map layer using the same color. For example, the roads layer includes two different classes of roads. You may want to show each class in a different color, with a different road line thickness. Or you may not want to show one of the classes at all.

This road data includes an attribute that tells you what class each segment of line is. To use the values of this field to color the lines differently, you can use the Classify button on the tool bar, shown in Figure 8-9. It is a button with the letter C inside it.

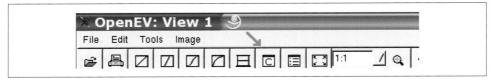

Figure 8-9. OpenEV's classify button

Click on this button, but remember to have the layer you want to classify (e.g., Roads) selected in the Layers window. The Layer Classification window appears (see Figure 8-10) and makes a basic set of classes for you.

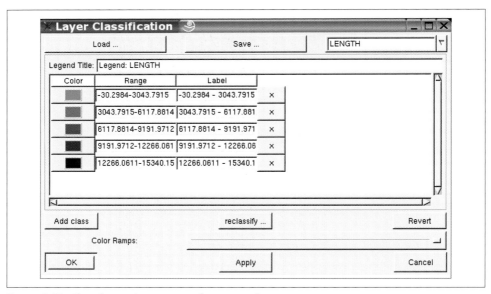

Figure 8-10. Classifying a layer using a feature attribute

For the road data it uses the LENGTH attribute by default because it is the first attribute. Switch the drop-down list in the top-right corner of the window to another field and see how it recreates the classification on the fly. Change this setting to the attribute ROAD_CLASS. This yields several values in a list, as shown in Figure 8-11.

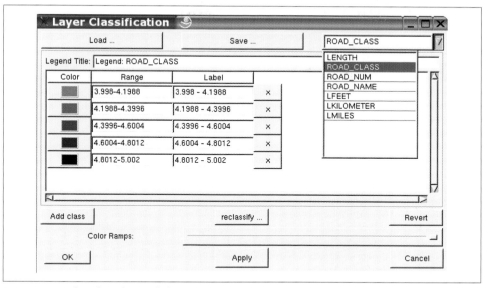

Figure 8-11. Classifying by road class

The default method for classifying these values isn't appropriate because it uses a range of values. There are only two road classes: integer numbers 4 and 5. You can change the way the classifier works by selecting the reclassify button. Change the Type to Discrete Values and press OK. This gives each distinct value in the ROAD_CLASS field a different color, as shown in Figure 8-12.

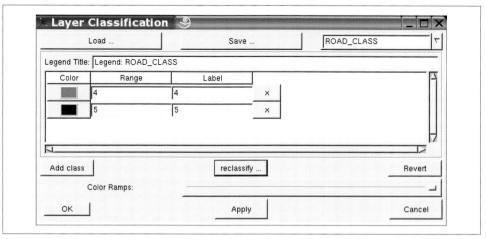

Figure 8-12. Classifying roads into two road classes

Notice how there appear to be some primary roads (class 4) and secondary roads (class 5). You can change the colors for each class until you are satisfied. Hit the Apply button to draw the roads using these colors, as shown in Figure 8-13. Remember that if one of the colors is black, it won't show against the black background in the view window.

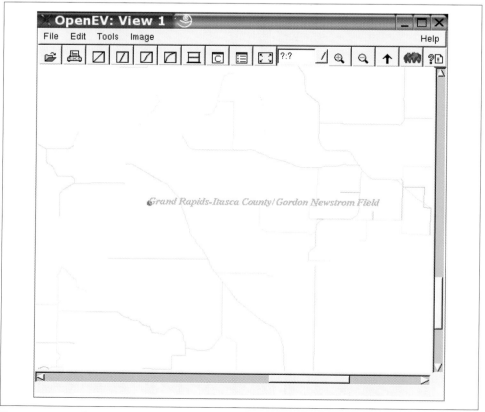

Figure 8-13. Applying color-theming using the road class attribute

There are several other options available in the classifier. One that is handy is the default set of Color Ramps in the drop-down on the Layer Classification window, shown in Figure 8-14.

You can quickly classify, reclassify, and set various color themes. Just select an item from the Color Ramps dropdown list, and hit Apply. Don't like it? Change it, and apply again. If you only have a couple values in your classification, these color ramps won't be as valuable, but they are particularly useful for raster data. When you are happy with the results, press the OK button to close the classification window.

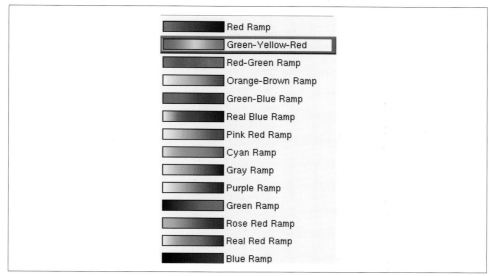

Figure 8-14. Selecting a color ramp to classify features

 In some case the vector layers may not draw properly after applying a color ramp. The workaround is to remove the layer and then add it again.

Loading a Raster

Adding a raster layer can often be easier than adding vector themes, because common raster formats are usually a single file with colors already assigned. The raster used in this example is a land cover dataset that covers the earth, but for this example it's focused on Itasca County, Minnesota. You can download the image from this book's O'Reilly web site at *http://www.oreilly.com/catalog/webmapping*.

This is a GeoTiff image, also known as a TIFF file. The *.tif* extension is the common filename suffix. Add the image to the OpenEV view by selecting File → Open and browsing your filesystem to find the *landcover.tif* file. Double-click on the filename or press the OK button. Notice that the layer is added to the list in the Layers window, but is currently not visible on the map (we'll come back to this point). It automatically becomes the topmost layer. Select the layer from the list and use the down arrow at the bottom of the layer window. This will move that layer to the bottom so that the vector data (airport points) will show on top of the other layer when it is ready.

If you right-click on the layer in the layer list, there are some options to select and change, just as with vector data, but the options are very different. The General tab is the only similarity. Some tabs are for information only; others will alter how the raster is displayed.

Reprojecting Data to Match Another Layer

Even if you press the Fit All Layers zoom button, you won't see the land cover layer because the workshop dataset and the land cover dataset aren't in the same map projection. This is a common problem when taking data designed for a county or region and using it in a global map.

In this case, the workshop datasets are in the UTM projection. The land cover raster isn't projected and uses geographic coordinates, specifically latitudes and longitudes measured in degree units. More information about map projections is available in Appendix A.

OpenEV doesn't itself have the ability to reproject data layers. The tools introduced in Chapters 3 and 7 can be used to reproject a layer so that OpenEV can display it the way you want.

 This chapter discusses map projections but shows only one real-world example of their utility. For more in-depth explanations and examples of map projections, see Appendix A.

In this example, ogr2ogr (introduced in Chapter 2) is used to reproject or transform the coordinates of the airport data from one spatial reference system to another:

```
> ogr2ogr shp_geo airports.shp airports  -t_srs "+proj=latlong" -s_srs "+proj=utm
+zone=15"
```

There are four parts to this command. The first section is the parameter that specifies the output dataset name. In this case, it creates a folder called *shp_geo* to put the translated files into.

The next section specifies what the input data is going to be. ogr2ogr reads in the *airports.shp* dataset and, specifically, the airports layer in that shapefile.

The next part starting with -t_srs specifies what target (or output) spatial reference system (t_srs) to put the data into. Without going into detail, the projection is set by +proj=, to output the data into latlong coordinates.

The final section -s_srs defines what the source spatial reference system (s_srs) is. Because the *airports.shp* file doesn't have projection information included in it, you have to know what it is and specify it here. This allows ogr2ogr to calculate what transformation to use. In this case, +proj=utm +zone=15, the projection is UTM, and the UTM zone is 15.

These are the most basic projection settings and will work for you, but you should be aware that to more accurately describe your data, you may need to specify more projection details such as datum, ellipsoid, or units.

When specifying projections you can use the EPSG code number as a shortcut. These are integer numbers. You can do so using the +init setting, not +proj. For example, you can specify:

```
-s_srs "+init=EPSG:26915"
```

for the UTM, zone 15 projection and:

```
-t_srs "+init=EPSG:4326"
```

for lat/long coordinate system.

Continue this conversion exercise for all the other workshop datasets (i.e., ctyrdln3. shp) so you can use them in your map. Just change the source and destination dataset/layer names in the ogr2ogr command example.

Add the newly created *shp_geo/airports.shp* file to the view. To quickly see their locations, remove the old UTM-based airports layer from the view, then click the Fit All Layers button to zoom out to the whole earth. Zoom in to the United States, and see where the airports fall. They are located around -93.54E, 47.53N degrees. You may need to resize or recolor the airport point symbols so that they are visible on top of the image, as in Figure 8-15. The locations are now shown to be on top of the land cover image, in northern Minnesota, because they are both in the same map projection. Figure 8-16 shows the map zoomed in to the area.

Creating a 3D View

OpenEV can render simple 3D perspectives of data. This is done using two input layers. One image shows the elevation surface—this is often called a Digital Elevation Model or DEM—where dark to light colors represent low to high elevations, respectively. The other input layer is the image you would like draped over the DEM. This can be thought of as a sheet being draped over a basketball, where the ball represents the elevation model.

Acquiring or creating these two layers can be tedious and frustrating. You need data colored a specific way to make it work. The images also need to have matching spatial reference systems so they overlap geographically. There are also several options which, if specified incorrectly, can produce inaccurate or unusable results.

Preparing the Digital Elevation Model

The first image you need is a DEM. If you don't have this kind of image, you can't create a useful 3D perspective of your data. If your target application is the United States, a lot of DEM datasets are available. They can often be used in OpenEV without any data conversion.

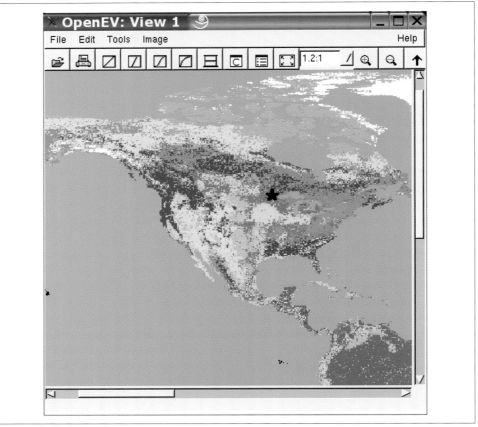

Figure 8-15. Land cover image with general location of airports shown by a black star

Here are some sites that have elevation datasets available:

GTOPO: Global digital elevation model
   http://edcdaac.usgs.gov/gtopo30/gtopo30.html

SRTM: Global coverage from Shuttle Radar Topography Mission
   http://srtm.csi.cgiar.org/Index.asp

USGS DEM: Digital elevation models for the United States
   http://edcsgs9.cr.usgs.gov/glis/hyper/guide/1_dgr_demfig/states.html

U.S. National Geophysical Data Center: Various types of data
   http://www.ngdc.noaa.gov/mgg/bathymetry/relief.html

The image used in this example is called `hibbing-w` and was downloaded in the USGS DEM data format from *http://edcsgs9.cr.usgs.gov/glis/hyper/guide/1_dgr_demfig/states/ MN.html*.

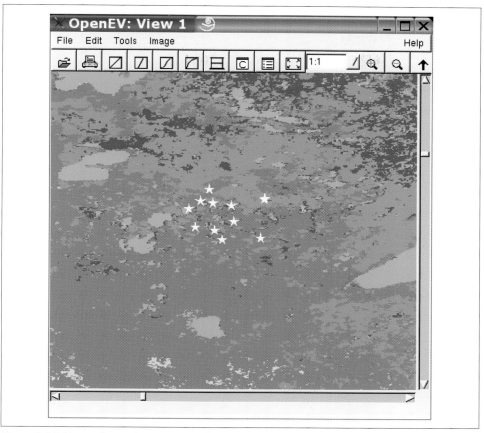

Figure 8-16. Zoomed in to the airports with the land cover image shown in the background

OpenEV and GDAL-based applications can read this image format. Add the image to a normal OpenEV view, and you will see that the image is grayscale—sometimes referred to as black and white (though that isn't technically correct). When you switch into 3D mode, black represents the lowest elevations in your model, and white represents the highest elevations.

The hibbing-w image is a good example of a smooth progression of shades from black to white, as shown in Figure 8-17 (in normal 2D mode). This is ideal. A DEM that has a very limited color gradient, with sharp contrasts, produces a chunky and unrealistic-looking surface. It would ultimately be useless unless you wanted an unnatural appearance.

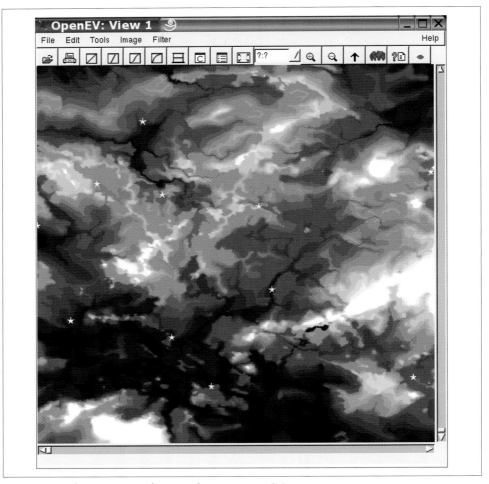

Figure 8-17. The DEM image for part of Minnesota, U.S.A.

Preparing the drape image

The other image you need is called the drape image. It's overlaid or draped on top of the DEM. The DEM surface itself isn't visible except by seeing the shapes and contours of the drape image laying on it.

Any image can be draped on the DEM, but it's not as easy as it sounds. There are some strict requirements you need to follow to get meaningful results.

The drape and DEM image sizes or extents must match, or the coordinate systems must be identical and overlap each other. You can have a high-resolution DEM with a lower resolution drape image, but the drape image must fall on top of the DEM to be shown properly.

One way to ensure that your drape image is useful is to have OpenEV output snapshots of your DEM and drape image to new files. In this example, the drape and DEM images are created by turning on various layers and printing them into new TIFF images.

You start by loading OpenEV with the DEM image and some of the workshop data layers. Remember to use the data in lat/long coordinates described earlier so it matches the DEM projection.

Now, with all layers except the DEM turned off, zoom in to the image. To take a snapshot of this DEM, use the Print command under the File menu. In the Print window, set the following:

```
Driver: TIFF
Device: FILE
File: <path to a local folder>/dem.tif
Output Type: Greyscale
Resolution: 1
```

Figure 8-18 shows how to put these values into the print window.

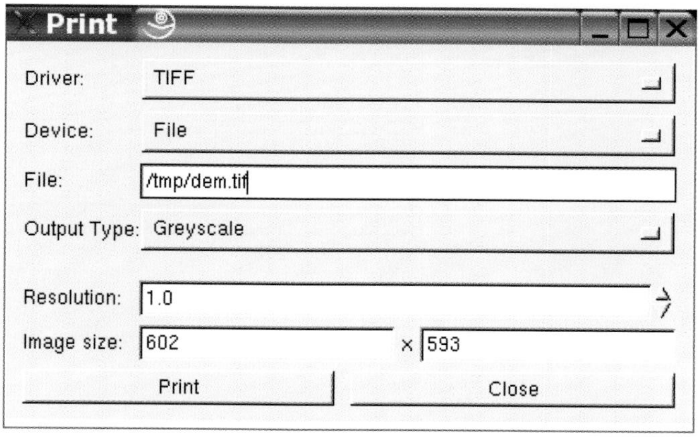

Figure 8-18. Printing the DEM map into an image file

When you press the Print button, OpenEV takes the contents of the View and outputs it to the new image file you specify. The same thing is done to create the drape image.

The main thing to remember when creating your drape image is not to move around in the view. Don't zoom in or out but keep looking at the same location that was used to print the DEM image. Turn on different layers: water, roads and the land cover image for example, as shown in Figure 8-19. Then go through the same print process as earlier, changing the File setting to call the file *drape.tif* instead of *dem.tif*. Be sure to switch Output Type to color if applicable.

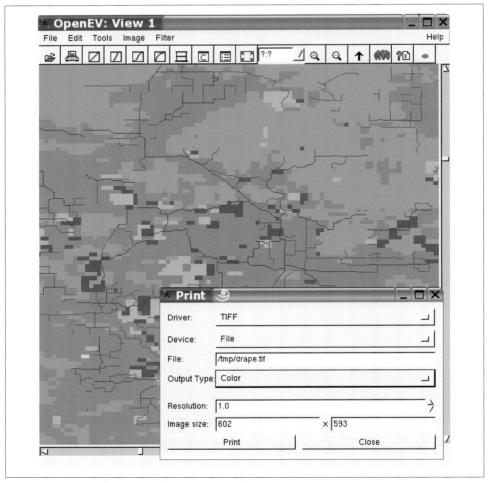

Figure 8-19. Using the print window to output a drape image

Initiating the 3D view

You are now ready to combine the DEM and drape images to create a 3D perspective. Select New View from the File menu to create a new working space without closing View 1. Then, in that new view, select Open 3D from the File menu. This displays a new window (see Figure 8-20), prompting you to select two different images: the DEM in the upper selection box and the Drape image in the lower one. Find the images you created earlier, and enter them into the filename selection boxes. Leave the rest of the options with their default settings, and press OK.

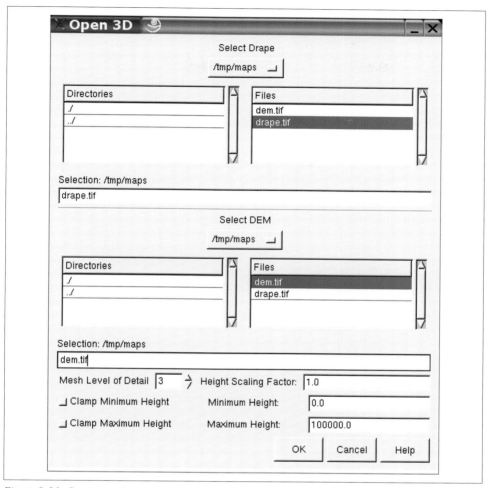

Figure 8-20. Creating a 3D view

OpenEV then creates the default perspective of your 3D view as shown in Figure 8-21.

The background is black, and the color drape image is shown with dips and bumps conforming to the DEM underneath. You can now navigate your way through the image and also raise or flatten the DEM further.

Navigating the 3D view

The controls for navigating in the 3D view aren't always easy to use but are sufficient for getting a quick perspective of your data. Navigating the 3D view isn't very

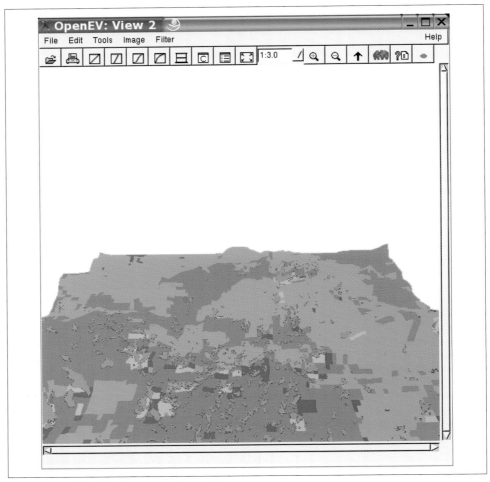

Figure 8-21. The default 3D view of a model

intuitive if you are new to the concept. Keep in mind that OpenEV is tracking several things about your 3D model and your location. The view acts like a camera, which requires you to look through a viewfinder. The camera is always looking at the subject, in this case the 3D model, from a certain location in space. By default, the view camera is positioned higher than the model and not right over it. A specific part of the model is in the center of the view, and the camera is tilted to a certain angle.

As in the normal 2D view, you zoom in to the model by holding down the left mouse button. Where the cursor is pointing is irrelevant. It always zooms in to the center of the view.

Moving the mouse while holding down the left mouse button the pivots the camera—both horizontally and vertically. This is where navigation can become a bit tricky. If you pause for a split second while pivoting your camera, OpenEV will start zooming again right away.

To drop the camera up and down or slide it left or right, hold down the control (CTRL) key while dragging with the left mouse button. Again, be aware that zooming will begin if you stop moving and continue to hold down the left mouse button.

There are some other keyboard controls that do the same tasks as the mouse commands. Page Up/Page Down zooms in/out. Pressing Shift while doing this makes it zoom faster. The keyboard arrow buttons move the camera up/down and left/right. The Home key returns you to the initial 3D view. This is especially useful if you get lost or are still learning to navigate.

It is possible to know the exact location of the camera and to change it manually by setting the camera coordinates. This is helpful if you want to recreate a scene at a later date. To do so, use the 3D Position options, found under the Edit menu. As seen in Figure 8-22, it lists the X,Y, and Z position of your camera as well as where the camera is looking on the model in the center of your view. These position values refer to pixel row and columns. You can change any of these values and the view will be updated. Simply change the value, and press Enter or Tab into the next field.

Every 3D model has a setting for a height or Z scaling factor. This is the amount that the DEM is stretched vertically, giving it the 3D appearance. Other applications and cartographic processes refer to this type of setting as *vertical exaggeration*. The default in OpenEV is 1.0 and is set in the Open 3D window before initiating your 3D view. If the setting is too low, your model will look flat; if too high, your model will look jagged or meaningless. This setting can be changed while viewing your 3D model using the plus + or minus - keys. Combining them with the Shift key allows you to rapidly increase or decrease the scaling factor. In Figure 8-22, the Z scaling factor is reduced to make the landscape look more realistic.

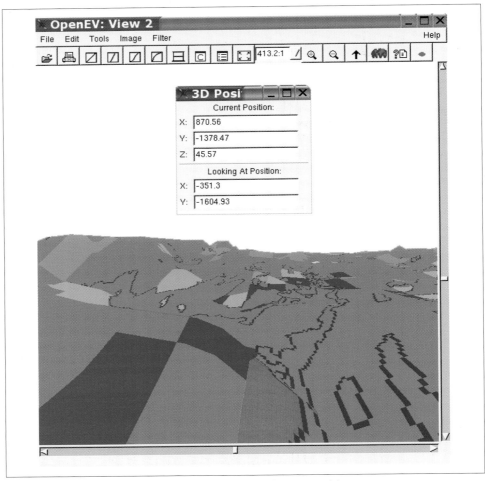

Figure 8-22. The 3D position window showing camera location and focus

## CHAPTER 9

Create and Edit Personal Map Data

Some projects have more than enough data available to create a useful map, but there are often times when you need to create your own data. This chapter will help guide you through the process of creating your own data from scratch. A few simple tools are all you need to get started. You will learn to use OpenEV with a simple base map to create your own map layers.

Planning Your Map

Planning your map at the outset can save you tremendous amounts of time later. Evaluating what you want to do, what you have to work with, and what you need to collect will help you make realistic decisions about your project.

Choosing a General Scale and Extent

The size and scale of the map you are making will affect various parts of your project. If you want a wall-size map covering your neighborhood, you will have very different requirements than someone planning a world map for a small book. You need to ensure that the data you create will work well with your intended map. Here are some questions to consider:

What part of the world do you want your map to cover?
  You may need global, regional, or local-scale data.

What size of map do you want?
  The larger the size, the more detailed the information you will probably want. A small map doesn't show a lot of detail. A large one does.

Will it be interactive or designed for a hardcopy print?
  An interactive map gives the reader more options and flexibility. You have to make sure your data can support those options. If you have a global-scale map and the reader can zoom in to their town, will you have detailed data available at

that scale? A hardcopy print is less flexible but easier to manage because you work with one scale all the time.

How accurate does the data need to be?

Will the product need to be used for precise navigation, or can you handle some error in your data? You need to know your limits so that you don't disappoint your readers.

Identifying Data Requirements for Your Base Map

When creating new or customized data it helps to have a base map to start with. You need data in the correct scale, covering the right area. You can then draw features on top of the base to create custom data. The data itself is the goal of this chapter, not a final map product.

The base map gives you a reference to the real world. You may have an air photo you can scan or a topographic map image downloaded from the Internet. Your base data doesn't necessarily need to look good if you are just using it as a reference for creating data. For example, highway data can be the reference for roughly locating towns. Since all highways won't be visible at a country-wide map scale, they won't end up on your final map.

When considering your base map requirements, keep in mind that global scale datasets are available but are often very coarse. There are a lot of detailed air photo and road line files available for the United States. You can probably even locate your house. Canada has a handful of satellite images available for most of the country but not to a scale you can use to locate a home. Other countries have varying levels of data available.

Chapter 5 has a list of data sources that can help you find useful base map data.

What Are Your Sources?

Once you've figured out your base map requirements, you need to find the appropriate data so, where do you go to get data? There are many options.

GPS

Global positioning system receivers can be an excellent source for getting locations of interest on to a map. However, receivers don't always come with programs for getting data out of them in a digital form. If you can get your GPS data into a text file, or better yet a GIS shapefile, you can start using it pretty quickly in your maps. You can even read coordinates off the screen of a receiver and type them into a spreadsheet or text file. You'll find some ways to access data from a GPS receiver in the O'Reilly book *Mapping Hacks*.

A comma-separated values (CSV) file can be converted using the GDAL/OGR utility `ogr2ogr`, or used in MapServer without conversion. However, it requires the use of the Virtual Data Source driver for OGR. See the Virtual Data Source section in Appendix B to learn how to do this.

See Chapter 7 for general data conversion examples using `ogr2ogr` and Chapter 10 for how to set up a MapServer application to access OGR data sources.

Air photo interpretation

Air photos can be an excellent source for both a base map or locating features of interest. Digital air photos are ideal for getting started quickly. If they aren't available don't despair; you might be able to just scan a printed air photo. A printed air photo can usually be obtained for a reasonable price from a local government map/ photo sales office. Purchasing digital images (e.g., satellite imagery) is also possible but often at a premium price.

A digital photo doesn't have to be sophisticated to be useful. You may find a photo or image of a scanned map on the Internet. If it provides a good frame of reference as a base, it can work.

Your photo image will need to be geo-referenced. *Geo-referencing* is the process of taking an image or other map data and giving it coordinates. You might specify what the coordinates of the corners of the image are. When you use it as a base map, your new data will be positioned somewhere in the real world. Other geo-referenced data will then be displayed in the same position. More on this is discussed in the "Preprocessing Data Examples" section later in this chapter.

Some photos are unsuitable for base maps. Oblique air photos (taken from an angle other than straight down) or those taken from the ground can't be geo-referenced.

When creating new data using a photo base, you go through a process of digitizing a feature. *Digitizing* is the process of identifying features on the photo base by drawing points, lines, or polygons showing their location. Information is then assigned to those features to identify them later, such as a road name.

Derived products

Sometimes your data is almost exactly what you need, but it requires some modifications. For example, you might have data for all the counties in your state, but only need data for three. You need to remove the unwanted parts. Utilities such as `ogr2ogr` and `gdal_translate` allow you to select portions of data and put it into new files, which make your work more efficient and reduces computing resources required for the task. See Chapter 4 for more on these utilities.

Your information may also need further analysis. For example, you want to map features within a certain distance of a stream. If you already have the stream line data, you can create a buffer or area around them to show your area of interest. Two datasets might also be overlaid or intersected to create a new set of information. Deriving products from a more basic source is typical for custom mapping projects.

 A powerful new mapping tool from Google has recently been unveiled that includes street level mapping and satellite imagery (*http://maps. google.com*).

Local knowledge

Sometimes the most satisfying map projects involve taking personal knowledge or experiences and putting them on a map. This is information that no one else may be able to map (or want to).

You can represent this information in several ways, including drawing on a photo, listing a set of coordinates, referring to place names, postal codes, etc.

For mapping street addresses, online street mapping applications such as MapQuest (*http://mapquest.com*) can serve as a useful point of orientation. MapQuest produces a map image showing you the location of a certain street address. There are limitations to using this in your own projects, but it is a great tool for getting your bearings or comparing one address to another. O'Reilly's *Mapping Hacks* also has some great examples that use these kinds of data.

Ultimately, to map these locations you need some coordinates or a GIS data file. Compiling a list of coordinates can be as easy as putting them into a text file or spreadsheet. If you plan to use MapServer, you can also put coordinates right in the configuration map file. If you can do some programming, various tools are available that allow you to create GIS data files from other sources. For example, you could use MapServer MapScript and write a Python script to convert a text file into a shapefile.

Preprocessing Data Examples

Projects in this chapter focus on the city of Kelowna, Canada. In the summer of 2003, there were massive fires in the area. It was a very destructive fire season, destroying many homes. This area is used as a case study throughout the rest of this chapter as you work through a personal mapping project in the area. Many of the typical problems, like trying to find good base map data, are discussed.

In order to use base map data, you need to do some data preprocessing. This often involves clipping out areas of interest or projecting information into a common coordinate system.

Clipping Out an Area of Interest

The satellite image used for this project covered a much broader area than was needed. Unnecessary portions of the image were clipped off, speeding up loading and making the image a more manageable size.

 Satellite imagery of Canada is readily available from the government's GeoGratis data site (*http://geogratis.cgdi.gc.ca/*). The scene for Kelowna is path 45 and row 25; you can grab the image file from the Landsat 7 download directory (*/download/landsat_7/ortho/geotiff/utm/ 045025/*). The files are organized and named based on the path, row, date, projection, and the band of data in the file. The file *...743_ utm10.tif* contains a preprocessed color composite using bands 7, 4, and 3 to represent red, green, and blue colors in the image.

I used OpenEV to view the file and determine the area of interest. Figure 9-1 shows the whole image or *scene*.

The large lake in the bottom half of the image is Okanagan Lake. After zooming in to the general area of interest, the Draw Region Of Interest (ROI) tool is used to select a rectangle. The Draw ROI tool is on the Edit Toolbar, which can be found in the Edit menu. To use the ROI tool, select the tool and drag a rectangle over the area. It creates an orange rectangle and leaves it on the screen, as shown in Figure 9-2.

This area is then exported to a new file. To do this, use the File → Export tool. The Export window provides several options as shown in Figure 9-3. There is a small button near the bottom of the window that shows Advanced Options.

The filename of the image that will be created is entered into the Set Output box. This tool automatically exports the whole image to a new file, but only the selected region needs to be exported. To do this, select the Window Input File button. The four text entry boxes in the Input Window area show numbers that correspond to the pixel numbers of the image that will be exported. Only the pixels in the portion of the image identified as the ROI should be used.

 A bug with the software sometimes requires you to redefine your ROI after the Window Input File option is selected. If you want to use the ROI that is already drawn, you can click on one edge of the ROI box in the view; the text boxes are then updated.

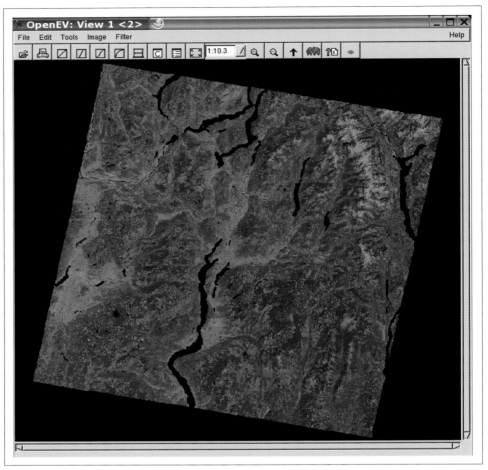

Figure 9-1. Landsat image of the Kelowna, Canada area

When you press the Export button, it creates the image using only the region you specify.

Now the original image isn't needed, and the new image can be loaded into OpenEV. Figure 9-4 shows the new image being displayed.

Now you have a more manageable image to work with, and it is nicely clipped to the area of interest. You can clearly see changes in vegetation cover and urban areas. The urban areas are gray, thicker forests are a darker green, brighter green are thinned forests, etc. The data is fairly low resolution, but if you zoom in to the city you can almost find your way around the main streets. The lower part of the image shows some hilly landforms; this is the area of Okanagan Mountain Park, where the fire began. The image shows this area before the fire occurred.

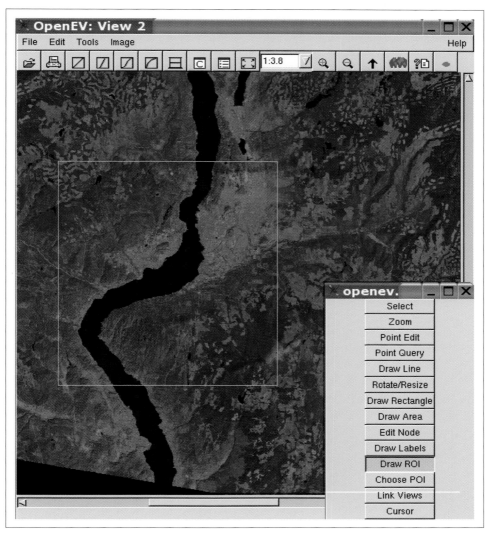

Figure 9-2. Defining a region of interest using the Draw ROI tool

This project will use a coordinate of a location from a GPS receiver. Because it is a single point, it is easy to just write down the coordinate off the receiver's screen rather than exporting it to a file.

The point was recorded using latitude and longitude geographic coordinates. The image is in a different spatial reference system that uses the UTM projection. The coordinates can be converted into UTM, or the image can be transformed into geographic coordinates (e.g., decimal degrees). The latter can be easiest because you

![GDAL Export Tool interface screenshot]

```
GDAL Export Tool                                                    _ □ X

Data Files
  [  Set Input  ]  /data/045025_0100_010703_l7_743_utm10.tif
  [  Set Output ]  /data/kelowna.tif

Basic Options
  Output Format:        GTiff                              ▾
  Output Resolution:    Full                               ▾

  ☐ Advanced Options
  Input Window
  Start Line:    4687          Start Pixel:    2321
  Num. of Lines: 1206          Num. of Pixels: 1168

  Interactive Options
  ☐ Window Input File
  ☐ Scale to View Settings
  [    Active Layer->Input Filename    ]  [    Draw ROI mode    ]
  [           Export            ]         [         Close        ]
```

Figure 9-3. Using the Export option in OpenEV

may end up using other data from global datasets, which are typically stored in decimal degrees.

Use the GDAL utility gdalwarp to transform the image. It is a Python script that can transform rasters between different coordinate systems, often referred to as reprojecting. The *kelowna.tif* image must be removed from OpenEV before reprojecting.

 GDAL utilities, including gdalwarp, are available in the FWTools package. Instructions for acquiring and installing FWTools can be found in Chapter 6.

The options for this command are formed in a similar way to projection exercises elsewhere in this book (e.g., Chapter 7 and Appendix A). From the command line specify the command name, the target spatial reference system (-t_srs), and the source/target filenames.

```
> gdalwarp -t_srs "EPSG:4326" kelowna.tif kelowna_ll.tif

Creating output file that is 1489P x 992L.
:0...10...20...30...40...50...60...70...80...90...100 - done.
```

Figure 9-4. Viewing the clipped image

The EPSG code system is a shorthand way of specifying a projection and other coordinate transformation parameters. The EPSG code 4326 represents the lat/long degrees coordinate system. Otherwise, you would have to use the projection name and ellipsoid:

```
-t_srs "+proj=longlat +ellps=WGS84 +datum=WGS84"
```

To transform data between coordinate systems, programs such as gdalwarp must know what the source coordinate system is and what the output system will be. This often requires the -s_srs (source spatial reference system) option. Because the source image has this coordinate system information already encoded into it, you don't need to explicitly tell gdalwarp what it is. It will find the information in the file and automatically apply it.

There is more information on projections, ellipsoids, and EPSG codes in Appendix A.

The resulting image looks slightly warped. Instead of being in UTM meter coordinates, all points on the map are in latitude/longitude decimal degree coordinates. Figure 9-5 shows the new image. When you move your cursor over the image, the coordinates show in the status bar at the bottom of the View window.

This image is now ready to use as a base map for creating your own data.

Starting to Draw Your Map Features

Once the base map is ready to be used, you can start to create new map data. This following example results in a simple map showing a home in Kelowna and the driving path to the fire burning in a nearby park. This involves a few different types of data: a point location of the home, a road line, and the area encompassing the fire.

Mapping locations of interest (point data)

With OpenEV open and the satellite image as the background layer, you are almost ready to start drawing points (a.k.a. digitizing). First you need to create a new vector layer that will store the point locations. This is done by clicking the New Layer button in the Layers window. It is the bottom-left button that looks like a page, as shown in Figure 9-6.

When the new layer is created, it is given the default name UserShapes_1. This layer is saved as a shapefile. Shapefiles are limited to holding one type of data at a time including points, lines, or polygons. If you create a point, it only stores points. Right-click on the new layer, and rename it Home in the properties window. You may need to turn the layer off and back on for the title to change.

Next, open up the Edit Toolbar from the Edit menu. The tool called Point Edit allows you to draw points on the map and store them in the currently selected layer. In Figure 9-7, the tool was selected and then used to identify a location near downtown Kelowna. The location was based on the coordinate: 119.491°W, 49.882°N. To find this location, you move your pointer over the map and watch the coordinates in the status bar change. When you get to that coordinate, click the mouse button. The location is drawn as a green square, according to the default properties of the new layer.

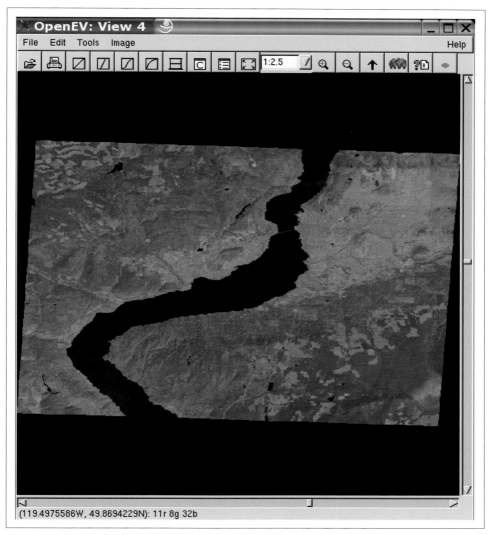

Figure 9-5. Image of Kelowna transformed from UTM to geographic coordinates

To save the new location to a shapefile, make sure the layer is still selected or active in the Layers window. From the File menu, select Save Vector Layer. A dialog box pops up asking for the location and name of the file to create. Store the file in the same folder as the satellite image so they are easy to find. Call the layer home.shp. To test that the layer saved properly, turn off the new layer you have showing and use File → Open to open the shape file you just saved. To remove points or move existing points, use the Select tool, and click on the point. You can click and drag to move the point.

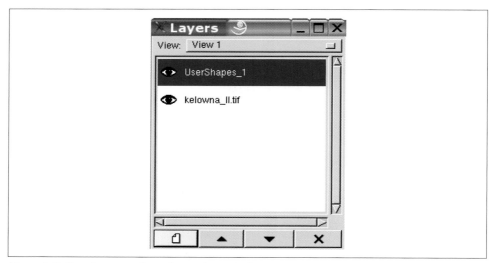

Figure 9-6. Creating a new layer for storing point locations

 Don't remove your new temporary working layer from the layer list yet. Loading in the saved shapefile is only a test to show you that saving works. In the next section, you will still need access to the new layer you create, not the saved shapefile.

Creating and saving tabular attributes

The geographic location isn't the only thing you'll want to save. Sometimes you will want to save an attribute to identify the point later on.

 An attribute is often called a field or column and is stored in the *.dbf* file associated with a shapefile.

With the new layer selected, go to the Tools menu, and select Tabular Shapes Grid. This shows an empty attribute table for the layer. If you do this with another vector layer that already has attributes, it will show those values. Your point will have a number identifier (e.g., 0) but nothing else to describe what the point represents. You can create a new attribute by clicking inside the Tabular Shapes Attribute window. A menu pops up giving you the Edit Schema option, as shown in Figure 9-8.

 You can only edit the schema of a new layer—one that hasn't been saved yet. It is often best to set up your attributes before saving the vector layer to a file.

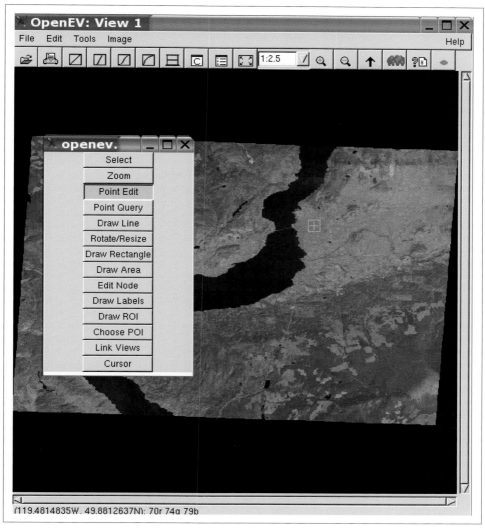

Figure 9-7. Using the Point Edit tool to draw a location on the map

The Schema window that appears allows you to create a new attribute. In Figure 9-9 a new attribute has been created, called Placename. This is done by typing the name of the new attribute into the Name box near the bottom of the window, then pressing the Add button (leaving the default type as string and width as 20). The description of the attribute is listed at the top of the window.

Close the Schema window, and you are brought back to the attribute listing. Now there is a new column, as in Figure 9-10. You can click inside that column and type in a value for the Placename attribute for the point created earlier. Try typing in My

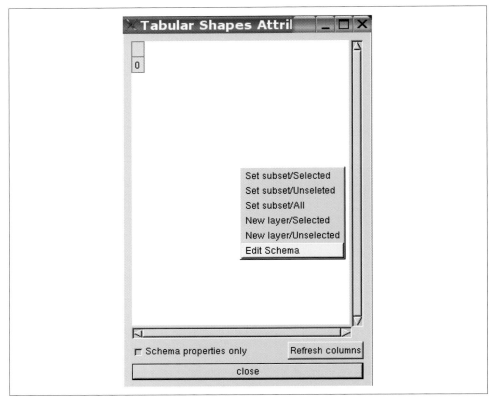

Figure 9-8. Viewing the attributes of your shape

Place and then press Enter to save the change. This change is saved automatically, and no manual resaving of the file is required.

You can test out this attribute by using it to label your new point. To enable labels, right-click on the layer name in the Layers window. This brings up the properties of the layer. Now, select the Draw Styles tab. Near the bottom is an option called Label Field. You should be able to change this from disabled to Placename. As shown in Figure 9-11, your view window should now display the label for the point you created.

Mapping roads and transportation paths (linear data)

Now that you have a point showing where the house is you're ready to draw some more details about the transportation infrastructure. This is a bit more complex because line features are more than just a point. In fact, line features are a series of points strung together and often referred to as line strings. Mapping road lines involves drawing a series of points for each line and saving them to a new shapefile.

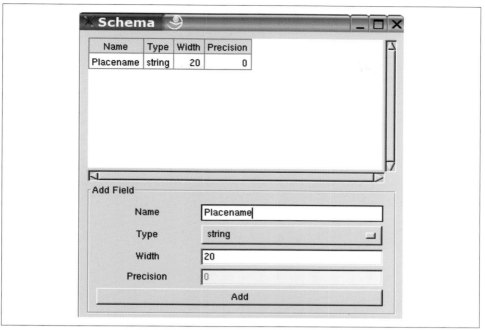

Figure 9-9. Adding a new attribute using the Schema editor

Figure 9-10. A new attribute added to the point

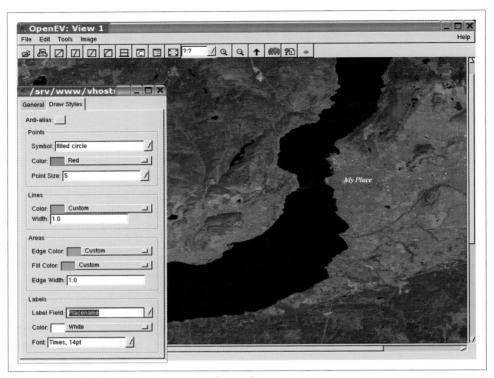

Figure 9-11. Labeling the new point using the attribute

Open the Layers window again, and click the New Layer button shown by the white-page icon. The typical new layer is created with a basic name such as UserShapes. Change the name to reflect the type of data being created, such as Roads.

From the Edit Toolbar (activated under the Edit menu), you will find a Draw Line tool. This is much like the Point Edit tool, but is made for lines, not points. In this project, a line is drawn showing the rough driving path from a park to the house (My Place). A base map of the area from a government web site helps show where the driving path should be drawn.

With the additional base map showing road lines, you can now draw on top of those lines, following the path to the park. Figure 9-12 shows the rough red line drawn as a path. Each point clicked becomes a vertex in the line. OpenEV shows these as squares. After the last vertex is created, press the right mouse button to finish drawing. That line is now complete. You can modify the settings for the Roads layer to draw the line a bit thicker, making it easier to see on top of the busy base map. Note that the base map image is fairly poor resolution. That doesn't matter because it will be tossed away when finished drawing; it's used here as a temporary reference.

Grabbing a Base Map Layer from a WMS

To get this base map you must use a WMS request through a URL (as discussed in Chapter 12), and feed it the extent coordinates of the *kelowna_ll.tif* file. You can get the coordinates by using the gdalinfo command and then create a World File for the image to geo-reference it. Here is the command used to grab the image (some layer names are removed and spaces added to try to keep it simple. It is all one line, with no spaces):

```
> wget -O msrm_wms.jpg
"http://libcwms.gov.bc.ca
/wmsconnector/com.esri.wsit.WMSServlet
/ogc_layer_service?request=GetMap
&version=1.1.1&srs=EPSG:4326
&format=image/jpeg
&layers=NTS_BC_RIV_LAKE_WET_POLYS_125M,
NTS_BC_CONTOUR_LINES_125M,
NTS_BC_TRANSPORT_LINES_125M,
NTS_BC_WATER_LINES_125M,
NTS_BC_ANNO
&bbox=-119.8232227,49.6477753,
-119.3140010,49.9870285
&width=745&height=496
&styles"
```

Of course, if you want to use this data in a MapServer application, you don't have to download the image and can have the image requested in real time from the WMS service. A WMS tool is currently being developed for OpenEV.

For more on world files and map projections see Appendix A. See Chapter 12 for using web services like WMS.

Now that you have a road line, you can save it to a shape file. As with the point data, just select that layer from the Layers window, and then use the Save Vector Layer option under the File menu to save it as *roads.shp*.

Mapping regions of interest (area/polygons data)

The third part of this mapping project is to draw the area of the forest fire. This won't be a point or a line, but a polygon or area showing the extent of a feature. To help with this task, a few satellite images that were taken during or after the fire are used. Two main barriers come up, one of resolution and the other a lack of geo-referencing information. Both images and their shortcomings are presented to give you an idea of the thought process and the compromises that need to be made.

The first image is from *http://rapidfire.sci.gsfc.nasa.gov/gallery/?2003245-0902/ PacificNW.A2003245.2055.250m.jpg.* An overview of this image, with the point from home.shp, can be seen in Figure 9-13.

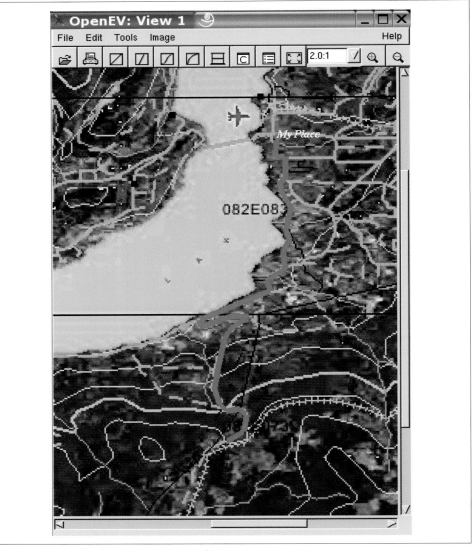

Figure 9-12. Road line/path drawn on top of base map

The web site at *http://rapidfire.sci.gsfc.nasa.gov/gallery/* is a great resource! It includes various scales of real-time imagery showing thousands of events from around the globe.

Figure 9-13. A real-time image of fires in the Pacific Northwest

The great thing about this image was that you can download the world file for the image too. This is the geo-referencing information needed to geographically position the image in OpenEV (and other GIS/mapping programs). The link to the world file is at the top of the page. Be sure to save it with the same filename prefix as the image. For these images, the filename suffix, or extension, is *jgw*. Be sure to save it with the proper name, or the image won't find the geo-referencing information. The only problem with this image is that it's very low resolution. My search for a better image led to:

http://earthobservatory.nasa.gov/Newsroom/NewImages/Images/okanagan_ast_ 2003245_lrg.jpg

It's good and has much higher resolution, showing the fire very well, as seen in Figure 9-14.

This image isn't geo-referenced. Because only the general extent of the fire is needed, it isn't worth the trouble of geo-referencing. It is possible to do so using the gdal_ translate utility with the -gcp option, but it can be very tedious.

Figure 9-14. A higher resolution image of the Okanagan Mountain Park fire

The final decision is to use the first image. It is lower resolution, but with little effort, it's ready to work with OpenEV.

Add the fire image layer, and you will see that it overlaps the Kelowna Landsat image very well. Because the base data is no longer in UTM projection, it lines up with this image without any more effort. This image is fairly low resolution, but it does show the rough area of the fire as well as smoke from the eastern portion as it still burns.

Create a new layer to save the polygon data to, and call it Fire_Area. Then from the Edit Toolbar, select the Draw Area tool. Draw the outline of the burned area. Don't be too worried about accuracy because the end product isn't going to be a highly detailed map—just a general overview. Figure 9-15 shows the process of drawing the polygon.

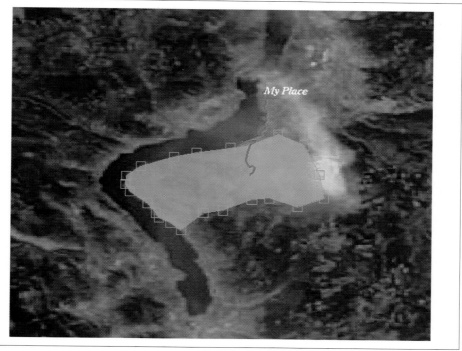

Figure 9-15. An area drawn to shown the extent of the fire

Each vertex helps to define the outer edge of the area. When done, press the right mouse button to complete the drawing. Then use Save Vector Layer to put the Fire_ Area layer into a shape file called *fire_area.shp*.

> You may notice that the extent of the fire shown on this image is quite different from the image in Figure 9-14. This is because Figure 9-15 was taken at an earlier time.

These examples have produced a few different images and three vector data shape-files. These can now be used in a MapServer-based interactive web map (Chapters 10 and 11), or the data can be made available to others through a web service (Chapter 12). Either way, you have made the basic map data and have the flexibility to use it in any program that supports these data formats.

CHAPTER 10

Creating Static Maps

Putting map data into an Internet page or interactive web site may be easier than you think. MapServer is often all you need to make it happen. This chapter shows you how to use MapServer to get your data up on a web site as quickly as possible. Even if what you really want is interactive maps, using MapServer to create static maps may be useful at times, and it's a good way to learn about the program.

MapServer is best known for its web mapping capabilities, but it also comes with a set of standalone command-line tools for personal use. These can be used to create static map images for web pages, documents, or email. This chapter starts with a description of each utility, then walks you through several common mapping tasks using a simple map file. Chapter 4 discussed the process of installing or compiling these utilities while Chapter 11 focuses on using MapServer as an interactive web mapping solution.

MapServer Utilities

MapServer comes with much more than the standard *mapserv* executable file. The following programs are compiled at the same time as the *mapserv* file and are usually included in any MapServer installation package. MapServer is more than just a web mapping program. To demonstrate this, the chapter begins with an introduction to some command-line tools. They can be used as standalone applications for making maps without a web server. Details about each program are included.

legend

> Creates a graphic image of a legend based on the symbols used to draw layers specified in a map file.

scalebar

> Produces a graphic image of a scalebar based on the options in a map file, using the map extent as set in the map file.

shp2img

Produces a map image based on a map file. Map extents and desired layers can be set. The options are robust enough that a simple desktop custom application could use this tool to create maps. Similar to *shp2pdf*, which outputs a PDF rather than just an image.

shp2pdf

Produces an output PDF file that includes a map based on the input map file. This requires that MapServer was compiled with PDF support and has similar syntax as shp2img.

shptree

Adds an index (quad-tree based) to a shapefile that can improve performance when creating maps from large shapefiles. More information about the different options can be obtained from the mailing list archives or online documentation, but are outside the scope of this chapter.

tile4ms

Creates an overview shapefile that points to the location of individual files and their extent rectangles. This output shapefile can be used by MapServer to reference a large number of shapefiles (or other support data formats) that are in multiple pieces. This is helpful because you don't have to append them all together or add dozens of layers in the map file. Instead, the tile index tells MapServer what layers are available and where they are geographically. It is more efficient because the extent rectangles are used as an index to find only those tiles of interest within the current map extent. It is recommended to also run shptree on the index that you create. ogrtindex and gdaltindex, part of the GDAL/OGR packages, are similar. These are highly recommended because they can index more than just shapefiles.

sortshp

Sorts a shapefile using a field in the table, rearranging the physical order of features in the file. This can be helpful when order is important for display or query optimization.

For historical reasons, the prefix shp is used for some of the programs. They were originally created to convert shapefiles into images. Now they take a MapServer map file and output an image. Therefore, in most cases the shp prefix is a misnomer because shapefiles may not actually be involved; MapServer can access dozens of different types of data.

Sample Uses of the Command-Line Utilities

When MapServer runs as a web mapping application it produces various graphic images. A map image is one of them. It can also produce an image of a scale bar, a reference map, and a legend. The command-line utilities let you create these manually (or scripted through your favorite scripting language). The following examples give a feel for the process of creating some basic results using these programs. These examples use the utilities from a typical MapServer installation as described in Chapter 4.

Acquire Some Mapping Data

A simple world map boundary dataset will be used for this example. This shapefile contains boundaries of the country borders for the world and are available from the FreeGIS (*http://www.freegis.org*) web site at *http://ftp.intevation.de/freegis/worlddata/ freegis_worlddata-0.1_simpl.tar.gz.*

This version contains simplified, lower-resolution boundaries and are about 3.7 MB in size. The full resolution boundaries take more effort for MapServer to display and are a larger file at over 30 MB.

You can use the full resolution data for the exercises in this chapter, but the files are large enough to require optimization to be effective. The exercises will run more slowly than with the simplified boundaries. For further exploration of MapServer, the higher resolution boundaries make a great dataset to work with. You can download them from *http://ftp.intevation.de/freegis/worlddata/freegis_worlddata-0.1.tar.gz.*

The first thing to do is check out the data. This is done using the `ogrinfo` tool as described in Chapter 6. This isn't a MapServer utility but is a valuable tool for getting started, as shown in Example 10-1.

Example 10-1. Using ogrinfo to examine the contents of the world countries shapefile

```
> ogrinfo countries_simpl.shp -al -summary
INFO: Open of 'countries_simpl.shp'
using driver 'ESRI Shapefile' successful.

Layer name: countries_simpl
Geometry: Polygon
Feature Count: 3901
Extent: (-179.999900, -89.999900) - (179.999900, 83.627357)
Layer SRS WKT:
(unknown)
gid: Integer (11.0)
cat: Integer (11.0)
fibs: String (2.0)
name: String (255.0)
f_code: String (255.0)
total: Integer (11.0)
```

```
male: Integer (11.0)
female: Integer (11.0)
ratio: Real (24.15)
```

This example shows several key pieces of information prior to building the MapServer map file.

```
Geometry: Polygon
```

The shapefile holds polygon data. MapServer can shade the polygon areas or just draw the outline of the polygons. If the geometry was line or linestring, it wouldn't be possible to fill the polygons with a color.

```
Feature Count: 3901
```

The feature count shows that there are many (3,901 to be exact) polygons in this file. If it said there were no features, that would tell me there is something wrong with the file.

```
Extent: (-179.999900, -89.999900) - (179.999900, 83.627357)
```

ogrinfo shows that the data covers almost the entire globe, using latitude and longitude coordinates. The first pair of numbers describes the most southwestern corner of the data. The second pair of numbers describes the most northeastern extent. Therefore when making a map file, set it up so that the map shows the entire globe from -180,-90 to 180,90 degrees.

```
Layer SRS WKT:
(unknown)
```

There is no spatial reference system (SRS) set for this shapefile. By looking at the fact that the extent is shown in decimal degrees, it is safe to say that this file contains unprojected geographic coordinates.

```
gid: Integer (11.0)
cat: Integer (11.0)
fibs: String (2.0)
name: String (255.0)
f_code: String (255.0)
total: Integer (11.0)
male: Integer (11.0)
female: Integer (11.0)
```

This is a list of the *attributes* (or fields) that are part of the file. This is helpful to know when adding a label to your map to show, for example, the name of the country. It also indicates that the field called name holds up to 255 characters. Therefore some of the names can be quite long, such as "Macedonia, The Former Yugo. Rep. of".

With this information you are ready to put together a basic map file.

If you want to have a quick look at what countries are included in the shapefile, some common text processing commands can be used to quickly filter the output from ogrinfo. This process is described further in Chapter 6. Here is a short example:

```
> ogrinfo countries_simpl.shp -al | grep name | sort | uniq
Layer name: countries_simpl
  name: String (255.0)
  name (String) = Afghanistan
  name (String) = Albania
  name (String) = Algeria
  name (String) = American Samoa
continued...
```

Creating a Simple MapServer Map File

The map file is the core of MapServer applications. It configures how the map will look, what size it will be, and which layers to show. There are many different configuration settings. Map file reference documents on the MapServer web site are a necessary reference for learning about new features. You can find the documents at *http://mapserver.gis.umn.edu/doc/mapfile-reference.html*.

Map files are simple text files that use a hierarchical, or nested, object structure to define settings for the map. The map file is composed of objects (a.k.a. sections). Each object has a keyword to start and the word END to stop. Objects can have other subobjects within them where applicable. For example, a map layer definition will include objects that define how layers will be drawn or how labels are created for a layer. Example 10-2 shows the most basic possible definition of a map file, using only 15 lines of text.

Example 10-2. A basic map file with one layer and showing the object start and end lines

```
MAP                     # Start of MAP object
  SIZE 600 300
  EXTENT -180 -90 180 90
  LAYER                 # Start of LAYER object
    NAME countries
    TYPE POLYGON
    STATUS DEFAULT
    DATA countries_simpl
    CLASS               # Start of CLASS object
      STYLE             # Start of STYLE object
        OUTLINECOLOR 100 100 100
      END               # End of STYLE object
    END                 # End of CLASS object
  END                   # End of LAYER object
END                     # End of MAP object and map file
```

There are only four objects in this map file:

- MAP object map-wide settings for the whole file
- LAYER object to define the layer to draw in the map
- CLASS object to define classes of settings for the layer
- STYLE object to define how features will be drawn in the class

Figure 10-1 is a graphical representation of the nested hierarchy of objects and properties.

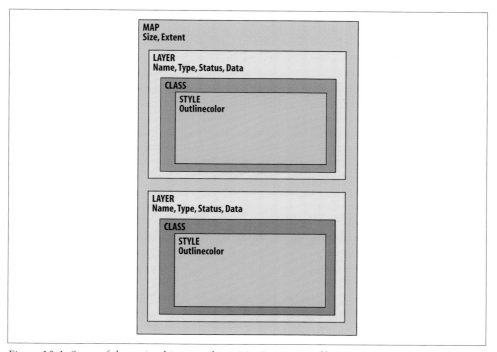

Figure 10-1. Some of the main objects used in a MapServer map file

These objects are nested within each other. Each object has different types of settings. The SIZE and EXTENT settings are part of the MAP object. The LAYER object has a NAME, TYPE, STATUS, and DATA setting. The CLASS object has no settings in this example, but holds the STYLE object, which defines what OUTLINECOLOR to draw the lines.

The DATA setting gives the name of the dataset used for drawing this layer. In these examples, the data is a shapefile called *countries_simpl*. The examples assume that the map file is saved in the same location that you are running the commands from. For more information on other data formats and how to use them in MapServer, see Appendix B.

Map File Rules and Recommendations

Comments can be interspersed throughout the map file using the # symbol. Everything written after the symbol, and on the same line, is ignored by MapServer. Example 10-2 uses comments to show the start and end of the main objects.

Indenting lines is optional but recommended to make your map file more readable. This structure is treated hierarchically by indenting the start of an object and un-indenting the end of the object.

Keywords in the map file can be upper, lower, or mixed case. It is recommended to write object names (such as MAP) and other keywords (such as DATA, COLOR) in upper-case and any items that are values for settings in lowercase (such as filenames, layer names, and comments). This is personal preference, but the convention can make it easier to read.

The text of the map file must be saved into a file on your filesystem. The filename of a map file must have a map suffix. The map file in Example 10-2 was saved as a file named *global.map*.

Values needing quotations can use either single or double quotes. In many cases, quotes are optional. Filenames are a good example. They can be either unquoted, single quoted, or double quoted.

Creating Your First Map Image

The MapServer command shp2img takes the settings in the map file and produces a map image. Example 10-3 and the later Example 10-4 show the syntax of the command as well as an example of how to run it with the *global.map* map file.

Example 10-3. Syntax for using the shp2img command

```
> shp2img
Syntax: shp2img -m [mapfile] -o [image] -e minx miny maxx maxy
                -t -l [layers] -i [format]
  -m mapfile: Map file to operate on - required.
  -i format: Override the IMAGETYPE value to pick output format.
  -t: enable transparency
  -o image: output filename (stdout if not provided)
  -e minx miny maxx maxy: extents to render - optional
  -l layers: layers to enable - optional
  -all_debug n: Set debug level for map and all layers.
  -map_debug n: Set map debug level.
  -layer_debug layer_name n: Set layer debug level.
```

Only the first two options (-m and -o) are used in the following example:

```
> shp2img -m global.map -o mymap.png
```

The *global.map* file assumes that the shapefile *countries_simpl* is located in the same folder as the map file.

This example produces a new file called *mymap.png,* shown in Figure 10-2.

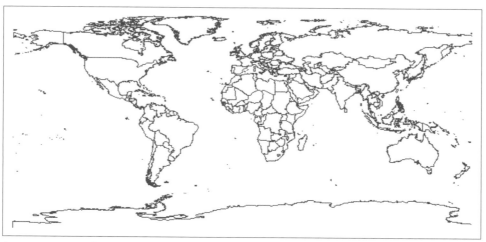

Figure 10-2. Initial map image of country boundaries

When the image is created, you can view it with any image viewing software. Internet web browsers can usually view PNG, JPEG, GIF, and others.

PNG is the Portable Network Graphics image format, and is much like a GIF or JPEG. For more information on the PNG format, see *http://libpng.org/pub/png/.*

Depending on where you got MapServer from or how you compiled it, the images you produce might not be PNG format by default. To explicitly request PNG output files, use the -i option, like:

```
> shp2img -m global.map -o mymap.png -i PNG
```

If you get an error or an image that isn't viewable, your copy of MapServer might not support PNG output. If so, try a JPEG or GIF format. Make sure you change the file extension of the output image to reflect the image format you choose, for example:

```
> shp2img -m global.map -o mymap.jpg -i JPEG
```

For more assistance see the Setting Output Image Formats section at the end of this chapter.

Adding Labels to the Map

The simple map outline used in the previous example is great for new users. With some simple additions to the map file, you can easily add labels to your map. Example 10-4 shows the additional lines required to do this.

Example 10-4. Adding labels to a map

```
MAP
  SIZE 600 300
  EXTENT -180 -90 180 90
  LAYER
    NAME countries
    TYPE POLYGON
    STATUS DEFAULT
    DATA countries_simpl
    LABELITEM 'NAME'
    CLASS
      STYLE
        OUTLINECOLOR 100 100 100
      END
      LABEL
        MINFEATURESIZE 40
      END
    END
  END
END
```

Four more lines were add to the country LAYER object.

```
    LABELITEM 'NAME'
```

This setting tells MapServer what attribute to use to label the polygons. Each country polygon has a set of attributes that can be used to create labels. The LABELITEM setting specifies which one is used. ogrinfo, discussed in Chapter 7, can output a list of the attributes available in the file.

The additional lines were very simple:

```
    LABEL
        MINFEATURESIZE 40
    END
```

The second line is optional but makes the map more readable. There are a lot of ways to control how labels are drawn by MapServer. The MINFEATURESIZE option allowed me to specify a minimum size (number of pixels wide) that a country has to be before it will have a label created for it. Therefore smaller countries don't get labeled because they would be unreadable at this scale anyway. Playing around with the value used for MINFEATURESIZE will yield very different results; try changing it from 40 to 20 or even down to 10.

If the EXTENT line is changed to zoom in to a smaller part of the world, more labels will show because the size of the countries will be larger.

When you rerun the shp2img command as in Example 10-4, it now produces a world map with a few labels, as seen in Figure 10-3.

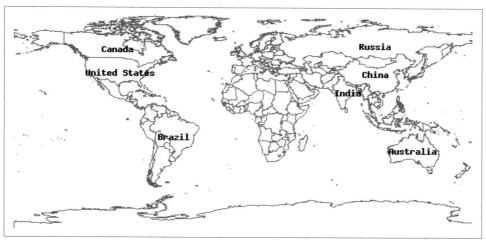

Figure 10-3. World map with country names as labels

Determining the Extent of a Country

The shp2img utility has several other options. One allows you to select a different map EXTENT to override what is defined in the map file. This is very handy because you don't need to change the map file. Simply modify your command by adding the -e parameter and specify an extent as in the map file.

Before using the -e parameter you must choose an area to zoom in to. You can use the ogrinfo utility in concert with the ogr2ogr conversion tool. The ogrinfo command gives you only the overall extent of a given layer; it doesn't report on the extent of a single feature. Therefore, you might want to extract only the features of interest and put them into a temporary shapefile. You can use the ogrinfo command on the new file and then throw the data away.

 You can also open the shapefile with a tool like OpenEV and find the coordinates of an area by zooming in.

Example 10-5 shows an example of this utility assessing the extents of a country.

Example 10-5. Selecting Bulgaria from the countries and putting it into its own shapefile

```
> ogr2ogr -where "name='Bulgaria'" bulgaria.shp countries_simpl.shp
> ogrinfo bulgaria.shp -al -summary

INFO: Open of 'bulgaria.shp'
using driver 'ESRI Shapefile' successful.

Layer name: bulgaria
Geometry: Polygon
Feature Count: 1
Extent: (22.371639, 41.242084) - (28.609278, 44.217640)
continued...
```

Using the -where option with ogr2ogr allows you to convert from one shapefile to a new one, but only transfer certain features, e.g., the boundary of Bulgaria. By running ogrinfo on that new file, you can see what Extent you should use in your map file to focus on that country. You can then use this extent in the shp2img command to create a map, as seen in Figure 10-4.

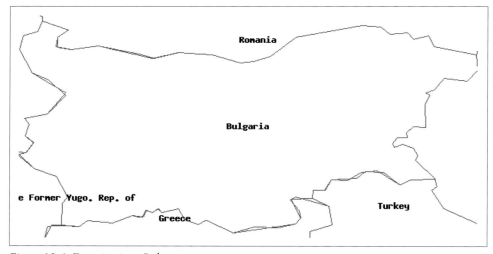

Figure 10-4. Zooming in to Bulgaria

 Beware of using this method with other countries that may not be as neatly packaged as Bulgaria. For example, the United Kingdom has lands outside of the British Isles, so if you create a new file with just the U.K. features in it, you may wonder why the extent is well beyond Europe. If you get an extent that looks wrong to you, consider foreign lands that belong to that country.

Here is an example that uses this information with the -e option:

```
> shp2img -m global.map -o mymap.png -e 22.371639 41.242084 28.609278 44.217640
```

This map shows Bulgaria and some of the surrounding countries.

If you want to zoom out further, decrease the minimum coordinates (the first pair of numbers) and increase the maximum coordinates (the second pair) by one or two degrees like this:

```
> shp2img -m global.map -o mymap.png -e 19 39 31 46
```

The map in Figure 10-5 is zoomed out further, giving a better context for Bulgaria.

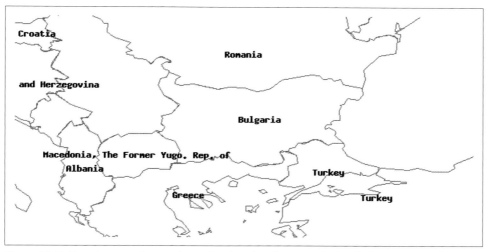

Figure 10-5. Zooming out of a map image by changing the extent in the shp2img command

Color Theming the Map

With a few more lines in the map file, as shown in Example 10-6, you can create a better looking map. Here is a modified map file with a few lines added and a couple changed.

Example 10-6. Color theming a map by creating multiple CLASS objects in a map file

```
MAP
  SIZE 600 300
  EXTENT -180 -90 180 90
  IMAGECOLOR 180 180 250
  LAYER
    NAME countries
    TYPE POLYGON
    STATUS DEFAULT
    DATA countries_simpl
    LABELITEM 'NAME'
    CLASSITEM 'NAME'
    CLASS
      EXPRESSION 'Bulgaria'
      STYLE
```

Example 10-6. Color theming a map by creating multiple CLASS objects in a map file (continued)

```
        OUTLINECOLOR 100 100 100
        COLOR 255 255 150
      END
      LABEL
        SIZE LARGE
        MINFEATURESIZE 40
      END
    END
    CLASS
      EXPRESSION ('[NAME]' ne 'Bulgaria')
      STYLE
        OUTLINECOLOR 100 100 100
        COLOR 200 200 200
      END
    END
  END
END
```

The shp2img command is the same as in the previous example, but produces a colored map showing Bulgaria more clearly. The command is:

```
> shp2img -m global.map -o example6b.png -e 19 39 31 46
```

The extent given by the shp2img command is still zoomed in to Bulgaria. Remember that the -e option overrides the EXTENT setting in the map file.

The result of this map file is shown in Figure 10-6.

Figure 10-6. Simple color theming of countries, highlighting a particular polygon and setting a background color

A few things to notice are three different COLOR settings and the single label:

```
IMAGECOLOR 180 180 250
```

This setting basically makes any place blue where there were no country polygons in the shapefile. IMAGECOLOR is the background color of the map image, which is white by default. In this case it makes an interesting background simulating water.

You may notice that in the map file there are two CLASS...END objects. One tells how to color and label Bulgaria. The other tells how to color all the other countries.

    CLASSITEM 'NAME'

This line sets you up to use multiple classes in your map file. In this case, it says that the NAME attribute is going to be used to filter out certain features on the map. This is done by specifying an EXPRESSION (more on expressions in the next section) for each class, like in the first class:

```
CLASS
    EXPRESSION 'Bulgaria'
    STYLE
        OUTLINECOLOR 100 100 100
        COLOR 255 255 150
    END
    LABEL
        SIZE LARGE
    END
END
```

When drawing this class, MapServer draws only the polygons that have a NAME attribute of 'Bulgaria'. All other polygons or countries aren't drawn in this class. The COLOR setting tells MapServer to fill Bulgaria with a color, and not just draw the outline as before. The only other change in this class is that the label size has been explicitly set a bit larger than the default.

> The default types of MapServer labels (a.k.a. bitmap type font) can be TINY, SMALL, MEDIUM, LARGE, or GIANT. It is also possible to use TrueType fonts, which produce higher quality labels. This requires a few more settings and some font files.
>
> With TrueType fonts you can specify a particular point size (e.g., 12) rather than a subjective size like TINY or LARGE. You have probably encountered TrueType fonts when using a word processing application. You might know a font by its name such as Arial or Times New Roman; these are usually TrueType fonts.

The second class tells how to draw all countries other than Bulgaria.

```
CLASS
    EXPRESSION ('[NAME]' ne 'Bulgaria')
    STYLE
        OUTLINECOLOR 100 100 100
        COLOR 200 200 200
    END
END
```

Notice that there is a more complex expression set for this class. This one ignores Bulgaria but draws all the other countries. The next section discusses expression concepts in more detail.

Understanding Operators

The FILTER and EXPRESSION keywords can use simple or complex expressions to define the set of features to draw. Example 10-6 showed the simple way to use EXPRESSION to define the features for a CLASS. In the example, a single text string is provided. It is quoted, but doesn't need to be. MapServer will look for all occurrences of that string in whatever attribute is set by CLASSITEM.

Logical expressions can also be defined where more than one value in a single attribute needs to be evaluated. Ranges of values and combinations of attributes can be given. Table 10-1 gives a summary of the types of expressions that can be used.

Table 10-1. Logical expression operators and syntax

Operator	Comments	Examples
= eq	Equals or is equal to	('[NAME]' eq 'Canada') ([TOTAL] = 32507874)
ne	Not equal to	('[NAME]' ne 'Canada')
> gt	Greater than	([TOTAL] gt 1000000) ([TOTAL] > 1000000)
< lt	Less than	([TOTAL] lt 1000000) ([TOTAL] < 1000000)
>= ge	Greater than or equal to	([TOTAL] ge 1000000) ([TOTAL] >= 1000000)
<= le	Less than or equal to	([TOTAL] le 1000000) ([TOTAL] <= 1000000)
AND	Where two statements are true	(('[NAME]' ne 'Canada') AND ([TOTAL] > 1000000))
OR	Where one or both statements are true	(('[NAME]' eq 'Canada') OR ('[NAME]' eq 'Brazil'))

There are some exceptions to this table's above rules when using the FILTER option with some data sources, particularly with database connections such as PostGIS:

- The operators eq, ne, gt, lt, ge, and le aren't available.
- Attribute names aren't enclosed in quotes or square brackets. For example: (TOTAL > 1000) is valid, and so is (NAME = 'Canada').

Creating expressions isn't always easy. Here are a few rules to keep in mind:

- Don't put quotes around the whole expression such as "('[COUNTRY]' = 'Canada')".

- Fields holding string/text values must have both the field name and the value quoted, such as: (`'[COUNTRY]' = 'Canada'`).
- Fields holding numeric values must not have their field names or their values quoted, such as (`[TOTAL] = 1000`).

Creating a Map Legend

An important part of any map is the legend describing what colors and symbols mean. MapServer can create legends in realtime when a map is produced, or as a separate image.

To add a legend to your map, you must add a LEGEND...END object to your MAP. Note that this isn't part of a LAYER object. It is part of the overall map object settings. Example 10-7 shows the first few lines of the map file (for context) with a few legend-specific settings highlighted.

Example 10-7. Embedding a legend in a map

```
MAP
  SIZE 600 300
  EXTENT -180 -90 180 90
  IMAGECOLOR 180 180 250

  LEGEND
    STATUS EMBED
    POSITION LR
    TRANSPARENT TRUE
  END
...
```

The status setting can be set to ON, OFF, or EMBED. The EMBED option is a great way to add the legend directly to the map. If you don't use EMBED, then you must create the legend as a separate image (as you will see in a moment). Setting the legend to have a transparent background is also a nice option. If you don't want it to be transparent, then you can remove the TRANSPARENT TRUE line. A default white background will be drawn behind the legend.

One more change is required to make the legend draw. You must have NAME settings for each class. The name given will be the text shown in the legend next to the symbols for that class. For example, add NAME 'Bulgaria' to the first class and NAME 'All Countries' to the second class as in Example 10-8. Until you do so, no legend will be created.

Example 10-8. Add a name to the class so that it shows in the legend

```
...
  CLASS
    NAME 'Bulgaria'
    EXPRESSION 'Bulgaria'
```

Example 10-8. Add a name to the class so that it shows in the legend (continued)

```
    STYLE
      OUTLINECOLOR 100 100 100
      COLOR 255 255 150
    END
    LABEL
      SIZE LARGE
      MINFEATURESIZE 40
    END
  END
  CLASS
    NAME 'All Countries'
    EXPRESSION ('[NAME]' ne 'Bulgaria')
    STYLE
      OUTLINECOLOR 100 100 100
      COLOR 200 200 200
    END
  END
...
```

Rerunning the `shp2img` command as before creates the image shown in Figure 10-7.

Figure 10-7. An embedded legend on the map

The POSITION setting has a few basic options that tell MapServer where to place the legend on the map using a two-letter code for the relative position: lower-right (LR), upper-center (UC), etc.

The legends so far have been embedded in the map image, but you can also create a separate image file that just includes the legend. This is done with the `legend` command:

```
> legend global.map legend.png
```

The legend command creates an image that has just the legend in it as shown in Figure 10-8. It takes two parameters after the command name: first, the map file name and then the output image filename to be created.

Figure 10-8. A legend image created by the legend command

The legend is created according to the settings in the LEGEND object of the map file. You can change certain settings, but the POSITION and EMBED options are effectively ignored. Those options are intended for use with shp2img or with the mapserv web application.

Adding a Scale Bar Using the scalebar Command

A scale bar is a graphic showing the relative distances on the map. It consists of lines or shading and text describing what distance a segment of line in the scale-bar represents. As with legends in the preceding examples, it is simple to add scale-bar settings to your map file. All the options for scale-bar settings are listed in the MapServer map file documentation, under the scale-bar object at *http://mapserver. gis.umn.edu/doc/mapfile-reference.html#scalebar*.

Example 10-9 highlights the eight lines added to the map file in previous examples.

Example 10-9. Adding scale-bar settings to the map file

```
MAP
  SIZE 600 300
  EXTENT -180 -90 180 90
  IMAGECOLOR 180 180 250

  UNITS DD

  SCALEBAR
    STATUS EMBED
    UNITS KILOMETERS
    INTERVALS 3
    TRANSPARENT TRUE
    OUTLINECOLOR 0 0 0
  END

  LEGEND
    STATUS EMBED
...
```

A scale bar converts the map distances (centimeters, inches, pixels) to real-world distances (kilometers, miles), as seen in the lower-left corner of Figure 10-9.

Figure 10-9. Map image with an embedded scale bar

The same method used in previous examples using shp2img created this map with the embedded scale bar:

```
> shp2img -m global.map -o mymap.png -e 19 39 31 46
```

The first line added to the map file is the UNITS keyword. DD tells MapServer that the mapping data is represented in decimal degree coordinates/units. This setting affects the whole map file and isn't just scale bar–specific, which is why it isn't inside the SCALEBAR...END object.

 The topic of map units, coordinate systems, and map projections is beyond the scope of this chapter. It is important when you start to work with data from different sources, or when you want to make your maps for different purposes. For more on projections, see Appendix A.

The SCALEBAR object of the map file has several options. A few, but not all, of the options are used in this example. These are just enough to make a nice-looking scale bar without a lot of fuss. The STATUS EMBED option is just like the one used in the legend example earlier. It puts the graphic right on the map, rather than requiring you to create a separate graphic. The UNITS KILOMETERS specifies what measurement units are shown on the scale bar. In this case each segment of the scale bar is labeled in kilometers. This can be changed to inches, feet, meters, etc.

INTERVALS 3 makes three segments in the scale bar. The default is four segments. This is a handy option, allowing you to have control over how readable the resulting scale bar is. If you have too many segments crammed into a small area, the labels can become hard to read.

There is one important option not shown in the earlier example. SIZE x y is an option that explicitly sets the width (x) and height (y) of the scale bar. You can accept the default to keep it simple. Note that when specifying the number of segments using INTERVALS, it subdivides the width accordingly. If you want a large number of INTERVALS, you will probably need to increase the SIZE of the scale bar to make it readable.

The last two options in Example 10-9 are aesthetic. TRANSPARENT makes the background of the scale bar clear. OUTLINECOLOR creates a thin black outline around the scale bar segments.

If you don't want to embed the scale bar in your map, change STATUS EMBED to STATUS ON and use the scalebar command-line utility to create a separate graphic image. It is used like the legend utility in previous examples. The following example shows how you use the command:

```
> scalebar global.map scalebar.png
```

The command takes two parameters, a map filename and an output image name. Note that scalebar doesn't have the same options as shp2img.

Figure 10-10 shows the image created by the command.

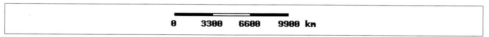

Figure 10-10. A simple scale bar graphic produced by a map file and the scalebar utility

Be sure not to scale the graphics if you are going to manually pull together the scale bar and map images for something like a publication or web page. If you change the size or scale of the scale bar and don't adjust the map image accordingly, your scale bar will be inaccurate.

The Final Map File

The final map file created for this example is shown in Example 10-10. The EXTENT value has been changed to reflect the extents used in the shp2img command in earlier examples.

Example 10-10. The final map file with all the changes and updates shown

```
MAP                        # Start of MAP object
  SIZE 600 300             # 600 by 300 pixel image output
  #EXTENT -180 -90 180 90  # Original extents ignored
  EXTENT 19 39 31 46       # Final extents
  IMAGECOLOR 180 180 250   # Sets background map color
  UNITS DD                 # Map units
  SCALEBAR                 # Start of SCALEBAR object
    STATUS EMBED           # Embed scalebar in map image
    UNITS KILOMETERS       # Draw scalebar in km units
```

Example 10-10. The final map file with all the changes and updates shown (continued)

```
    INTERVALS 3            # Draw a three piece scalebar
    TRANSPARENT TRUE       # Transparent background
    OUTLINECOLOR 0 0 0     # Black outline
  END                      # End of SCALEBAR object
  LEGEND                   # Start of LEGEND object
    STATUS EMBED           # Embed legend in map image
    POSITION LR            # Embed in lower-right corner
    TRANSPARENT TRUE       # Transparent background
  END                      # End of LEGEND object
  LAYER                    # Start of LAYER object
    NAME countries         # Name of LAYER
    TYPE POLYGON           # Type of features in LAYER
    STATUS DEFAULT         # Draw STATUS for LAYER
    DATA countries_simpl   # Source dataset
    LABELITEM 'NAME'       # Attribute for labels
    CLASSITEM 'NAME'       # Attribute for expressions
    CLASS                  # Start of CLASS object
      NAME 'Bulgaria'      # Name of CLASS
      EXPRESSION 'Bulgaria' # Draw these features in class
      STYLE                # Start of STYLE object
        OUTLINECOLOR 100 100 100
                           # Color of outer boundary
        COLOR 255 255 150  # Polygon shade color
      END                  # End of STYLE object
      LABEL                # Start of LABEL object
        SIZE LARGE         # Size of font in label
        MINFEATURESIZE 40  # Min. sized polygon to label
      END                  # End of LABEL object
    END                    # End of CLASS object
    CLASS                  # Start of CLASS object
      NAME 'All Countries' # Name of CLASS
      EXPRESSION ('[NAME]' ne 'Bulgaria')
                           # Draw features in class
      STYLE                # Start of STYLE object
        OUTLINECOLOR 100 100 100
                           # Color of outer boundary
        COLOR 200 200 200  # Polygon shade color
      END                  # End of STYLE object
    END                    # End of CLASS object
  END                      # End of LAYER object
END                        # End of MAP object and map file
```

Setting Output Image Formats

MapServer can produce map images, legends, and scale bars in different image formats. Throughout this chapter, the PNG format is shown in the examples because it is the default image format. MapServer packages can have different default image formats. PNG format is commonly supported by many MapServer packages, but in some cases MapServer may not be able to produce PNG files or doesn't produce them by default.

MapServer can be compiled using many different options. The term "MapServer package" refers to the set of programs, e.g., shp2img, that you are using. The capabilities of these programs depend on how they are compiled. Some packages will have more features enabled than others.

The output image format can be explicitly set in the map file. This requires adding a single line specifying the output format you are requesting. Example 10-11 shows the additional line added to the earlier example map file.

Example 10-11. Specifying the output image format as JPEG

```
MAP
  SIZE 600 300
  EXTENT -180 -90 180 90
  IMAGECOLOR 180 180 250
  IMAGETYPE JPEG

  UNITS DD
...
```

This setting can be overridden when using the shp2img command with the -i option. It can't be overridden when using commands such as scalebar or legend, as mentioned earlier in "Creating Your First Map Image."

The IMAGETYPE specified must be one supported by the MapServer package you are running. To check what output formats your installation supports, run the mapserv file (or mapserv.exe on Windows) with the -v option. This option tells you what input and output formats are supported by the utilities in your MapServer package. The following example shows the output from the MapServer used in this chapter, with the output image formats highlighted:

```
> mapserv -v
MapServer version 4.4.1 OUTPUT=PNG OUTPUT=JPEG OUTPUT=WBMP SUPPORTS=PROJ
SUPPORTS=FREETYPE SUPPORTS=WMS_SERVER SUPPORTS=WMS_CLIENT SUPPORTS=WFS_SERVER
SUPPORTS=WFS_CLIENT INPUT=EPPL7 INPUT=POSTGIS INPUT=OGR INPUT=GDAL INPUT=SHAPEFILE
```

This listing shows that this installation of MapServer can only output PNG, JPEG, or WBMP format files. That means the IMAGETYPE could be set to either of those three. Therefore it can't output GIF, TIFF, PDF, or any other formats.

WBMP images produced by MapServer appear to be unreadable. This may only be a problem for non-Windows environments.

For many vector-mapping applications, the PNG output format is sufficient. In many cases it will be the default output format. If you have a raster layer with more than 256 colors, it will probably not look right using the default PNG image type. Usually, all that is needed is to increase the depth of colors that MapServer creates in the output image. This can be set by requesting a 24-bit version of the PNG output format such as:

```
IMAGETYPE PNG24
```

Be warned: increasing the color depth also increases the file size of your images. This can be a major performance issue when sending graphics across the web.

More specific output image format settings can be made using an OUTPUTFORMAT object in your map file. This is an advanced topic and isn't described here. Please refer to the MapServer documentation at *http://mapserver.gis.umn.edu/doc/mapfile-reference.html#outputformat.*

## CHAPTER 11

Publishing Interactive Maps on the Web

MapServer is typically used through a web server such as Apache or IIS. Any web server that supports CGI applications can use MapServer. The web server passes along the map-related requests and returns the results to the browser. Chapter 4 describes how to compile or download binary versions of the MapServer CGI program called mapserv. This is the main MapServer program discussed in this section. The mapserv executable, not the command-line tools described earlier (Chapter 10), is used for web server applications. When this book refers to "integrating MapServer with a web server," it means using the mapserv executable (mapserv.exe on Windows) with a web server.

MapServer also has a scripting environment called MapScript. MapScript provides application programming interfaces for several programming languages. This is covered in Chapter 14. If you are a programmer and want to incorporate MapServer functionality into an application, MapScript is for you.

The CGI version of MapServer discussed in this chapter is for those who want MapServer up and running right away, without programming.

Preparing and Testing MapServer

A few things need to be set up before using MapServer. There are some differences between operating systems such as the name of your MapServer executable, where files are stored, etc.

MapServer for Windows (MS4W)

Chapter 4 described how to access and install the MS4W package. You might want to look at the MS4W portion of that chapter and review how to start the web server. A custom application will be built later in this chapter, but first you need to understand how MapServer works in the MS4W environment.

MS4W comes with a version of the Apache HTTP web server. The MapServer program is stored in Apache's *cgi-bin* folder, the main location for many web programs. If you were compiling your own *mapserv.exe* file, you install it by copying it into the *cgi-bin* folder. By default, this folder is located in the *\ms4w\Apache\cgi-bin* folder on the drive MS4W is installed on (e.g., *C:* or *D:*). There may be several versions of MapServer located there. For example, *mapserv_36.exe* is MapServer Version 3.6 (very out of date) and *mapserv_44.exe* is the most recent Version 4.4. Usually the more recent version will just be called *mapserv.exe*.

MapServer on Linux with Apache

Preparing MapServer on Linux is also described in Chapter 4. Installing the MapServer CGI program is similar to how you do so for MS4W. The mapserv executable is simply copied (or linked) to Apache's *cgi-bin* folder. For example, on SuSE Linux, the web server's *cgi-bin* folder is located at */srv/www/cgi-bin*. The mapserv application must be copied into this folder so it is accessible to the web server. These instructions also apply to non-MS4W installations of Apache on other platforms.

Configuring Apache

Configuring Apache to use MapServer doesn't have to be complicated. If you put the mapserv/mapserv.exe program into the web server's default *cgi-bin* location, there may not be much more to do to get the program running. The next section gives a couple of example tests to see if it is running properly.

There are other settings you will need in order to access maps produced by MapServer. When MapServer runs, it needs a temporary area to create the images for maps, legends, scale bars, etc. This temporary folder must also be accessible to the web so that users can view the images created by MapServer.

Windows temporary image folder location

MS4W comes with a temporary folder already set up. This folder is *c:\ms4w\tmp\ms_tmp*. The Apache configuration file at *c:\ms4w\Apache\conf\httpd.conf* sets this folder up with an *alias* called */ms_tmp*. This means that when a web application requests a file in */ms_tmp*, Apache looks for the file in *c:\ms4w\tmp\ms_tmp*. For example, if MapServer created a map image at *c:\ms4w\tmp\ms_tmp\mymap.png*, the web application would request to see the image by using a URL like *http://localhost/ms_tmp/mymap.png*.

The key thing to remember is that MS4W creates all the temporary map image files in this folder.

Linux temporary image folder location

If you are using a fresh install of Apache, you need to set up your temporary location and alias in the configuration files manually. There are several ways to configure settings. One method that uses Apache 2 on SuSE Linux is discussed here. You can set up your MapServer temporary folder anywhere on your filesystem. To keep it simple, you can put it directly under the *htdocs* root folder. This means that you don't need to create an alias for Apache because the folder is a child of the web server's root folder.

For example, the root web folder may be set in the */etc/apache2/httpd.conf* file and specified as *DocumentRoot /srv/www/htdocs*.

You can create your temporary image folder in */srv/www/htdocs/ms_tmp* so that MapServer will be able to find it when it is set to look in *http://localhost/ms_tmp*. As a quick test, if your earlier image *mymap.png* is placed in */srv/www/htdocs/ms_tmp*, you should be able to see it at *http://localhost/ms_tmp/mymap.png*.

Permissions for the *ms_tmp* folder must be set properly for MapServer to be able to save the map images. The trick is to have the web server user and group assigned as owner of the folder. You can then run the command:

```
> chown wwwrun.www /srv/www/htdocs/ms_tmp
```

This should make it accessible to the web server and, in turn, to MapServer. This process will vary on other platforms, depending on how your web server is being used, but the concepts are the same.

The distinction between the filesystem path to the *ms_tmp* folder (it doesn't have to be called *ms_tmp* by the way; call it whatever you like) and the online URL is very important to understand when setting up your MapServer applications. MapServer needs to know where on the filesystem it can write the map image files to. It will also need to know what URL to send back to the web browser for loading the map images into the web page.

 It may help to think of these two different ways of locating the folder by thinking of the filesystem path as the internal or private folder in which only the web server can create files and the URL as the public folder where anyone can view the files but not change them.

Testing and Troubleshooting

You can run a few tests to check that the MapServer program is properly set up. The set up of MS4W and Linux running Apache is very similar, but there are some differences worth mentioning.

Testing mapserv.exe on Windows

The first step for testing MS4W assumes that the web server is running as described in Chapter 4. To test that the MapServer executable (`mapserv.exe`) is available, you make a direct request to it without any parameters. For example, point your web browser to *http://localhost/cgi-bin/mapserv.exe*. You should get a message like this:

```
No query information to decode. QUERY_STRING is set, but empty.
```

This is a good thing. It is a message coming directly from MapServer. You didn't pass any of the required details to MapServer for processing, but the message confirms that you were able to make a request. It is also a reminder that you won't be running MapServer this way. If you get any other errors, there is either a permissions problem and Apache can't access the requested file, or the web server isn't up and running properly.

Testing mapserv with Apache on Linux

The MapServer program on Linux can be tested the same way you do MS4W. The only difference is that the name of the program is slightly different.

With Linux, there are no standard filename suffixes such as *.exe* to tell you which files are executable and which aren't. Instead, there are file permissions. On Linux the main MapServer program is simply called `mapserv`. This is the same file that was discussed earlier in this chapter and copied into the *cgi-bin* folder of the web server.

Test the `mapserv` executable on a Linux and Apache system by going to the URL *http://localhost/cgi-bin/mapserv*. Notice there is no *.exe* suffix. You should get the same notice from MapServer as with the MS4W examples earlier:

```
No query information to decode. QUERY_STRING is set, but empty.
```

Testing the MapServer Setup Using a Demo Application

To test that MapServer can actually create maps, you will build on the demonstration map files used with the command-line tools in Chapter 10.

The *countries_simpl* shapefile dataset can be downloaded as a compressed archive file from *http://ftp.intevation.de/freegis/worlddata/freegis_worlddata-0.1_simpl.tar.gz*.

The map file example from Chapter 10 will be customized further and made into a web-based application. To do so, there are three files involved:

Map file
> Stores all the settings required for drawing the map

Start page
> Creates initial settings and launches the first map

HTML template page
> A template MapServer fills in to show the current map, legend, etc.

Figure 11-1 illustrates how the basic application begins, with a start page sending settings to the CGI to produce a map.

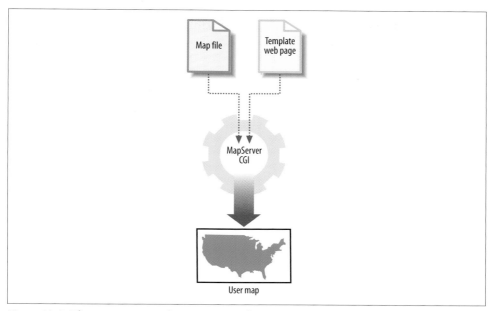

Figure 11-1. The start page initializes MapServer by passing it a map file and an HTML template document

Example 11-1 takes the demonstration map file *global.map*, used in the previous chapter, and adds the settings required to make it a web map. The additional settings are highlighted.

Example 11-1. Sample of global map application's map file

```
MAP
  SIZE 600 300
  EXTENT -180 -90 180 90
  IMAGECOLOR 180 180 250

  UNITS DD

  SCALEBAR
    STATUS EMBED
    UNITS KILOMETERS
    INTERVALS 3
    TRANSPARENT TRUE
    OUTLINECOLOR 0 0 0
  END

  LEGEND
    STATUS EMBED
```

Example 11-1. Sample of global map application's map file (continued)

```
    POSITION LR
    TRANSPARENT TRUE
  END

  WEB
    TEMPLATE global.html
    IMAGEPATH "/srv/www/htdocs/tmp/"
    IMAGEURL "/tmp/"
  END

  LAYER
    NAME countries
    TYPE POLYGON
    STATUS DEFAULT
    DATA countries_simpl
    LABELITEM 'NAME'
    LABELMAXSCALE 50000000
    CLASSITEM 'NAME'
    CLASS
      NAME 'Bulgaria'
      EXPRESSION 'Bulgaria'
      OUTLINECOLOR 100 100 100
      COLOR 255 255 150
      LABEL
        SIZE LARGE
        OUTLINECOLOR 255 255 255
        MINFEATURESIZE 40
      END
    END
    CLASS
      NAME 'All Countries'
      EXPRESSION ('[NAME]' ne 'Bulgaria')
      OUTLINECOLOR 100 100 100
      COLOR 200 200 200
    END
  END
END
```

Only a few lines were added to make the map file work with the web server instead of command-line tools.

 If using MS4W, the WEB object looks slightly different:

```
WEB
TEMPLATE global.html
IMAGEPATH "/ms4w/tmp/ms_tmp/"
IMAGEURL "/ms_tmp/"
END
```

A whole new object called WEB was added. There are three parts to the web object:

TEMPLATE global.html

The TEMPLATE file is specified by an HTML/web page document. It has some placeholders set to take the data created by MapServer and embed it into an output web page. The HTML in this page should be customized for your particular application. The examples shown in this chapter are some of the simplest possible. The options are endless, and this page can look as good or as bad as you want.

IMAGEPATH "/srv/www/htdocs/tmp/"

IMAGEPATH is the location on the local filesystem where MapServer can store its temporary images. The web server must be able to write new files into that folder.

IMAGEURL "/tmp/"

IMAGEURL tells the user's web browser where the output map image is to be located. This isn't the filesystem location, but a pointer to the same location as IMAGEPATH through an Internet URL. In this case */tmp/* comes off of the Apache DocumentRoot which is */srv/www/htdocs/*. No special alias is set up, just the relative path to the location of the map file.

LABELMAXSCALE 50000000 was also added to the countries layer. This sets the map to show labels only when zoomed in to a certain map scale. The scale of the initial map is so small that Bulgaria is barely visible. Having a label on top of the country makes it harder to see; instead, as you zoom in to a more readable scale, the labels will appear.

With these map file settings in place, you can set up an initialization page. This page will be called *index.html* and its contents are listed in Example 11-2. The page can be called whatever you want.

To keep the examples simple, you can put all the files introduced here into the main web server document folder. You will probably want to move these to another location in the future, but for now put them in:

- On Linux: */srv/www/htdocs/*
- On Windows with MS4W: *\ms4w\apache\htdocs*

Example 11-2. Listing of the index.html MapServer initialization page

```
<HTML>
<HEAD><TITLE>MapServer Test</TITLE></HEAD>
<CENTER><H2>MapServer Test</H2>

<FORM method=GET action="/cgi-bin/mapserv">
  <INPUT type="hidden" name="map" value="/srv/www/htdocs/global.map">
  <INPUT type="hidden" name="layer" value="countries">
```

Example 11-2. Listing of the index.html MapServer initialization page (continued)

```
  <INPUT type="hidden" name="zoomdir" value=1>
  <INPUT type="hidden" name="zoomsize" value=2>

  <INPUT type="hidden" name="program" value="/cgi-bin/mapserv">

  <INPUT type="submit" value="Start MapServer">
</FORM></CENTER></BODY></HTML>
```

This example is almost as stripped down as it can be. There is a title and heading on the page. Other than that, the rest of the HTML code is for starting MapServer. This page can be completely customized as long as the form and its variables are maintained.

All this page shows is a single button: Start MapServer. Behind the page are a bunch of hidden settings that are passed to MapServer when the form is submitted. This starts the first map. After the application is started, the *index.html* page isn't used.

 CGI applications operate like stock brokers. Stock brokers receive certain requests, information, and a commission. In exchange, they provide some stocks for the client.

MapServer CGI applications receive requests for maps, including information like geographic extent, layers to show, etc. They then return a web page showing the requested map content. Fortunately, CGI applications don't require a commission.

The *index.html* page isn't essential to the application, but does make it a lot easier to get started. If you know how to form the proper request manually, you can put together a URL that requests the map from the MapServer CGI. After the initial request, all the settings and request information are stored in the URL and sent back to the CGI upon further requests.

The MapServer CGI application sends the viewer a new web page. The URL to that web page contains several variables (like the ones defined in *index.html*). When a user requests a change to the map, it then sends those variables back to the CGI for reprocessing. The purpose of the *index.html* page is to get the whole process started without forcing you to have a complex-looking initial URL.

As you saw in Example 11-1, a template file called *global.html* is specified in the map file. This template file is also a web page written in HTML. MapServer takes this page and populates portions of it before sending it back to the user's web browser. Example 11-3 shows my *global.html* code.

Example 11-3. Listing of the global.html MapServer template file

```
<HTML>
<HEAD><TITLE>MapServer Test</TITLE></HEAD>
<CENTER><H2>MapServer Test</H2>
```

Example 11-3. Listing of the global.html MapServer template file (continued)

```
<HR>

<FORM method=GET action="/cgi-bin/mapserv">
  <INPUT NAME="img" TYPE="image" SRC="[img]" width=600 height=300 border=0
            ALT="Map Image">

  <INPUT type=hidden name=zoomdir value=1 [zoomdir_1_check] >
  <INPUT type=hidden name=zoomsize size=4 value=[zoomsize]>

  <INPUT type="hidden" name="imgxy" value="[center_x] [center_y]">
  <INPUT type="hidden" name="imgext" value="[mapext]">
  <INPUT type="hidden" name="map" value="[map]">
  <INPUT type="hidden" name="savequery" value="true">
  <INPUT type="hidden" name="mapext" value="shapes">

</FORM></CENTER></BODY></HTML>
```

If you are familiar with HTML forms and tags, you may notice that the only objects visible on this page are the heading and title and an image. The image source (SRC) is filled in by MapServer in real time when the page is generated.

When MapServer populates *global.html*, it checks for any MapServer-specific variables, such as [img]. MapServer replaces this text with the URL to the map image on the web site. This is the temporary map image that MapServer created.

 There are many other MapServer variables that can be used in template documents. The [legend] and [scalebar] variables are discussed later in this chapter.

Figure 11-2 shows the output web page created by the *global.html*.

The map will look exactly like some of the map output from the command-line tools in Chapter 10. The only difference is that this map is being created by MapServer when requested, and automatically embedded into a web page.

The basic *global.html* template has virtually no controls, or at least none that are apparent. *Controls* refers to the buttons and check boxes you see on many web maps. These were deliberately left out so that this example would be simple to implement, and the HTML code wouldn't be more confusing than necessary.

To interact with this map, just click on the map, and it will zoom in towards that location. Click once on the map, and then wait for the map to update. Once the image is updated, click again. Notice that if you zoom in toward Bulgaria, the label starts to appear. The results of clicking twice on the map are shown in Figure 11-3.

Because the number of controls has been kept to a minimum, there are no zoom-out buttons. In a web-mapping application this simple, the only way to zoom out is for

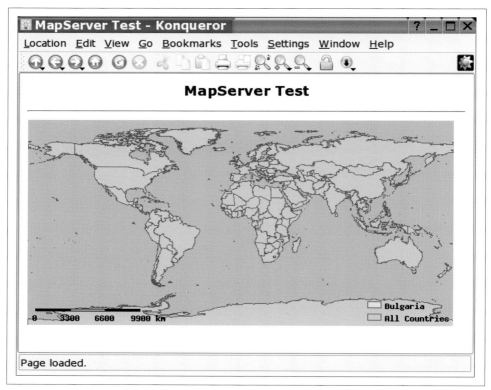

Figure 11-2. The basic global web map example

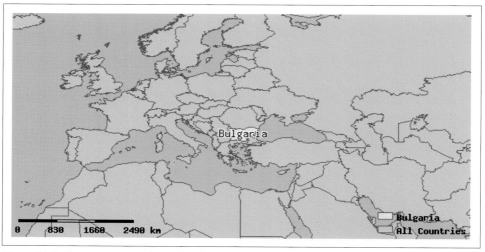

Figure 11-3. Zooming in to Bulgaria by clicking two times on the map

the user to go back in the web browser. This actually works reasonably intuitively because web page users are used to going back to previous pages.

If you've made it this far with your application, MapServer is set up and running well. Of course there are many other options and settings you can use. Some of these are covered in the next section when you start to make further customizations to the global map example.

Create a Custom Application for a Particular Area

MapServer has many different settings you will want to learn more about as you develop your skills. A very small, core subset of options are used in the examples in this chapter. For a complete listing of map file settings, see the map file reference document at *http://mapserver.gis.umn.edu/doc/mapfile-reference.html*.

Also note that there are several MapServer CGI variables used in this chapter. For more information see the current MapServer CGI reference document at *http://mapserver.gis.umn.edu/doc/cgi-reference.html*.

Changing the Initial Extent of the Map

In Chapter 10 you learned how to change the extents of the map when using the `shp2img` command-line utility. With an interactive map the extents can be changed by zooming in, just like the test example with the global map application. The initial map shown by that application covers the whole world. If you are interested only in a map covering a certain area, you will want to change the initial extent of the map to suit your area of interest.

You will continue to build on the previous examples in this chapter, including the *global.map* file. The EXTENT line in the map file specifies what the initial extent of the map will be when MapServer starts up. This was set to:

```
EXTENT -180 -90 180 90
```

which covers the whole world. Now you will set this to zoom in to a new area, to make a map of Canada. You will do so by continuing to use the *countries_simpl.shp* shapefile, and also use the `ogr2ogr` and `ogrinfo` tools to assess what extent you need. Please see the procedures for using `ogr2ogr` and `ogrinfo` in Chapter 10. Example 10-5 shows the same methodology for determining the extent of Bulgaria.

These command-line programs aren't part of MapServer. They are part of the GDAL/OGR package described in Chapter 3. The `ogr2ogr` utility extracts the shapes of Canada and saves them in to a new shapefile. `ogrinfo` is then run to see what the coordinate extents of Canada are.

The OGR utilities are available as part of the FWTools package. You can download it from *http://fwtools.maptools.org*.

The new shapefile is used only as a temporary means of determining the coordinates of the area of interest. These coordinates are then set in *global.map* so that MapServer focuses on Canada.

The extent of Canada, as returned from `ogrinfo`, is:

```
Extent: (-141.000000, 41.675980) - (-52.636291, 83.110458)
```

You can put this extent into the *global.map* file and see how things look. Simply copy/paste this text right into the map file and then clean it up, removing brackets and commas. Example 11-4 shows how the first few lines of the changed application look.

Example 11-4. A modified map file to include the extent of Canada instead of the whole world

```
MAP
  SIZE 600 300
  EXTENT -141 42 -52 83
...
    CLASS
      NAME 'Canada'
      EXPRESSION 'Canada'
      OUTLINECOLOR 100 100 100
      COLOR 255 255 150
    END
...
```

In this example, exact coordinates aren't required. You can round them off or drop the decimals. Note the changes to the LAYER object. The class that highlighted Bulgaria now highlights Canada instead. The LABEL object has been removed from the CLASS object. Figure 11-4 shows the initial map produced by using these new extent settings.

The extents of this map are so tight that it is hard to really get the context of the map. It is zoomed in so tightly to Canada that it's difficult to see any of the neighboring countries.

 MapServer has been very accurate about displaying the map according to the requested extent. That's a good thing. Some mapping programs always add on an extra bit of space around the feature you have asked to display. While this is usually helpful when creating a quick graphic, it isn't always helpful when you are trying to be accurate.

To make the map look a little nicer, increase the extent settings by five degrees. Here are the the initial and final extents:

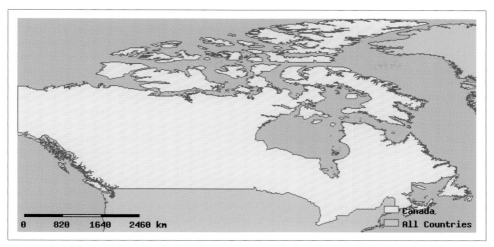

Figure 11-4. The initial map with Canada's extents specified in the map file

Initial extents
```
EXTENT -141 42 -52 83
```
Final extents
```
EXTENT -146 37 -47 88
```

The values of the new extent aren't just all increased or decreased. The minimum values (the first two numbers) are decreased because I want more of the south and west of the map to be shown. The maximum values (the last two numbers) are increased to show more of the north and east parts of the map. Increased here means made more positive, not just increasing the absolute value. This holds true for the western hemisphere north of the equator, and when using latitudes and longitudes. Figure 11-5 shows where the extents are on a map. Figure 11-6 shows the resulting map that uses the final extent.

 A grid line dataset was added to the map to help show the effects of the projection change in the next section. Notice the grid is rectangular, and all lines meet at right angles

Changing the Map Projection

If no PROJECTION objects are set for the map or the layers, MapServer assumes they are all in the same coordinate system. Therefore, no reprojection is required. For data in decimal degrees, MapServer uses a default map projection (a.k.a. Plate Caree). This default projection isn't the best way to display this map because it distorts several properties of the map. A large part of Canada is in the polar region, which this projection specifically distorts.

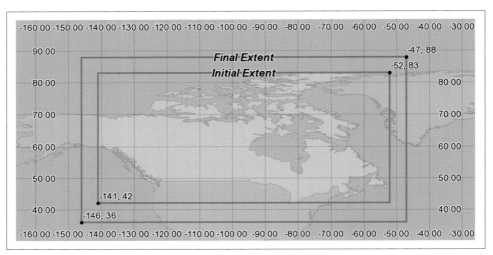

Figure 11-5. Map of showing the initial and final extents used for a map of Canada

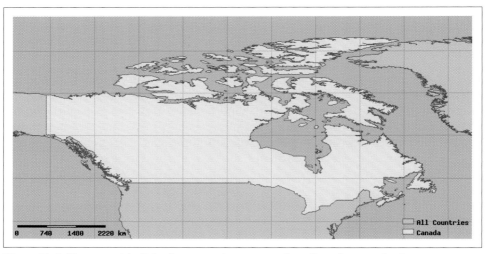

Figure 11-6. The map with slight changes to the extent to show Canada more clearly

 Some examples of changing projections are discussed here. Appendix A discusses map projections in more depth.

Setting the map and layer projections

The first thing you must know is that each layer can have a projection set for it, and the overall map can have a projection as well. If the data in the layers is a different projection than what you want displayed, MapServer will have to reproject the source data. You have to set each layer with a projection so that MapServer knows how to reproject the data into the desired output projection for the map.

Reprojecting Map Analogy

Reprojecting source data on a map in a different destination projection can be compared to planning airplane travel for a holiday. In order to plan which flights are required to get to the destination, the source (or origin) airport must be known. The connecting flights between the source and the destination can then be determined. So it is with projections. The source and destination projections must both be known in order to change one to another. If the source and destination projections are the same, no computation is required because, following the analogy, you've already arrived at your destination.

The first PROJECTION object in the map file is often called the map file's global projection setting. It is part of the MAP object. The other place projections are set is within the LAYER object. This tells MapServer what projection the map data within the data source of that layer uses. If it is different than the MAP projection, MapServer will reproject the source data into the output projection.

The *global.map* example has not required any projection information because the output map and source data are both in geographic, decimal degree coordinates. If another layer is added to the map and isn't in the same coordinate system, they will not be displayed properly. Likewise, the output map projection can be changed but if the input layer projections aren't set, MapServer won't be able to transform features from one projection to another. Example 11-5 shows the projections for the map and for the layer being explicitly set.

Example 11-5. Setting projections for the map and source layers

```
...
 UNITS DD

 PROJECTION
   "proj=latlong"
   "ellps=WGS84"
 END

 SCALEBAR
 ...
 LAYER
   NAME countries
   TYPE POLYGON
   ...
   CLASS
     NAME 'All Countries'
```

Example 11-5. Setting projections for the map and source layers (continued)

```
      OUTLINECOLOR 100 100 100
      COLOR 200 200 200
    END
    PROJECTION
      "proj=latlong"
      "ellps=WGS84"
    END
  END
END
```

Notice that in Example 11-5, the map and layer projections are identical. This is virtually the same as not setting a projection because no reprojection is necessary. It is a good habit to set these even if they aren't needed at the moment, so that adding in new layers using different coordinate systems can be done easily at a later time.

Choosing an output map projection

What if you want a different output map projection? There are two things to consider when setting the output projection. First, you need to update the map object's projection setting (the first projection object in Example 11-5). Determining what projection to use is beyond the scope of this chapter, but you need to keep in mind what geographic area your web map is being designed for. Is it for a global-scale, continental, or regional-scale application?

The Atlas of Canada has a good site discussing mapping theory, projections, their web mapping design, and more at *http://atlas.gc.ca/site/english/learningresources/carto_corner/index.html*.

This example will focus on mapping Canada. If using a Canada-specific projection, you need to be sure users won't be going outside of Canada. This is because the projection won't display maps of other countries very well.

The second thing to consider when setting up your map projection is the coordinate units used in the projection. Decimal degrees have been used in these examples, but other projections may use meters or feet as units of measure. This becomes important when you have to change your extent settings. The values for extents must be specified in the units of the map. So far, the examples have used decimal degree representations of the extent. In the next example the units will be in meters.

Layer projection settings will never change once properly set unless the data itself changes, or you set it wrong in the first place. You will usually only want to change the map's output projection and not the source data layer's projection.

The following example will use the Lambert Conformal Conic projection (LCC)—a projection commonly used by the Atlas of Canada. This projection is used with specific settings that center the projection in Canada, therefore making maps in that area more accurately displayed than maps that fall outside the area. This projection isn't suitable for users wanting to view areas outside of Canada.

EPSG projection codes versus project details

There are two ways to specify projections in MapServer. One uses a number identifier that refers to details stored in another file. This is using the standard code identification method of the European Petroleum Survey Group (EPSG). The EPSG is a numeric index code number referring to several projection-related settings. These codes are part of a text file called *epsg*. It comes as part of the PROJ.4 libraries that enable MapServer to project coordinates. More on using EPSG codes and PROJ.4 is covered in Appendix A.

The other method is to enter the details (which can sometimes appear very cryptic) directly into the map file. Example 11-6 shows how to set the map projection using both the EPSG code and detailed descriptive methods. You should specify the projection only once, using just one of these methods. You can use either method for layers or the map projection and mix them as desired.

Example 11-6. Specifying projection information using the EPSG code for LCC projection

```
PROJECTION
  "init=epsg:42304"
END

PROJECTION
  "proj=lcc"
  "ellps=GRS80"
  "lat_0=49"
  "lon_0=-95"
  "lat_1=49"
  "lat_2=77"
  "datum=NAD83"
  "units=m"
  "no_defs"
END
```

As you can see, the EPSG code can be much simpler to use, as long as the projection library requirements are properly installed.

Deciding which projection or EPSG code to use can take a bit of work. For the map of Canada, a good way to decide is to see what other people are using. For example, the Atlas of Canada web site describes what they use. If you go to the web page, it describes how their web mapping service is set up, including which EPSG codes they use; see *http://atlas.gc.ca/site/english/dataservices/web_map_service.html*.

PROJ.4 comes with a master list of EPSG codes you can augment with your own codes. Some of these Canada-specific codes, such as 42304, aren't official codes developed by the EPSG organization. Instead, other organizations have created their own codes where necessary. If you are looking for codes of the 42xxx series, you can download a new EPSG definitions file from *http://maptools.org/dl/proj4-epsg-with-42xxx.zip.*

You can review the EPSG file to see what the detailed projection settings are for a given EPSG number. The definition of the 42304 code is shown in the following example. The file will be located in the *proj* folder. On MS4W, it's at */ms4w/proj/nad/epsg;* on Linux, it's at */usr/local/share/proj/epsg.*

```
<42304> +proj=lcc +ellps=GRS80 +lat_0=49 +lon_0=-95 +lat_1=49 +lat_2=77 +datum=NAD83
+units=m no_defs <>
```

This output is all one line. Notice the <42304> at the beginning of the line. This is the EPSG code number. The rest of the line lists the details of the projection.

If you refer back to Example 11-6, you'll see how the details of the projection are put into a format acceptable to MapServer. You can take these details, remove the preceding addition signs (+), wrap them with double quotation marks, and put them on separate lines in the map file to make it more readable.

The various settings tell MapServer all the critical information it needs to know to reproject the data:

- Projection: proj=lcc
- Ellipsoid: ellps=GRS80
- Latitude of origin: lat_0=49
- Central meridian: lon_0=-95
- First/second standard parallels: lat_1=49/lat_2=77
- Datum: datum=NAD83
- Units of measure, in meters: units=m

See Appendix A for more information on map projections and these settings.

Modifying the map extent

Just changing the map projection won't give you a working map. You still need to change the extent settings for the map. These need to be set in meter units because the projection in the example uses meter units (units=m) rather than decimal degrees. How do you choose what extent to use? This is where it helps to know a bit about map projections, although some simple guessing and testing of extent values is perfectly valid too.

Here is one way to help determine what extent you want to have. The extents will be set in meter units, relative to the latitude of origin and central meridian of the projection. These details are listed in Example 11-6. The central meridian is -95° longitude, and the latitude of origin is 49° north. When the extent of the map is set, the southwest and northeast corners will be the distance, in meters, from the central point: -95°, 49°. For example

```
EXTENT -3000000 -1000000 3000000 1000000
```

sets the extent to start at 3,000 km west and 1,000 km south of the central point, and extend to 3,000 km east and 1,000 km north. If you go back to Figure 11-5, you can use the map grid to help determine where the center point is. It is centrally located but south of the center of the country, along the U.S. border. Now you can decide how wide and tall you want your extent to be. Figure 11-6 is a good map to give you an idea of distances. The scale bar provides a reference for the width of Canada. Setting an extent that is 6,000 km wide isn't unreasonable. Figure 11-7 shows the resulting map using the above extents.

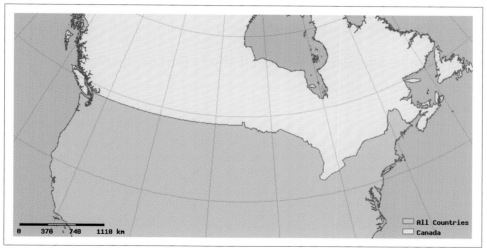

Figure 11-7. An initial guess for setting the map extents using an LCC projection of Canada

The initial guess wasn't too bad, though you can see that the map is shifted too far south and not far enough east. Through a process of tweaks and changes, you can determine an optimal extent to use. For example, you can decrease the minimum y and increase the maximum y values in the extent. Test out a few variations. Here is one extent that works well:

```
EXTENT -2400000 -900000 3100000 4000000
```

With these extents, MapServer produced the map shown in Figure 11-8. Grid lines were added to the map to show the difference in the shape of features that the projection change makes. Compare it to the regular rectangles in Figure 11-6.

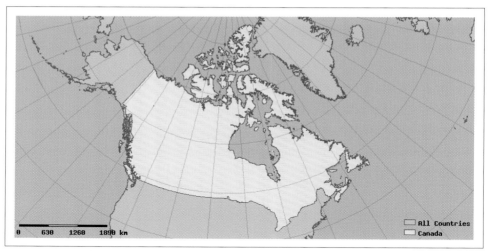

Figure 11-8. Final map extents set for a map of Canada

Modifying Image Size to Better Fit the Extent of the Map

There is a lot of extra space on the left and right sides of the map in Figure 11-8. This can be easily fixed by changing the size of the map image.

This mapping application was originally set up to show the whole world using a global project, which works great assuming the world map is twice as wide as it is tall. The map SIZE setting has been 600×300 throughout these exercises. That's a width to height ratio of 2 to 1. The previous map shows that Canada is roughly square using that LCC map projection. You can change the size of your map to be roughly 1 to 1, and the map will fit much better to the extents of Canada. Change the size setting to something like 400×400 or 600×600, and see how it looks. This is done by changing the SIZE setting near the beginning of the map file: SIZE 600 600.

The resulting map is shown in Figure 11-9. Notice how much better Canada fits into the map image.

Before you can start mapping this, you need to change the image dimensions used in the HTML template file, *global.html*. The image width and height was hardcoded. To make the map more flexible, you can replace the hardcoded image dimensions with MapServer variables. This allows the HTML template to dynamically set the image dimensions based on the settings in the map file.

To use the MapServer variables instead, change line 7 in *global.html*. Replace the width and height numbers with the [mapwidth] and [mapheight] variables. It should look like this:

```
<INPUT NAME="img" TYPE="image" SRC="[img]" width="[mapwidth]" height="[mapheight]"
border=0 ALT="Map Image">
```

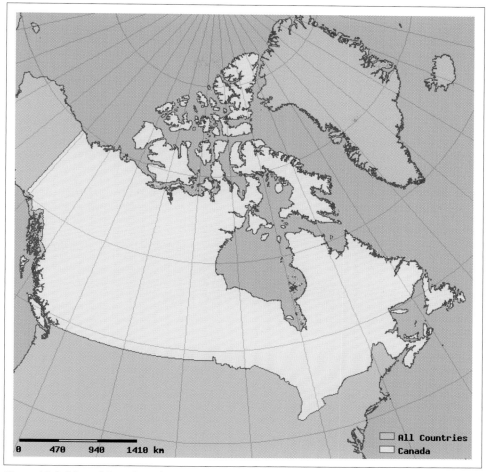

Figure 11-9. Map of Canada with a map SIZE setting ratio of 1:1

Likewise, you need to change the `imgxy` variable to automatically use the center of the image instead of the hardcoded center pixel value:

```
<INPUT type="hidden" name="imgxy" value="[mapcentroidx] [mapcentroidy]">
```

In cases where you need to hardcode the dimensions into the HTML template file, you must remember to keep the same dimensions in the HTML template and the map file. If the dimensions differ, it may not be apparent, but if you change the width/height ratio of the image enough, you will get a stretched or compressed map.

Adding Zoom and Recenter Tools to the Web Page

So far, the application has only one real tool. You can point and click to zoom in to an area. You haven't been able to zoom out (other than by hitting the Back button in your web browser) or move the map sideways to recenter your view. Now you'll add add three options to the web page, one for zooming in, another for zooming out and one to recenter the map on a new location.

If you are already familiar with HTML forms, this will be a snap. All you're doing is adding an HTML form control that passes another CGI variable to the MapServer program. In the application so far, zooming was hardcoded. Instead, you will make a three-way option using three radio buttons.

Radio buttons are different from check boxes and normal buttons. When multiple radio buttons have the same name, only one can be selected at a time. This works perfectly for the task of selecting a single tool or option.

Example 11-7 shows the modified HTML template file, *global.html*, and Figure 11-10 shows the resulting web page from the exercise.

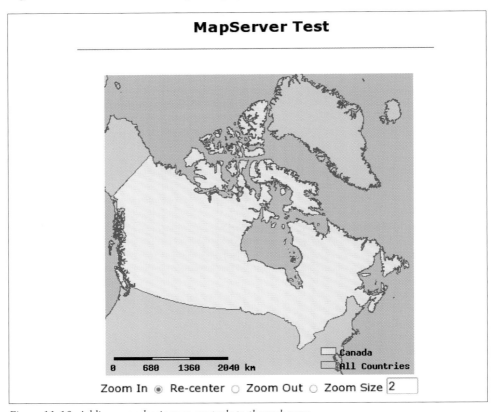

Figure 11-10. Adding some basic map controls to the web page

Example 11-7. Adding zoom and recenter tools to the basic application

```
<HTML>
<HEAD><TITLE>MapServer Test</TITLE></HEAD>
<CENTER><H2>MapServer Test</H2>
<hr>

<FORM method=GET action="/cgi-bin/mapserv">
  <INPUT NAME="img" TYPE="image" SRC="[img]" width="[mapwidth]" height="[mapheight]"
            border=0 ALT="Map Image">
  <BR>

  Zoom In
  <INPUT type=radio name=zoomdir value=1 [zoomdir_1_check] >

  Re-center
  <INPUT type=radio name=zoomdir value=0 [zoomdir_0_check] >

  Zoom Out
  <INPUT type=radio name=zoomdir value=-1 [zoomdir_-1_check] >

  Zoom Size
  <INPUT type=text name=zoomsize size=4 value=[zoomsize]>

  <!-- Remove the following three lines
  <INPUT type=hidden name=zoomdir value=1 [zoomdir_1_check] >
  <INPUT type=hidden name=zoomsize size=4 value=[zoomsize]>
  -->

  <INPUT type="hidden" name="imgxy" value="[center_x] [center_y]">
  <INPUT type="hidden" name="imgext" value="[mapext]">
  <INPUT type="hidden" name="map" value="[map]">
  <INPUT type="hidden" name="savequery" value="true">
  <INPUT type="hidden" name="mapext" value="shapes">

</FORM></CENTER></BODY></HTML>
```

First, the radio button settings were added to the form. These are spaced out in the code example to try to show them more clearly. All three are very similar. Text will be shown beside the button, and the form code defines what each button does. The first two changed lines are formatting and labeling of the button:

```
<BR>
Zoom In
```

The <BR> tag acts as a new line, so that the tools are displayed underneath the map image. The words Zoom In start on a new line and are next to the radio button itself. The radio button is defined by the tag:

```
<INPUT type=radio name=zoomdir value=1 [zoomdir_1_check] >
```

The <INPUT...> tag is part of the CGI form on this page. It has three settings:

type=radio
> This defines what kind of control is put on the form. So far in these examples, type=hidden has been used. This doesn't put a control on the form for the viewer but keeps a setting behind-the-scenes as if the control was invisible. In this case radio specifies that you want a radio button in this location. There are three radio buttons added on this page. They are all part of the same group, but only one can be selected at a time.

name=zoomdir
> This is the name of the variable. This variable will hold the value defined in the next option. The name (and value) is passed on to the MapServer program and used to create the next map, depending on what button was selected.

value=1
> This is the value the button has. Each button has a different value (-1, 0, 1). This value is sent with the above name, which is passed to the MapServer program to interpret. If zoomdir=1, MapServer zooms in to the map. If it is -1, it zooms out. If it is 0, it recenters the map to the location that is clicked.

The final piece of text in the INPUT tag is: [zoomdir_1_check]. This is a piece of text that is replaced by MapServer when the HTML page is created. This is similar to the [img] variable used to draw the map in the page. MapServer replaces these place-holders with values after creating the map. In this case, it replaces the text with the word checked beside the button that was pressed last. If you click on Zoom In, then click on the map, it should zoom in to where you clicked on the map. At that point the Zoom In tool will still be selected. That is because it is now marked as checked. You can see this in the HTML behind the page showing the map:

```
<INPUT type=radio name=zoomdir value=1 checked >
```

If you select the Re-center button, it marks the second radio button with the checked setting:

```
<INPUT type=radio name=zoomdir value=0 checked >
```

This allows the web browser to maintain the options you selected when it draws a new map or refreshes the page.

The only other line added was to enable the box to enter in a Zoom Size:

```
Zoom Size
  <INPUT type=text name=zoomsize size=4 value=[zoomsize]>
```

This setting tells MapServer how much to zoom in (or out) when a user clicks on the map. For example, a zoom size of 2 doubles the scale and makes features on the map appear twice as large. This was hardcoded into a hidden variable before adding the controls. These lines can now be removed from the HTML template. The zoomdir setting was also hardcoded to value=1, so that any time a user clicked on the map it only zooms in. With the new controls just added, these lines are no longer required:

```
<INPUT type=hidden name=zoomdir value=1 [zoomdir_1_check] >
<INPUT type=hidden name=zoomsize size=4 value=[zoomsize]>
```

One change is also required in *index.html*. In the earlier examples, the default action was to zoom in. You had to set the hidden zoomdir variable to value=1, which MapServer interprets as zoom in. By changing this to value=0 (zero), it makes the default action be recenter instead of zoom. This will become more important by the end of this chapter when we study the redraw button. If you hit redraw, and zoom in is selected by default, the map will not only redraws, but also zooms in. Here is the changed line in *index.html*:

```
<INPUT type="hidden" name="zoomdir" value=0>
```

 It is a good idea to move your HTML code around so it is the most readable to you. Putting in spaces makes clear breaks for discussion here, but HTML has very few formatting rules. You can add or remove spaces between lines and words and even put the code into one long line if you really want to. Indenting can help keep it readable as well. Using the break tag <BR> or paragraph tag <P> is needed for putting different controls onto different lines. Try putting <BR> before each of the INPUT radio buttons.

Adding a List of Layers to Choose From

Zoom and recenter features are critical for most web mapping applications. Many users also like the ability to control what layers they see. Those using the application will need some level of control. Being able to turn layers on and off is a key part of many MapServer applications. Try to give users as much freedom to explore their maps as possible, but also try to prevent them from making major mistakes. For example, if you give complete control and allow them to turn off every layer, the map will be empty. They got what they asked for but may think that your application is broken. You will have to decide how important complete control is versus having things a bit more restrictive but predictable.

Before you get into setting up layer selection options, you need to create a new layer in the global mapping application. You could find some images to include or another shapefile showing the locations of places of interest. To keep it simple, the following example is going to create a layer that shows text labels for the countries. You can do this using the same *countries_simpl* shapefile dataset that is already being used in the application. Example 11-8 shows the new layer created in *global.map*. The new layer is called country_labels. Instead of drawing polygons or lines, tell it to only draw labels by setting TYPE ANNOTATION.

Example 11-8. Adding a layer of labels to the map

```
LAYER
  NAME country_labels
  TYPE ANNOTATION
  STATUS DEFAULT
  DATA countries_simpl
  LABELITEM 'NAME'
  CLASS
    LABEL
      COLOR 255 255 255
      OUTLINECOLOR 0 0 0
      POSITION CC
      MINFEATURESIZE 100
    END
  END
  PROJECTION
    "proj=latlong"
    "proj=WGS84"
  END
END
```

With MapServer, you can set layers to be drawn two ways. One way is to force the map to always draw the layer. This is done by setting the layer to STATUS DEFAULT. The other way is to have it turned on only when requested. In this case you can set it to STATUS OFF. If a layer is set to OFF in the map file, it doesn't mean it will never be drawn. If the layer is requested to be drawn by the web page, then it will be.

Right now there are two layers in the map file: countries and country_labels. To have the country boundaries always shown, leave the countries layer STATUS set to DEFAULT. But for country_labels, set it to STATUS OFF. This allows the user to turn off the labels.

There is a third option, STATUS ON, which confuses many new MapServer application developers. For the purposes of this tutorial, and if you are just beginning, it's probably a good idea to stick with using OFF or DEFAULT. The ON setting will become more useful if you use MapScript. For more about MapScript see Chapter 14.

The next place you make changes is in the *index.html* page. The settings in this page tell MapServer which layers to draw when drawing the first map. This is different from setting the layer to be on by default in the map file. Instead, the *index.html* page will pass a list of layers to draw through to the MapServer program. If the layers are available in the map file, it will request to see them. You will see the names of the layers embedded in the URL as CGI values (e.g., &layers=countries). MapServer uses these parameters to determine which layers to draw.

Back in Example 11-2 you saw the initial settings for *index.html*. That included this line:

```
<input type="hidden" name="layer" value="countries">
```

Having this line as part of the initialization form meant that MapServer would be requested to draw the countries layer when the first map is drawn. Considering that the layer is already set to draw by default, this setting becomes redundant. countries will be drawn all the time anyway, and the user won't be able to turn it off. However, keep this line, and copy it for use with the new layer that shows the labels:

```
<input type="hidden" name="layer" value="country_labels">
```

Now when the map starts up, both layers will be drawn. If you don't want any layers other than those set with STATUS DEFAULT to be drawn, just remove any of the lines in *index.html*, where name="layer".

The third place to set up layer options is in the HTML template file (*global.html*). MapServer puts the map image into this HTML page and displays any of the controls you want to have in your application, including a list of layers to choose from. This is the most labor-intensive part of the exercise, but it is important. This is where the user will actually see some options. The settings in *global.map* and *index.html* are hidden from the user (except in the URL) but anything shown in the HTML template page will be for the user to see.

The HTML template page already has a form defined on it. All you need to do is add in a few more controls, also known as select options. To have these displayed on the right side of the map, put the code right after the <INPUT...> tag that draws the map. Make sure there are no line breaks <BR> between the select controls and the map if you want them to be side by side. Make sure that a <BR> tag follows the select list so that the zoom/recenter controls are below everything else. Example 11-9 shows the first few lines of HTML, including the start of the SELECT tag which is needed for the layer list.

Example 11-9. Starting to create the SELECT list for choosing which layers to view

```
...
<FORM method=GET action="/cgi-bin/mapserv">
  <BR> <INPUT NAME="img" TYPE="image" SRC="[img]" width="[mapwidth]" height="[mapheight]"
border=0 ALT="Map Image">
  <SELECT multiple name="layer" size=3>
  <!--the list of layers to chose from will go here -->
  </SELECT>
  <BR>
    Zoom In <INPUT type=radio name=zoomdir value=1 [zoomdir_1_check] >
...
```

The size=3 setting for the SELECT tag determines how many lines will be shown in the list. If you only have a few layers to put in the list, you can set the size to equal the number of layers you have available. If you have more than will easily fit in the list, the list will still include them, but you have to scroll through the list to find them. Using three makes it easier to see that this is a list.

So far the list won't do anything. Next you need to add an entry for the country_ labels layer. You should also add some text that will be displayed near the list to describe what the list is showing. Each layer that you want to show in the list needs an <OPTION...> tag like this:

```
<OPTION value="country_labels" [country_labels_select]> Country Names</OPTION>
```

The pieces specific to the application have been highlighted. The first setting, value="country_labels", is the name of the layer that will be drawn when this entry is selected from the list.

 If you are using groups in your map file, this could also be the group name. In addition to a NAME setting, each LAYER can have a GROUP setting. This allows you to control multiple layers using a single group name instead of many single layer names.

The second setting [country_labels_select] is necessary for the web page to highlight layers you have selected on previous maps. This is similar to the checked settings used when creating the radio buttons for zoom/recenter. This setting should be the same as the value setting, but with _select added to it.

 Typos in these two settings can really leave you confused and frustrated, so be careful to match the text to your layer name exactly.

The third item added is the text Country Names. This is outside of the <OPTION...> tag and is text to be written on the web page. The text put here can be whatever you want it to be. It will be used as a label for this layer in the select list on the web page. With all these changes, the new web page looks like Figure 11-11.

The complete *global.html* file looks like Example 11-10. In the final *global.html*, some text describing how to use the list and what it is for has been added. A few of the tags are moved around to make the page a bit more structured.

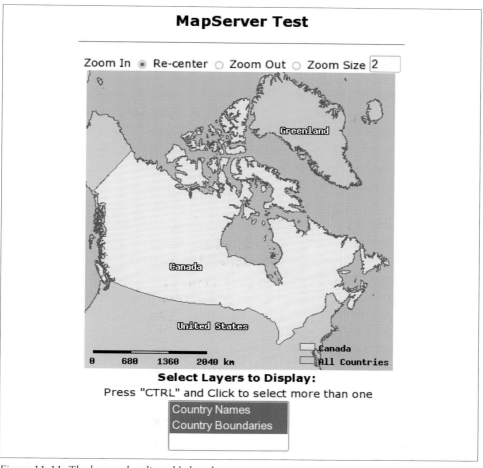

Figure 11-11. The layer select list added to the map page

Example 11-10. Two layers added to a list beside the map

```
<HTML>
<HEAD><TITLE>MapServer Test</TITLE></HEAD>
<CENTER><H2>MapServer Test</H2>
<HR>

<FORM method=GET action="/cgi-bin/mapserv">
    Zoom In <INPUT type=radio name=zoomdir value=1 [zoomdir_1_check] >
    Re-center <INPUT type=radio name=zoomdir value=0 [zoomdir_0_check] >
    Zoom Out <INPUT type=radio name=zoomdir value=-1 [zoomdir_-1_check] >
    Zoom Size <INPUT type=text name=zoomsize size=4 value=[zoomsize]><BR>
  <INPUT NAME="img" TYPE="image" SRC="[img]" width="[mapwidth]" height="[mapheight]"
border=0 ALT="Map Image"><BR>
  <B>Select Layers to Display: </B><BR>
      Press "CTRL" and Click to select more than one<BR>
```

Example 11-10. Two layers added to a list beside the map (continued)

```
<SELECT multiple name="layer" size=3>
  <OPTION value="country_labels" [country_labels_select]> Country Names</OPTION>
  <OPTION value="countries" [countries_select]> Country Boundaries</OPTION>
</SELECT>

<INPUT type="hidden" name="imgxy" value="[center_x] [center_y]">
<INPUT type="hidden" name="imgext" value="[mapext]">
<INPUT type="hidden" name="map" value="[map]">
<INPUT type="hidden" name="savequery" value="true">
<INPUT type="hidden" name="mapext" value="shapes">
```

```
</FORM></CENTER></BODY></HTML>
```

The natural next question is, how do you make the map redraw after choosing new layers? You can use the zoom or recenter tools, and it will update the map, reflecting this change, but this is hardly intuitive. The easiest way is to add a button to the page that requests a new map. HTML forms have a submit button you can use. Add this code to *global.html*, right after the end of the select list </SELECT>:

```
<BR><INPUT type="submit" value="Redraw/Update">
```

Now a button will appear right under the select list, as shown in Figure 11-12. You can select or deselect a layer, press the button, and see the change on the new map.

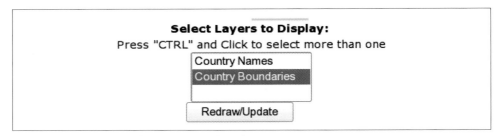

Figure 11-12. Adding a submit button to the web page to request a new map

Congratulations. You have created your own interactive web mapping applications. There is a lot more to learn but you know the basics of creating interactive maps. The rest of the chapter provides a few more tweaks and tips for further developing your application.

Adding a Legend to the Application

A legend is another key component of web mapping application and is very simple to add. It only takes a minute to modify your code to add a legend graphic to the page. The legend is a small graphic showing what colors and styles are being used to draw the map layers. So far in this example application you've used an embedded legend that is part of the map image. Now you will pull that legend out of the map image and have it drawn separately on the page. This requires two changes: one modification of the *global.map* file to remove the embedded legend and an addition to the *global.html* file to draw the legend on the page.

Removing the embedded legend from the map file

An embedded legend is often used for compactness and neatness, though a separate graphic showing the legend outside of the map image may sometimes be preferred. In order to do this, disable the embedded legend and set it to be a normal legend. This is done by changing the STATUS EMBED to STATUS ON in the LEGEND object of the map file. The POSITION and TRANSPARENT keywords are unnecessary because they don't really apply anymore, so they can be removed as well. Example 11-11 shows the original LEGEND object of the *global.map* file, followed by the modified version.

Example 11-11. Removing an embedded legend and setting the legend status to normal

```
# Original legend
  LEGEND
    STATUS EMBED
    POSITION LR
    TRANSPARENT TRUE
  END
#-------------------
# Modified legend
  LEGEND
    STATUS ON
  END
```

Behind the scenes, this will create a separate image file showing the legend graphic.

Adding the legend graphic to the web page

Making this new legend appear on the web page requires a small piece of code to be added to the map template. You can add the code in Example 11-12 to *global.html*, in any spot you like.

Example 11-12. Adding the legend code to the web page

```
<BR><HR>
<B>Legend</B><BR>
<IMG src="[legend]" alt="Map Legend"><HR>
```

 This web page isn't pretty, but it does work. Organize your page and add frames, HTML divs, etc. to make it look suitable for your audience.

This code places an image into the web page. It is very common in web publishing. For example, take your favorite web site that shows pictures and select the web browser's View → Page Source (or Document Source depending on which browser you use). This shows the underlying HTML code behind the page. Nine times out of ten there will be a similar <IMG> tag in there to display a graphic.

 The alt="Map Legend" part of the code can be omitted. However, to meet the HTML standards, you must have this attribute set. It provides a short, textual description of the image. This is used by people who can't render the images or who are using a text-only browser.

Put the code in Example 11-12 right after the redraw button. The magical piece of this code is the use of src="[legend]". The src setting, in other types of web pages, points to the location of an image file. Its usage is no different in this application, except that MapServer automatically fills it in for you. MapServer creates uniquely named temporary image files. MapServer creates this image file on the fly, as the map is created, and creates a new file every time. The [legend] code is replaced with the actual path and name of the legend image file that it created. It then sends this page to you, ready for your browser to load in the image. The final result is a web page that looks like Figure 11-13.

Adding a link to the legend image

The [legend] setting in *global.html* can be used as a URL to the legend graphic just as if it were the URL. This is useful if your legend is very long and doesn't fit well on the same page as the map. It is very simple to create a link a viewer can click to see the legend. This can save some space on the main map page. Using the <A> tag to create a simple link looks like this:

```
<A HREF="[legend]" TARGET="_blank"><B>View Legend</B></A>
```

The words View Legend appear as a link to the image file itself, as in Figure 11-14. When the user clicks on it, the image is viewed on its own page in the web browser.

Adding a Scale Bar to the Application

Scale bar images are created through the same process as legend images. When the scale bar isn't used as an embedded image, it is created as a separate image. MapServer then inserts it into the HTML template wherever it finds the [scalebar] variable.

To *global.html* add one simple line, just like with the legend. Place it below the map image so that it is near enough to be useful for measuring. This is shown in Example 11-13.

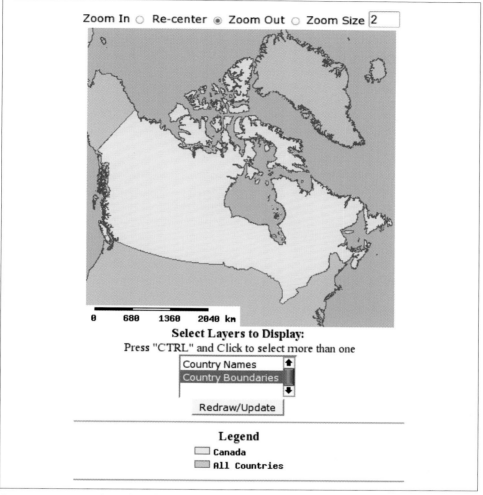

Figure 11-13. *Legend graphic added as a separate entity on the web page*

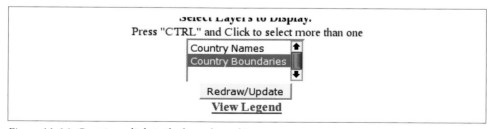

Figure 11-14. *Creating a link to the legend graphic*

Example 11-13. HTML for adding a scale bar image to the web page

```
<INPUT NAME="img" TYPE="image" SRC="[img]" width="[mapwidth]" height="[mapheight]"
       border=0 ALT="Map Image"><BR>

<IMG src="[scalebar]" alt="Map scale bar"><BR>

<B>Select Layers to Display: </B><BR>
```

In the SCALEBAR object of the *global.map* file, change STATUS EMBED to STATUS ON so that the scale bar is no longer shown on the map image itself.

The final outcome looks like Figure 11-15.

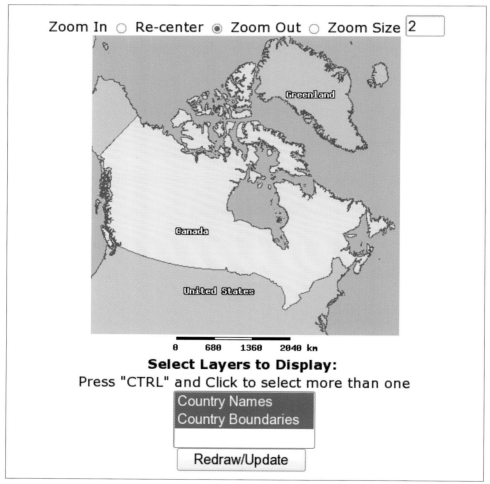

Figure 11-15. A scale bar graphic added to the web page

Adding an Overview/Reference Map to the Application

Just like a legend and scale bar, a reference map image can be created at the same time as a map and added to your application. This requires a bit more forethought and some preparation. You need to keep in mind the purpose of your reference map. Typically, it is used for two purposes.

The primary purpose is showing where you are zoomed in to, relative to the original extent of the map. For example, Figure 11-16 shows a MapServer-based web site (*http://www.gommap.org*) that uses a reference map to orient users to their current view of the map.

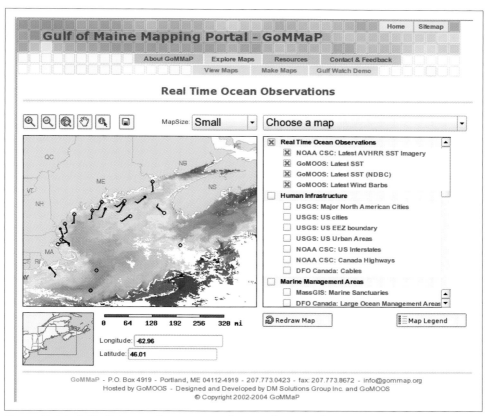

Figure 11-16. Gulf of Maine web mapping application showing reference map

Reference maps can also be used to recenter the main map. If you want to view a different area, just click on the reference map, and the main map will recenter on that location. This feature is particularly helpful when you want to maintain the scale of your map but move to another location. Rather than using the recenter tool on the main map over and over again, just one click in the reference map takes you there.

Adding a reference map to your application follows a similar process to adding a legend or scale bar. You add a REFERENCE object to your map file and some code to the HTML template (e.g., *global.html*). The only other requirement is an image file to use for the reference map. It isn't generated with a map file or layers but is a static background map image.

You can download a small world map image in PNG or GIF format from:

http://www.oreilly.com/catalog/webmapping

The image is shown in Figure 11-17.

Figure 11-17. A reference map image

Now, save the image in the same folder as the *global.map* map file. Add the code highlighted in Example 11-14 to the map file. I recommend you do so somewhere near the beginning. In this example, it is shown between the LEGEND and PROJECTION objects.

Example 11-14. Adding a REFERENCE object to the map file

```
...
  LEGEND
    STATUS EMBED
    POSITION LR
    TRANSPARENT TRUE
  END

  REFERENCE
    STATUS ON
    IMAGE keymap.png  # This could be keymap.gif instead
    EXTENT -180 -90 180 90
    SIZE 241 121
    COLOR -1 -1 -1
    OUTLINECOLOR 255 0 0
  END

  PROJECTION
    "proj=latlong"
...
```

The reference image file doesn't have geographic coordinates saved in the file. Instead, you must specify what the extent coordinates are using the EXTENT setting. This tells MapServer that the *keymap.png* image covers the globe. The SIZE setting tells how wide and tall the image is (in pixels). These two settings allow MapServer to find a specific coordinate location on the reference map image. If your reference map doesn't seem to work properly, one of these two settings may be incorrect.

When the reference map is used, it draws a rectangle on top of the *keymap.png* image. The COLOR setting sets what color that rectangle will be. It is red by default. COLOR -1 -1 -1 tells MapServer to not color the rectangle, but to make it transparent. The OUTLINECOLOR setting gives the rectangle a red outline.

The REFERENCE object doesn't have projection settings. This means that the EXTENT is always specified in the same units as the output map projection. This example really only works with a map that is displayed in the lat/long projection used at the beginning of this chapter. Also, the extents will not be specified in meter units for the LCC projection used earlier. Instead, the units must be set to UNITS DD for this example to work. The map EXTENT will need to be in decimal degrees.

The *global.html* template file needs to be modified as well. There are two ways to do this. The first is to include another <IMG> tag, like <IMG SRC="[ref]">. This creates a simple reference map. The other way to add the reference map lets you click on the reference map to recenter your map. Use this code instead of the previous:

```
<INPUT name="ref" TYPE="image" SRC="[ref]" width="241" height="121" ALT="Reference
map">
```

This shows the image and also sets it up to take a click and change the main map image. If you add it right after the main map image, you will have a web page that looks similar to Figure 11-18. All the layer controls have been removed, and the legend and scale bar were switched back to embed.

Continuing Education

The examples in this chapter barely scratch the surface of MapServer capabilities. You can get an idea of the other kinds of functions that are available by looking at other MapServer applications. The MapServer web site maintains an application gallery at *http://mapserver.gis.umn.edu/gallery.html*.

It shows several examples of applications people have built, including sites that allow querying, data entry, searching, etc.

There are also quite a few developments under way that will make MapServer applications easier to develop. These are often called *application development frameworks*. They require some more advanced setup to get started, because of their

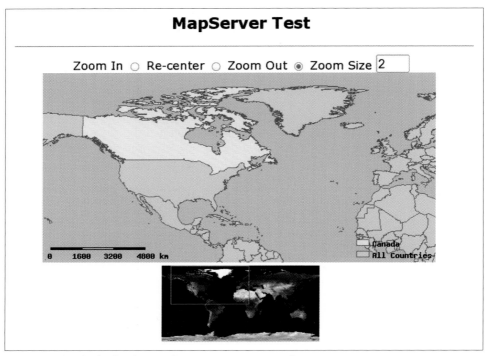

Figure 11-18. The final web page showing an interactive reference map

dependency on web programming languages (e.g., PHP). Here are a few application development tools:

- Chameleon and MapLab (*http://www.maptools.org*)
- Flexible Internet Spatial Template (FIST) (*http://datashare.gis.unbc.ca*)
- MapBender (*http://www.mapbender.org*)

There has also been increasing interest in integrating MapServer functionality with a content management system (CMS), groupware, or wiki. Tikiwiki (*http://tikiwiki.org/tiki-map.phtml*) is one example of this.

CHAPTER 12

Accessing Maps Through Web Services

While publishing maps to the traditional Web for human consumption is definitely one of MapServer's most attractive features, you may also want to share your data so that other programs can use it. To do this, you'll likely want to take advantage of web services. Ethan Cerami gives a good definition of a web service in the introduction to his book *Web Services Essentials* (O'Reilly):

> A web service is any service that is available over the Internet, uses a standardized XML messaging system, and isn't tied to any one operating system or programming language.

Similarly, Venu Vasudevan in his *A Web Services Primer*, defines a web service as "XML plus HTTP." See *http://webservices.xml.com/pub/a/ws/2001/04/04/webservices/index.html*.

The term *web service* typically refers to an Internet communication protocol between applications. Web services are built on the standard web HTTP protocol used for web browsing. HTTP is the transfer protocol coupled with XML as a communication language. These communication specifications allow the Internet to act as a communication network between applications—not just as a service for sharing web pages.

Web services are important because they play the integral part of interoperability between applications which were developed independently of each other and yet are able to communicate. The web services standards are independent of programming languages, operating systems, and platforms. They provide a standardized method of communicating between web-accessible applications, and are especially important to mapping applications that use the Internet to share data.

One of the great things about web services is that you don't need to understand all their ins and outs to use them. To use mapping-related web services, you just need to know how to point your application at a data source across the Internet. If you want to share your data with others, you need to know how to set up your applications so they are accessible.

Web Services for Mapping

While the internal details of web services—XML-RPC, UDDI, WSDL, SOAP (all covered in *Web Services Essentials*, from O'Reilly)—are interesting to developers, they aren't the focus here. There are services particular to mapping and, even though they may operate in a similar fashion, they are completely different from the general services a web developer may be familiar with. This chapter focuses on the web services MapServer supports.

What Do Web Services for Mapping Do?

Mapping web services has been developed independently of the Web. They use similar approaches and follow some common communication protocols, but the web services for mapping are maintained independent of web services in general.

Web services for mapping are the future of web mapping. Computing and network resources have reached the level of sophistication to make this possible. As data sources continue to expand, the demand to have access to them increases. Meeting this demand will only be possible using mapping web services.

Web services for mapping essentially fill two roles: accessing remote data sources as a consumer and serving up or sharing data as a provider for others. Web services for mapping are all about sharing information.

Accessing remote data sources requires some specific knowledge about the data source. Particulars may include the server address to connect to, the data layers available, or the format the data can be sent to you in. Once you know the details, you can set up your application to request exactly what you want. MapServer will add in its own pieces of information to each request so you get something logical back on a map.

Sharing (a.k.a. publishing) your own data is relatively easy to do. A few additions to your application will allow others to query it for such things as available layers and data format options. Once you've made a few modifications to your map file, other users can add your layers to their applications.

Web services for mapping don't require you to know a bunch of details about how requests are made or sent. MapServer will take care of the guts of the operation for you, such as sending HTTP or XML-based requests and receiving responses and data. You usually won't have to read XML when using these services. However, you might occasionally need to review an XML-based document to learn more about a service.

The examples in this chapter walk you through the steps of building your own request manually. You can then incorporate this technology into your own applications. If you are just planning to have MapServer broker requests to a WMS server, then you won't need to pay as much attention to the manual examples.

Just as telephones or CD players use common methods for sending or receiving information, so do mapping web services. Therefore, other products or applications can work together as long as they use the common standards or protocols.

Why Use These Services?

There are various reasons for sharing and accessing map data using web services. A government or large corporation may make map data available so that other divisions or departments don't need to store their data locally. Consider the cost savings often touted for centralizing data storage. If data is centralized, the users still need to access it. Web services for mapping make the data available.

Perhaps someone is willing to share data with you but can't allow you to have a complete copy, for whatever reason. A web service can facilitate that. Some map data, such as hurricane locations, is constantly changing. Downloading that data might not be possible or timely. Integrating a layer in your map that accesses a web service in realtime might be the answer. Some data repositories are so large that it would be unrealistic to copy them to your location. Web services can make that data available for you at the time you need it. This helps reduce the need for continual data storage upgrades. Figure 12-1 illustrates the basic function of a MapServer application accessing remote data through a web services request.

Whether sharing or accessing, it is all about making the most of our time and resources. Continually changing an application to point to new data can be inefficient. Storing large amounts of data locally may also be an unreasonable option.

Internal Versus External Needs

Some service providers sharing data will never use the information internally. For example, think of a government agency that makes mapping data available to the public. The public benefits by having free and open access to mapping information. The government benefits by successfully fulfilling their mandate. Providing web services for mapping data can require a serious commitment to openness and support for clients.

On the other end of the spectrum, a company might share data internally and never share it with the public. Web services don't require that the data be publicly accessible. Services can be securely guarded like any other web page or internal application. Large corporations may use services internally to make data broadly accessible

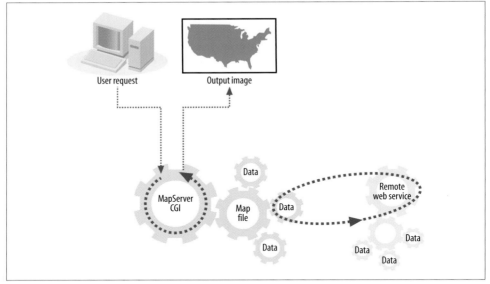

Figure 12-1. MapServer requesting map data from a remote web server

without having to maintain redundant hardware infrastructures across divisions. This can be a cost-reduction measure, but it can also improve service to users. Users need two things: access to information and access to information in the right format. The benefit of mapping services is that a data source can be made available, and how the data sources are formatted or presented can be managed as well.

Both internal and external needs scenarios can be handled equally well through web services for mapping with MapServer.

Using MapServer with Web Services

It isn't necessary to program applications to use web services. MapServer is already able to access and provide data using a web services framework. This chapter focuses on setting up your MapServer application to use these services and will show you how to define a layer in your map file (which uses data retrieved from a remote data source). You will also learn how to set up your own service to make your data available to others.

The web services specifications for mapping come from the Open Geospatial Consortium (formerly known as the Open GIS Consortium). The OGC has developed standards or specifications for web services for mapping. The goal of the organization is to improve interoperability between applications by creating some common interchange languages through common standards. The membership list is quite impressive, as are the goals. Here is a brief description from the About page at *http:// opengeospatial.org/about/*:

> The Open Geospatial Consortium, Inc. (OGC) is an international industry consortium of 270 companies, government agencies and universities participating in a consensus process to develop publicly available interface specifications. OpenGIS® Specifications support interoperable solutions that "geo-enable" the Web, wireless and location-based services, and mainstream IT. The specifications empower technology developers to make complex spatial information and services accessible and useful with all kinds of applications.

The focus here isn't on creating applications, but on specifications for sharing data. This makes sense when you consider that major mapping, GIS, and IT players sit together on this consortium (e.g., Autodesk, ESRI, MapInfo, Intergraph, and Oracle).

MapServer can implement many OGC specifications, in varying degrees of completeness, as summarized in Table 12-1.

Table 12-1. OGC specifications implemented by MapServer

Abbreviation	Name	Purpose
WMS	Web Map Service	Share and request vector and raster map data in plain image format
WFS	Web Feature Service	Share and request vector map data and attributes in GML format
WCS	Web Coverage Service	Share image/raster data with original data values
WMC	Web Map Context	Save and load views of a WMS application as XML
SLD	Styled Layer Descriptors	Request particular symbolization and styling from a WMS
GML	Geography Markup Language	XML-based format for spatial and tabular data interchange
Filter	Filter Encoding	XML-based format for defining queries on spatial data

Two of the more popular specifications are presented here: Web Map Service and Web Feature Service. Other specifications are useful, including some not used for mapping, but aren't discussed here. Information on all the OGC specifications can be found at *http://www.opengeospatial.org/specs/?page=specs*.

> A MapServer OGC Web Services Workshop package can be downloaded from *http://devgeo.cciw.ca/ms_ogc_workshop/index.html*. This demonstrates various ways to access services.

Reference and tutorial documents for WMS and WFS are available in the OGC Compliance section of the MapServer documentation page. See these documents for the most up-to-date, MapServer-specific information about WMS, WFS, and other web services at *http://mapserver.gis.umn.edu/doc/*.

These web sites may help you find a publicly accessible web service:

GeoConnections Discovery Portal
   http://geodiscover.cgdi.ca/gdp/search?action=searchForm&entryType=webService

Refractions Research: OGC Services Survey
   http://www.refractions.net/ogcsurvey/

National Geophysical Data Center: Interactive Map Services
   http://www.ngdc.noaa.gov/maps/interactivemaps.html

Web Map Service (WMS)

WMS provides a way to send map images over the Web. Your MapServer applications can request customized maps from remote sources that have a WMS available. Finding a WMS source isn't always easy. Others on the MapServer or OGC-related mailing list can point you in the right direction. Any web site you find that uses web mapping may also have a WMS available. For sites using MapServer, enabling this service can be simple.

A range of parameters and options are used when requesting a map, its content, and look. It works much like if you phoned a consultant and asked him to put together a map and email the image to you. How would you make the request? It might be something like this:

   Client: "Good morning. I need a map."

   Consultant: "Hello. What part of the world are you interested in?"

   Client: "Pretty much all of North America."

   Consultant: "Really? All Canada, United States, and Mexico?"

   Cl: "Actually, I'm interested in everything north of the equator."

   Co: "Okay, that's still pretty big. You want all the way to the North Pole?"

   Cl: "Yes, definitely."

   Co: "Okay, I'm going to give you a map that goes from the equator to the North Pole, and also covers Newfoundland in the east (50 degrees west) to the border of Russia in the west (170 degrees west). How big is the final map going to be?"

   Cl: "It's going to cover my entire wall from floor to ceiling."

   Co: "So about eight feet tall?"

   Cl: "Yes, I guess so."

   Co: "How wide do you think it will be?"

   Cl: "Probably half as wide: four feet."

   Co: "What print resolution are you going to use?"

   Cl: "Hmm, my printer supports up to 150 dpi."

   Co: "Okay, the image will be about 14,400 pixels high and 7,200 pixels wide. I hope you have lots of space in your email box. This is going to be a big file! Is there a particular map projection you want to use?"

   Cl: "I want it to be just like one I already have. Just a second, I'll see what it is. Okay, it says it is Plate Caree. Does that mean anything to you?"

Co: "Yep, no problem. I'll just use the EPSG projection code 4326 for the map, same thing. What do you want to see on your map?"

Cl: "Hmmm, the country boundaries, major highways, waterways, and capital cities."

Co: "Do you want any special styling for your layers, or should I just use the default way I usually do them?"

Cl: "Keep it simple; the usual way is fine."

Co: "Okay, I've got those. One last question. What type of image file would you like? I can give you JPEG or PNG."

Cl: "JPEG please."

Co: "Okay, I'll send you the file in a few minutes."

Cl: "Thanks a lot. Talk to you later."

All the crucial information needed to get started on a map was collected by the consultant. Now he can go away and create the map image for the client. A WMS request is virtually the same thing, except that there isn't as much two-way discussion going on. The client must know what to ask for. Asking for the wrong thing doesn't get you very far.

Specific WMS parameters are required for requesting a map. Table 12-2 briefly describes them, using the phone call analogy for examples.

Table 12-2. Required WMS parameters for a GetMap request

Common name	Description	WMS example
The type of service	Tell the server you want to make a WMS request. This is done automatically by MapServer.	`service=WMS`
Request a map	As opposed to requesting other types of WMS information. This is done automatically by MapServer.	`request=getmap`
Specify the version of the WMS to be used	Some WMS supports only certain versions.	`version=1.1.1`
Projection or spatial reference system (SRS)	Requested map projection using the EPSG projection code. SRS is going to be called CRS in future versions of the WMS.	`srs=EPSG:4326`
Image format	What image format the map will be sent back in.	`format=image/jpeg`
Layer names or data sources	Names used by the server to describe a layer or group of layers to be drawn. As a URL, the parameter is called `layers`. A map file uses the `wms_name` parameter to specify the layers.	`layers=Countries, road, water, cities`
Image size	Image size in width and height, pixel units. Many servers restrict the size of the image to 1024 × 1024 or 2000 × 2000.	`width="7200" height="14400"`
Geographic extent or bounding box	Two pairs of coordinates defining the southwest and northeast corners of the map.	`bbox=-170 0,-50 90`

Table 12-2. Required WMS parameters for a GetMap request (continued)

Common name	Description	WMS example
Choose styles for each layer	Layers can be drawn in different ways, e.g., using different datasets, if the server supports it. Leaving it blank selects the default style.	styles=

In many cases you may specify only the SRS, layer, and image type in your map file. The rest is taken care of by MapServer when it makes the actual request. For example, MapServer knows what size the map is and requests an image size that is the same. It also knows what area of the world the map is looking at, so it automatically passes the bounding box parameter with correct values. If you are building a URL manually, you will have to specify all these parameters.

The parameter names aren't case sensitive, but the values are. Depending on the server that receives the request, you may need to match their values exactly. For instance, some servers allow request=getMap, and others require request=getmap. Using the wrong case for layer names is also a common pitfall.

Checking the capabilities of a WMS provider

Once you've found a WMS source or a site offering WMS, you will probably be given an obscure URL to look at. This page (*http://www.refractions.net/ogcsurvey/index. php?country=US*) provides a comprehensive list of WMS (and other) services that are available. The URL given for each item doesn't take you to a web page. This is the reference to a WMS document (a.k.a. capabilities document). This may not mean much to someone just starting out with WMS, but this is the standard way of sharing connection information.

To understand what a WMS offers, you need to access this capabilities document. For these examples, you will use a popular WMS that provides global satellite imagery and various other layers for the United States. The URL for *wms.jpl.nasa.gov* is shown on the WMS listing as *http://wms.jpl.nasa.gov/wms.cgi?request=GetCapabilities*.

So what do you do with this URL? Depending on your web browser, clicking on the link may or may not be helpful. The result is an XML document with information in it about the WMS. If your browser doesn't automatically show the contents of the document, you may need to save it to a file on your system and open it with another program. It is sent in a WMS-specific XML format that most browsers won't recognize, though when you force it to load the file, it can render the XML just fine. You can also use the command-line tool wget to download the document directly to a file, like this:

```
> wget  -O jplwms.xml "http://wms.jpl.nasa.gov/wms.cgi?request=GetCapabilities"
```

This is all one line. The -O (capital letter o) option saves the results of the URL into a file. Otherwise it will list it on the screen instead. Any text editor such as Notepad,

Wordpad, or Emacs can open this document. A web browser should be able to as well. You should save this file using the *.xml* file extension.

Example 12-1 shows some pieces of the capabilities document. The document is usually rich with information and includes the names of those who maintain the service and any restrictions on use. The parts you are most interested in describe the available projections, layers, and image formats.

Example 12-1. Parts of a standard WMS capabilities document

```
...
<Title>OnEarth Web Map Server</Title>
  <SRS>EPSG:4326</SRS>
  <SRS>AUTO:42003</SRS>
...
<Layer queryable="0">
  <Name>global_mosaic</Name>
  <Title>WMS Global Mosaic, pan sharpened</Title>
  ...
  <LatLonBoundingBox minx="-180" miny="-90" maxx="180" maxy="90"/>
...
</layer>
...
```

Deciphering XML

The XML format for capability documents is text with a very specific structure. WMS information is encoded between pairs of markup tags, those pieces of text with words surrounded by less-than and greater-than signs <>. When you see a tag that has a preceding backslash /, it represents the end of a piece of information. For example, <Layer....> is the start of some layer information, and </Layer> is the end of the section. Notice that there are pieces of text indented and embedded within other sections. <Name> is within <Layer>, for example. This means that the name information pertains to that particular layer section. That's your short primer on XML. If you want to know more about the purpose and methods of using XML (in a much wider context), see other O'Reilly books such as *Learning XML* or *XML In A Nutshell*.

Capabilities documents play an integral role in effective web map services. They contain metadata (data about the data) that isn't obvious by looking at the data itself. These documents allow tools to search for the availability of information or catalog services, even by geographic location. Capabilities documents describe what information is available and how to access it. Without these documents, the implementation of OGC web services is hampered.

All you need to know is that each little section holds some information about the service. Much of the document may be meaningless to you, but the following paragraphs highlight the key things to look for.

Projections are especially important when using WMS layers in MapServer. The remote WMS source may provide maps in various projections. When you set up a layer, you need to decide which projection to request. This should be the same as the projection you are using in your application. The first three lines of Example 12-1 show the title of the service and two spatial reference system codes you can choose from. If the one you are using in your map isn't listed, you can still use the WMS but you'll have to tell MapServer to reproject the image to fit your other layers. The EPSG code for the example is 4326, a global coordinate reference system typically known as WGS 84. So you're in luck; it is listed as an option:

```
<SRS>EPSG:4326</SRS>
```

You can request this directly from the service provider, and MapServer won't have any additional overhead for reprojecting the map for your application.

The next section in Example 12-1 is the most important if you already know that the service will be useful to you:

```
<Layer queryable="0">
  <Name>global_mosaic</Name>
  <Title>WMS Global Mosaic, pan sharpened</Title>
  ...
  <LatLonBoundingBox minx="-180" miny="-90" maxx="180" maxy="90"/>
</layer>
```

The layer sections give you the critical pieces of layer connection information. The main item is the Name element.

```
<Name>global_mosaic</Name>
```

This element gives the layer a unique name that you will refer to in your application. The name here is global_mosaic. Layer names can be quite cryptic. The title element can help you understand what the name means. In this case, the title for the layer is WMS Global Mosaic, pan sharpened. Use the name and not the title of the layer in your MapServer map file.

The next section in Example 12-1 is the LatLonBoundingBox:

```
<LatLonBoundingBox minx="-180" miny="-90" maxx="180" maxy="90"/>
```

This is most useful if you are unfamiliar with the geographic area that a WMS covers. The coordinates represent a geographic rectangle that the service covers. If you are south of the equator, a quick look at this line tells you that the southernmost area covered is miny="-90" or 90 degrees *south* of the equator. It extends to maxy="90.0" or 90 degrees *north*. This service covers the globe, so you should be able to use it in any application you want, no matter where it is located.

There are other useful elements in the capabilities document, such as `<MinScaleDenominator>20000</MinScaleDenominator>`. You can use it as a guide to know what scale the layer is meant to mapped at. This value is set as the `MINSCALE` when adding the layer to the MapServer map file, which you'll see later in Example 12-4.

The layer name and other parameters are put into a URL and sent to the WMS provider, which then sends back a map image. If there is a problem with your request you will probably get an error message instead of an image. If you have the request right, but there is no data for that area, or at that scale, you will get an empty map and no error.

Manually requesting a map from a WMS source

Now you'll take this information and build your own URL from scratch. MapServer creates all of this automatically later on, but Example 12-2 gives you a taste of what is going on behind the scenes. This URL is all one line, with no spaces. It has been broken into multiple lines with space added to make it more readable. Figure 12-2 then shows the image that is returned from this URL.

Example 12-2. A basic WMS request from a handmade URL

```
http://wms.jpl.nasa.gov/wms.cgi
    ?request=GetMap
    &service=WMS
    &version=1.1.1
    &srs=EPSG:4326
    &format=image/jpeg
    &styles=
    &bbox=-180,-90,180,90
    &width=600
    &height=300
    &layers=global_mosaic
```

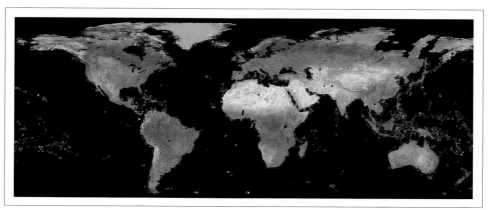

Figure 12-2. A global map image from a WMS request

This is a very simple example though it may look complicated. There are other parameters and options that can be used by some WMS providers, but these are just the most basic. The last four settings (layers, bbox, width, and height) can be easily changed to modify your map if you want a larger map, or a different layer.

The example can be spiced up a bit by simply adding more layer names to the layers parameter. Example 12-3 shows a map that adds another layer listed in the capabilities document. This layer helps fill in the background where the global_mosaic layer had gaps, in Antarctica and northeast Asia, for instance.

Example 12-3. Several layers requested in a URL to a WMS

```
http://wms.jpl.nasa.gov/wms.cgi
?request=GetMap
&service=WMS
&version=1.1.1
&srs=EPSG:4326
&format=image/jpeg
&styles=
&bbox=-180,-90,180,90
&width=600
&height=300
&layers=modis,global_mosaic
```

Very little effort is needed to change the URL and produce a map displaying more information. Figure 12-3 shows the map that is created and returned.

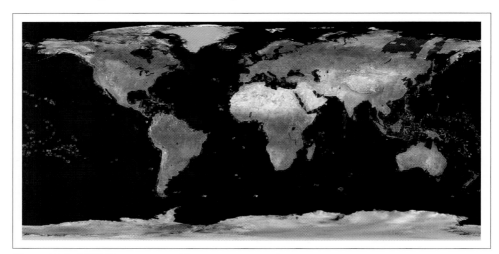

Figure 12-3. A WMS map returned from a remote service

A few minor modifications yield a much more complete-looking map. Notice that where there was no Landsat imagery in Figure 12-2, the gaps have been filled. Note that the modis layer was listed first in the layers parameter. This draws it first on the map, then the global_mosaic draws over top. If you put the modis layer after the global_mosaic, it will draw, but completely cover the global_mosaic.

If you want to experiment a bit, change the bbox setting to one of these, for interesting views of parts of the world. Be sure to keep the image size to 600×300 or at least keep the width/height ratio as 2:1.

Baghdad
&bbox=44.22252,33.24291,44.58252,33.42291

Gibraltar
&bbox=-6.825,35.3775,-4.575,36.5025

Panama Canal
&bbox=-80.30625,8.8725,-79.18125,9.435

You can also remove the global_mosaic layer and see how the global modis layer looks on its own.

All the other layers listed in the capabilities document can be added to the URL, but many won't show very well because they overlap each other and may only draw at certain scales.

One limitation with this WMS is that if you make requests too quickly, it may give you an error. If you get an error, wait a few seconds and try again. This is an experimental server and may be discontinued, modified, or become unsupported at any time.

Adding a WMS layer to a MapServer map file

Sending WMS requests through URLs in your web browser can be interesting, but WMS becomes much more powerful when you combine it with your own, locally stored, data. The remote source doesn't know anything about the other layers on your map, but can add to them. MapServer takes the image that results from the request and treats it as another layer to overlay. It is possible to have an application that uses only external WMS layers. The real power is in combining your own information with someone else's to produce a more effective map than you would have been able to do on your own.

A WMS layer in your map file has some more specific settings than other layers. Example 12-4 shows a layer defined using the data source in Example 12-2.

Example 12-4. A sample WMS layer in a MapServer map file

```
LAYER
  NAME global_landsat
  TYPE RASTER
  STATUS DEFAULT
  CONNECTIONTYPE WMS
  CONNECTION "http://wms.jpl.nasa.gov/wms.cgi?"
```

Example 12-4. A sample WMS layer in a MapServer map file (continued)

```
  MINSCALE 20000
  METADATA
    "wms_server_version" "1.1.1"
    "wms_srs" "EPSG:4326"
    "wms_format" "image/jpeg"
    "wms_styles" ""
    "wms_name" "modis,global_mosaic"
  END
END
```

You can add this layer to the *global.map* used in previous chapters. A couple other changes will be required to make it work in that environment. You will probably want to change MapServer's output image format to support more colors, because this WMS has a lot of different colors. Add IMAGETYPE PNG24 right after the IMAGECOLOR setting. You should also remove the COLOR setting from the countries layer so that you can see the WMS data underneath. A complete listing of the *global.map* file used for these examples is included at the end of the chapter in Example 12-13.

The settings in a map file are very similar to those used in the URL. The biggest difference is that several settings aren't required because MapServer generates them internally (e.g., width, height, bbox). MapServer can infer these settings based on the current map being viewed, its extent, size, etc.

The connection setting must be set to CONNECTIONTYPE WMS to tell MapServer to make a WMS request. Then the base URL is put in as the connection string. This URL goes up to and includes the question mark (as in Examples 12-2 and 12-3).

 If the server is based on MapServer, the path to the map file may also need to be specified in the CONNECTION string. In that case, the base URL will end at the ampersand (&) after this setting; for example, *http://spatialguru.com/cgi-bin/mapserv?map=/maps/globalwms.map&*.

All remaining parameters are put into a METADATA section for the layer. Each setting is named, and a value is given. For example "wms_name" is the setting, and the value is "modis,global_mosaic". These setting/value pairs are taken by MapServer and converted into the proper format to request the map image behind the scenes.

Most of the settings are self-explanatory if you compare them to the earlier examples. The main difference is the use of "wms_name" to provide the list of layer names. Instinct might tell you to use something like "wms_layers", but that won't work. All the layers that you are requesting need to be set in the wms_name setting. Multiple layers are listed in one long piece of text, separated by a comma.

Notice that you don't use any CLASS objects in a WMS layer. You can't change the way the WMS map is drawn unless you use another OGC specification called Styled Layer Descriptors (SLD). SLD allows you to request specific styling of a WMS layer if the WMS supports it. Using SLD is beyond the scope of this book. More information about using SLD with MapServer can be found at *http://mapserver.gis.umn.edu/doc/sld-howto.html*.

 It is possible to query WMS layers. Instead of a getMap request, it uses a getFeatureInfo request. Querying is more complicated than making basic map viewing requests. See the OGC WMS specification to understand more about what parameters it requires at *http://www.opengeospatial.org/specs/?page=specs*.

WMS is aimed at interoperability between applications; this includes MapServer and any other WMS-compliant mapping program. In the examples earlier in this chapter, you use MapServer as a client program to make requests from a WMS. The WMS is provided by a different web mapping package from MapServer. This is the power of WMS: application independence not being tied to one particular software package. It is the same when using MapServer as a WMS server; any other program that supports WMS can connect to it, and MapServer doesn't care.

There are many other tools that can act as WMS clients. Here are a few:

OpenEV WMS Tool (http://openev.sourceforge.net)
   A WMS Client tool for OpenEV that allows you to add WMS layers. It is also included with FWTools.

Intergraph OGC WMS Viewer (http://wmsviewer.com)
   A web-based WMS viewing tool that allows you to add your own WMS sources to their global mapping application

Refractions WMS Extension for ArcView 3 (http://refractions.net/arc3wms/)
   An extension that allows you to define and add WMS themes to ArcView 3

ESRI ArcMap (http://esri.com/software/arcgis/)
   A commercial desktop GIS program that supports connections to WMS data sources

Using MapServer as a WMS server

MapServer can also serve as a WMS server, allowing you to make your data available to others. There isn't a lot to it. You just need to add a few more settings to the map file, and then others can connect to your WMS with their applications.

Two parts of the map file need to be modified to support a WMS. Some changes need to be made in the WEB section of the map file; other changes need to be made in the layers you want to make available.

The WEB section defines some settings for the entire MapServer application. In this case, you add a few lines describing your application to external WMS clients. Example 12-5 shows what the WEB section looks like if you modify the *global.map* application. A full listing of *global.map* is shown in Example 12-13 at the end of the chapter. The highlighted sections were added to enable WMS server support.

Example 12-5. Modifying the WEB class to enable WMS server capabilities

```
WEB
  HEADER none
  TEMPLATE global.html
  FOOTER none
  IMAGEPATH "/srv/www/htdocs/tmp/"
  IMAGEURL "/tmp/"
  METADATA
    "wms_title" "My Global Map WMS Server"
    "wms_srs" "EPSG:4326"
  END
END
```

These values are used when a WMS client makes a GetCapabilities request to your server. It shows the title of your service and what projection it uses.

The other place to make changes is at the layer level. Again, we modify the METADATA section of a layer to add a few settings. Most settings merely describe your layer in more detail so that external users can request appropriate information. Example 12-6 shows what the definition for the WMS-enabled layer looks like, with the modifications highlighted. A full map file is listed at the end of the chapter in Example 12-14. The global_mosaic WMS layer was removed as well as the labels for the country layer, to keep this example short and simple.

Example 12-6. Making a layer available through WMS

```
LAYER
  NAME countries
  TYPE POLYGON
  STATUS ON
  DATA countries_simpl
  MINSCALE 1000
  MAXSCALE 1000000000
  CLASSITEM 'NAME'
  CLASS
    NAME 'Bulgaria'
    EXPRESSION 'Bulgaria'
    STYLE
      OUTLINECOLOR 100 100 100
    END
  END
  CLASS
    NAME 'All Countries'
    EXPRESSION ('[NAME]' ne 'Bulgaria')
    STYLE
      OUTLINECOLOR 100 100 100
    END
  END
  METADATA
    "wms_title" "Country boundaries"
  END
END
```

This layer makes the countries layer WMS-accessible.

By setting STATUS ON, this layer won't be drawn by default. WMS clients won't want default layers every time; they'll want to pick and choose.

MINSCALE and MAXSCALE settings prevent data from being used at unsuitable scales. If you don't set them, you may receive warnings. These warnings can be safely ignored, but it is good practice to set them anyway. In this example, it doesn't really matter, so the range is very broad.

Just as with the WEB object, you insert a METADATA object containing a wms_title for the layer. This title is displayed in the capabilities document for your WMS.

Checking your own WMS capabilities document

Once you have a WMS server up and running with the previous modifications to your map file, you can test it. The URL will point to the MapServer executable and the map file, using a request=GetCapabilities tagged on the end. The URL used to check is (again, all one line with no spaces) *http://spatialguru.com/cgi-bin/mapserv? map=/maps/global.map&request=GetCapabilities&service=WMS*.

If you are running the example on your own computer, you need to replace *http:// spatialguru.com/* with your hostname, e.g., *http://localhost/*. You also need to give it the path to the map file you have built.

You will get a lot of information back from the getCapabilities request, but all you need to know is that the layer you set up earlier is listed properly. It is in the XML file you downloaded using the earlier URL, shown here. The <Style> section was removed to show the main layer settings.

```
...
<Layer queryable="0" opaque="0" cascaded="0">
    <Name>countries</Name>
    <Title>Country boundaries</Title>
    <Style>
        ...
    </Style>
    <ScaleHint min="0.498903" max="498903" />
</Layer>
...
```

Now someone else can request data from the WMS running on your web server. The first three lines describe the group the layers are assigned to in the map file. The second <Layer...> tag in the file starts the actual countries layer section, which is shown. Notice how a lot of information is provided about the layer, including SRS and BoundingBox. These were not explicitly set in the METADATA; MapServer provides these important pieces of information automatically.

Web Feature Service (WFS)

Another increasingly popular service uses the WFS specification. It is implemented in several mapping applications; MapServer is just one example. WFS operates much like the WMS but has significant differences. With WMS, only a map image is returned to you; with WFS, actual feature data is returned to the client. The server sends back geographic coordinate data such as line, point, or polygon features.

In MapServer, the features can then be drawn like any other layer because it has a copy of the data to work with. The process is more labor-intensive than WMS. WMS is desirable because MapServer just overlays other layers on top of the image; you'll like WFS because it offers more flexibility and can, optionally, save features into a usable data file.

Checking the capabilities of a WFS provider

The capabilities of a WFS can be determined through a URL request. Here's a simple one:

> *http://map.ns.ec.gc.ca/envdat/map.aspx?service=WFS&version=1.0.*
> *0&request=GetCapabilities*

The results are given back to you in an XML file, similar to the WMS capabilities document format. Portions of the document are listed in Example 12-7.

Example 12-7. Sample WFS capabilities document

```
...
<Service>
  <Name>MapServer WFS</Name>
  <Title>ENVIRODAT - Atlantic Region Water Quality Chemistry Database</Title>
  <Abstract>ENVIRODAT is a repository of water quality information including chemical,
physical, biological, and selected hydrometric data which are stored for surface,
groundwater, wastewater, precipitation and various other water types</Abstract>
...
  <OnlineResource>http://map.ns.ec.gc.ca/envdat/map.aspx?</OnlineResource>
...
    <FeatureType>
      <Name>envirodat</Name>
      <Title>ENVIRODAT - Atlantic Region Water Quality Chemistry Database</Title>
...
      <SRS>EPSG:4326</SRS>
      <LatLongBoundingBox minx="-64.6622" miny="46.7594" maxx="-52.6808" maxy="55.2333" />
    </FeatureType>
```

The key pieces of information needed for this map file are the OnlineResource and the Name of the FeatureType.

Manually requesting data from a WFS source

Manual requests to a WFS source can also be made through a URL. Instead of getting a map back, you get an XML file with geographic and tabular data encoded in it. The file is in the OGC format, Geography Markup Language or GML. WMS gave you a map image back; WFS gives you raw data to work with.

The URL looks similar to the WMS URL, but is often much simpler. Because WFS sends you raw data to work with, you don't need to send the service any information such as the size of your map or the image format. The following example shows how to use the wget command to grab data and put it into a file:

```
> wget -O wfs_data.gml "http://map.ns.ec.gc.ca/envdat/map.aspx?service=WFS&version=1.
0.0&request=GetFeature&typename=envirodat"
```

Other services may be more strict, but this will at least get you started. The resulting file is 86 KB in size and over 2,000 lines long.

> If you have the ogrinfo utility handy, you can see summary details about the GML file by running:
>
> ```
> > ogrinfo wfs_data.gml envdat:envirodat -so
> ```
>
> Using the results, you can select one attribute to use to label these points. Remove -so to list all the feature details, or just open it in a text editor to see all the gory details.

This file can be used as a GML data source in your map file, but with WFS, you don't need this manual step. Instead you can encode the details from the URL into a connection string in the layer definition.

Adding a WFS layer to a MapServer map file

Adding the WFS from the previous section as a layer in the map file is fairly simple, as shown in Example 12-8. The key parts are highlighted, and the rest are just settings that make the points look better on the map. Certain parts of the URL used in Example 12-8 are split into METADATA parameters, as with WMS.

Example 12-8. Example map file layer that uses a remote WFS

```
...
EXTENT -64.6622 46.7594 -52.6808 55.2333
...
LAYER
  GROUP testing
  NAME wfs_test
  STATUS OFF
  TYPE POINT
  CONNECTIONTYPE WFS
  CONNECTION "http://map.ns.ec.gc.ca/envdat/map.aspx?"
  LABELITEM "envdat:Station_ID"
  CLASS
```

Example 12-8. Example map file layer that uses a remote WFS (continued)

```
    STYLE
      SYMBOL 'circle'
      SIZE 10
      OUTLINECOLOR 150 150 0
      COLOR 250 250 0
    END
    LABEL
      SIZE SMALL
      COLOR 255 255 255
      POSITION UR
    END
  END
  METADATA
    "wfs_version" "1.0.0"
    "wfs_srs" "EPSG:4326"
    "wfs_typename" "envirodat"
    "wfs_request_method" "GET"
    "wfs_service" "WFS"
  END
END
```

 If the WFS source is an older version of MapServer than yours, you have to include the last parameter: `wfs_request_method`. Otherwise, this parameter is optional. This may also be necessary for other vendors' map servers. The `wfs_service` also needs to be explicitly set in older versions of MapServer, unlike with a WMS layer. This bug was recently fixed.

As shown in Figure 12-4, part of the global mapping application produces a map of water quality points in Newfoundland, Canada. The EXTENT for the map was changed so that the map would focus on an area within the WFS data source bounding box. Example 12-15 shows the complete map file for this WFS client test. Several items were added to improve appearance. Notice that the COUNTRIES layer was shaded, and the WFS layer was added to the end of the map file so that the points draw on top of the COUNTRIES layer.

Figure 12-5 shows an example of a map with the WMS global_mosaic layer used earlier, in combination with the WFS layer and some local water and transportation layers. This shows just how well sources can be combined to provide valuable context.

Using MapServer as a WFS server

MapServer can be built to operate as a WFS server. It is then easy to make your vector data accessible to others. As with WMS, there are two places you need to add WFS settings.

The first place to add settings is in the WEB...METADATA section. Example 12-9 shows the WEB section of the map file, with some WFS METADATA added.

Figure 12-4. A map including water quality station points from a WFS data source

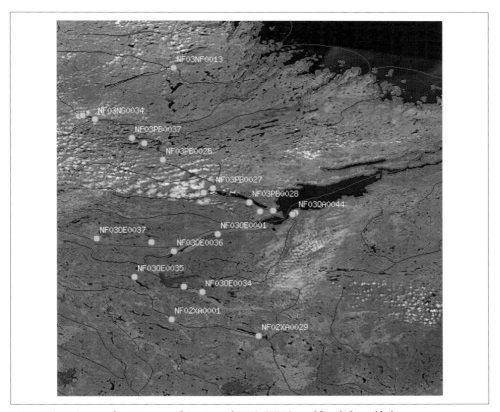

Figure 12-5. A map showing a combination of WFS, WMS, and local shapefile layers

Example 12-9. Modifying the WEB class to enable WFS server capabilities

```
WEB
  IMAGEPATH "/srv/www/tmp/"
  IMAGEURL "/tmp/"
  METADATA
    "wfs_title" "My Global WFS Map Service"
  END
END
```

The example shows the most basic settings possible, adding only a `"wfs_title"` parameter and a name value for the service. There are several other parameters you might choose to include. The `EXTENT` for the map file restricts any WFS request. In this example, set it back to a global extent (`EXTENT -180 -90 180 90`). If you keep the `EXTENT` used in the previous section, only features that overlap the `EXTENT` are returned.

The MapServer OGC Web Services Workshop is a good resource for seeing more complete examples of a map file configured for WFS; see *http://devgeo.cciw.ca/ms_ogc_workshop/index.html*.

For more information about these parameters, see the MapServer documentation for adding WFS support to your map files at *http://mapserver.gis.umn.edu/doc/wfs-server-howto.html*.

Other changes need to be made for each `LAYER` you want to make available. Keep in mind that only vector data layers can be used for WFS. GML supports vector data types, not imagery; if you need to serve up images, you should be using WMS or WCS (see Table 12-1). Example 12-10 shows the countries layer with the changes required to make it WFS accessible. The full map file is shown at the end of the chapter in Example 12-16.

Example 12-10. Making a shapefile layer available through WFS

```
LAYER
    NAME countries
    TYPE POLYGON
    STATUS ON
    DUMP TRUE
    DATA countries_simpl
    METADATA
      "wfs_title" "Country Boundaries"
    END
    PROJECTION
      "init=epsg:4326"
    END
END
```

Notice how all the styling `CLASS` objects and some other settings have been removed. If you only want to make your data available through WFS, these objects aren't required because they aren't being mapped. Only the feature data is being sent back to the client. You can still have layers set up to draw maps, and serve up WFS or WMS data as well.

Not all settings are made in the METADATA section. For instance, the DUMP parameter needs to be set to TRUE at the layer level. This gives MapServer permission to send raw data to those requesting it. Set this to FALSE for layers you don't want to share.

The only required METADATA setting is "wfs_title". It is good practice to use a lot more metadata than shown in these simplistic examples. In fact, you can use it to store whatever metadata you want. Metadata describes your information so that users who aren't familiar with it won't expect more from it than it can provide. It is also a critical tool for large organizations because it keeps track of and manages their spatial data infrastructure.

Checking your own WFS capabilities document

Testing your WFS server is much easier than testing a WMS server, because very few parameters are required. Example 12-11 shows wget downloading the capabilities document URL for the previous example. Parts of the results of the capabilities document are shown as well.

Example 12-11. Testing the WFS using a URL with the tool

```
> wget -O wfscapabilities.xml "http://spatialguru.com/cgi-bin/mapserv?map=/maps/globalwfs.
map&service=WFS&version=1.0.0&request=GetCapabilities"

...
<Service>
  <Name>MapServer WFS</Name>
  <Title>My Global WFS Map Service</Title>
  <OnlineResource>http://spatialguru.com:80/cgi-bin/mapserv?map=/maps/globalwfs.map&</
OnlineResource>
</Service>
...
<FeatureTypeList>
  <Operations>
    <Query/>
  </Operations>
    <FeatureType>
        <Name>countries</Name>
        <Title>Country Boundaries</Title>
        <SRS>EPSG:4326</SRS>
        <LatLongBoundingBox minx="-180" miny="-89.9999" maxx="180" maxy="83.6274" />
    </FeatureType>
</FeatureTypeList>
...
```

Notice that the file is full of many entries automatically generated by MapServer, i.e., not part of the WFS METADATA object. MapServer even calculated the LatLongBoundingBox for you. It also created a Name element based on the layer's name setting, which is something else you can set in the METADATA section using the wfs_ name parameter if you would like something different.

To grab the data from the test layer you have to change the type of request to &request=GetFeature and add &typename=countries based on the FeatureType Name for the layer in the capabilities document. The URL and a piece of the data output from the request is shown in Example 12-12.

Example 12-12. Testing the WFS by downloading feature data

```
> wget -O countries.gml "http://spatialguru.com/cgi-bin/mapserv?map=/maps/
globalwfs.map&service=WFS&version=1.0.0&request=GetFeature&typename=countries"
...
<gml:featureMember>
  <countries>
    <gml:boundedBy>
      <gml:Box srsName="EPSG:4326">
        <gml:coordinates>
            -57.336025,54.494965 -57.245407,54.577198
        </gml:coordinates>
      </gml:Box>
    </gml:boundedBy>
    <gml:polygonProperty>
      <gml:Polygon srsName="EPSG:4326">
        <gml:outerBoundaryIs>
          <gml:LinearRing>
            <gml:coordinates>
              -57.336025,54.494965 -57.330402,54.563805
              -57.245407,54.577198 -57.250492,54.506748
              -57.336025,54.494965
            </gml:coordinates>
          </gml:LinearRing>
        </gml:outerBoundaryIs>
      </gml:Polygon>
    </gml:polygonProperty>
    <gid>36354</gid>
    <cat>38</cat>
    <fibs>CA</fibs>
    <name>Canada</name>
    <f_code>FA001</f_code>
    <total>32507874</total>
    <male>16071958</male>
    <female>16435916</female>
    <ratio>97.799999999999997</ratio>
  </countries>
</gml:featureMember>
...
```

The list goes on and on, showing the data for every country polygon feature in the layer.

GML is a vector format that OpenEV can read, so Figure 12-6 shows a map made to test the downloaded data. Country boundaries were put on top of an earth image, and then some clouds were added. Now this file can be zipped and emailed to some-body else or connected to as a WFS layer in another MapServer application.

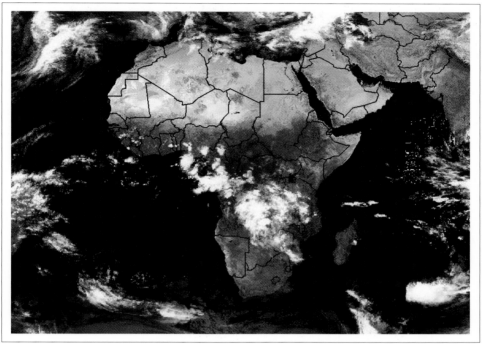

Figure 12-6. Map produced by OpenEV using the GML file downloaded from the WFS and some other imagery

Reference Map Files

This section includes the complete listing of map files (Examples 12-13 through 12-16) used in this chapter. Additions to the files are highlighted. Lines to be removed are commented out by the preceding # symbols.

Example 12-13. The global_mosaic WMS layer added to the global.map file

```
MAP
  SIZE 600 300
  EXTENT -180 -90 180 90
  IMAGECOLOR 180 180 250
  IMAGETYPE PNG24

  UNITS DD

WEB
  TEMPLATE global.html
  IMAGEPATH "/srv/www/htdocs/tmp/"
```

Example 12-13. The global_mosaic WMS layer added to the global.map file (continued)

```
      IMAGEURL "/tmp/"
    END

    LAYER
      NAME global_landsat
      TYPE RASTER
      STATUS DEFAULT
      CONNECTIONTYPE WMS
      CONNECTION "http://wms.jpl.nasa.gov/wms.cgi?"
      MINSCALE 20000
      METADATA
        "wms_server_version" "1.1.1"
        "wms_srs" "EPSG:4326"
        "wms_format" "image/jpeg"
        "wms_styles" ""
        "wms_name" "modis,global_mosaic"
      END
    END

    LAYER
      NAME countries
      TYPE POLYGON
      STATUS DEFAULT
      DATA countries_simpl
      LABELITEM 'NAME'
      LABELMAXSCALE 50000000
      CLASSITEM 'NAME'
      CLASS
        NAME 'Bulgaria'
        EXPRESSION 'Bulgaria'
        STYLE
          OUTLINECOLOR 100 100 100
#         COLOR 255 255 150
        END
        LABEL
          SIZE LARGE
        END
      END
      CLASS
        NAME 'All Countries'
        EXPRESSION ('[NAME]' ne 'Bulgaria')
        STYLE
          OUTLINECOLOR 100 100 100
#         COLOR 200 200 200
        END
      END
    END
  END
END
```

Example 12-14. Enabling a map file to serve up a layer using WMS

```
MAP
  SIZE 600 300
  EXTENT -180 -90 180 90
  IMAGECOLOR 180 180 250

  IMAGETYPE PNG24
  UNITS DD

  WEB
    TEMPLATE global.html
    IMAGEPATH "/srv/www/htdocs/tmp/"
    IMAGEURL "/tmp/"
    METADATA
      "wms_title" "My Global Map WMS Server"
      "wms_srs" "EPSG:4326"
    END
  END

  LAYER
    NAME countries
    TYPE POLYGON
    STATUS ON
    DATA countries_simpl
    MINSCALE 1000
    MAXSCALE 1000000000
    CLASSITEM 'NAME'
    CLASS
      NAME 'Bulgaria'
      EXPRESSION 'Bulgaria'
      STYLE
        OUTLINECOLOR 100 100 100
      END
    END
    CLASS
      NAME 'All Countries'
      EXPRESSION ('[NAME]' ne 'Bulgaria')
      STYLE
        OUTLINECOLOR 100 100 100
      END
    END
    METADATA
      "wms_title" "Country boundaries"
    END
  END
END
```

Example 12-15. Map file example showing a WFS data source added to the global map

```
MAP
  SIZE 600 300
  EXTENT -58 46 -54 52
  IMAGECOLOR 180 180 250
```

Example 12-15. Map file example showing a WFS data source added to the global map (continued)

```
IMAGETYPE PNG24
UNITS DD

WEB
  TEMPLATE global.html
  IMAGEPATH "/srv/www/htdocs/tmp/"
  IMAGEURL "/tmp/"
END

PROJECTION
  "init=epsg:4326"
END

SYMBOL
  NAME "circle"
  TYPE ellipse
  FILLED true
  POINTS
    1 1
  END
END

LAYER
  NAME countries
  TYPE POLYGON
  STATUS ON
  DATA countries_simpl
  MINSCALE 1000
  MAXSCALE 1000000000
  CLASSITEM 'NAME'
  CLASS
    NAME 'Bulgaria'
    EXPRESSION 'Bulgaria'
    STYLE
      OUTLINECOLOR 100 100 100
      COLOR 255 255 150
    END
  END
  CLASS
    NAME 'All Countries'
    EXPRESSION ('[NAME]' ne 'Bulgaria')
    STYLE
      OUTLINECOLOR 100 100 100
      COLOR 200 200 200
    END
  END
  PROJECTION
    "init=epsg:4326"
  END
END

LAYER
```

Example 12-15. Map file example showing a WFS data source added to the global map (continued)

```
      NAME wfs_test
      STATUS ON
      TYPE POINT
      CONNECTIONTYPE WFS
      CONNECTION "http://map.ns.ec.gc.ca/envdat/map.aspx?"
      LABELITEM "envdat:Station_ID"
      CLASS
        STYLE
          SYMBOL 'circle'
          SIZE 6
          OUTLINECOLOR 150 150 0
          COLOR 255 250 0
        END
        LABEL
          SIZE TINY
          COLOR 0 0 0
          POSITION CL
        END
      END
      METADATA
        "wfs_srs" "EPSG:4326"
        "wfs_version" "1.0.0"
        "wfs_typename" "envirodat"
        "wfs_request_method" "GET"
        "wfs_service" "WFS"
      END
      PROJECTION
        "init=epsg:4326"
      END
    END
  END
END
```

Example 12-16. Enabling a map file to serve up the countries layer through WFS

```
MAP
  SIZE 600 300
  EXTENT -180 -90 180 90
  IMAGECOLOR 180 180 250

  UNITS DD

  WEB
    TEMPLATE global.html
    IMAGEPATH "/srv/www/htdocs/tmp/"
    IMAGEURL "/tmp/"
    METADATA
      "wfs_title" "My Global WFS Map Service"
    END
  END

  PROJECTION
    "init=epsg:4326"
```

Example 12-16. Enabling a map file to serve up the countries layer through WFS (continued)

```
  END

  LAYER
    NAME countries
    TYPE POLYGON
    STATUS ON
    DUMP TRUE
    DATA countries_simpl
    METADATA
      "wfs_title" "Roads"
      "wfs_group_title" "North American Features"
    END
    PROJECTION
      "init=epsg:4326"
    END
  END
END
```

CHAPTER 13

Managing a Spatial Database

The previous chapters explained how to interrogate and convert data, and how to select subsets of it for more customized use. This chapter is for those who need a spatial database for creating, managing, and manipulating data. Spatial databases combine the power of a relational database with geographic and tabular information. The focus of this chapter is on getting some spatial data into a database, querying it, and using it in a map. It will also cover how to use PostGIS data in a few different applications and how to export it into other formats.

Introducing PostGIS

PostGIS is a spatial (or geographic) extension of the popular open source PostgreSQL relational database. This chapter focuses on using the normal tabular components of PostgreSQL in conjunction with the spatial data management functions of PostGIS.

> For more in-depth help with PostgreSQL, I recommend O'Reilly's *Practical PostgreSQL* (*http://www.oreilly.com/catalog/ppostgresql/*) and the PostgreSQL web site *http://www.postgresql.org*.

PostGIS is an open source extension developed by Refractions Research. Their web site (*http://postgis.refractions.net*) gives this summary of the product:

> PostGIS adds support for geographic objects to the PostgreSQL object-relational database. In effect, PostGIS "spatially enables" the PostgreSQL server, allowing it to be used as a backend spatial database for geographic information systems (GIS), much like ESRI's SDE or Oracle's Spatial extension.

What Is a Spatial Database?

A database is a tool for storing and accessing tables of information. Traditional databases store information in fields and records (columns and rows or attributes and values). The types of data that fields can hold varies across different types of databases but, generally speaking, they hold numeric and text data. The main feature of a database is that of querying, where you can retrieve information that meets your specific criteria. *Relational* databases allow you to join information from multiple tables using a common piece of information that is in both tables.

 To learn more about relational database management systems (RDBMS), see *http://en.wikipedia.org/wiki/RDBMS*.

A *spatial* database is much the same, but it can also store geographic data. Several databases and GIS products use the term *spatial database* to mean slightly different things. For example, ESRI's Spatial Database Engine (SDE) isn't a spatial database, but is advertised as an interface between client software and a normal database. It allows spatial data to be stored in SDE's format, in the database. To load and manipulate the spatial data, you need to have an ESRI product or access to an ESRI service.

ESRI's SDE product isn't the only option for spatially enabling a database. Despite the limited amount of marketing, there are other databases available that better fit the description of *spatial database*. Oracle has an extension called Oracle Spatial and IBM has a Spatial Extender for the DB2 database. MySQL database also has a spatial extension. All these are similar to PostGIS; they store and access the spatial data using database tools, without requiring specialized GIS software to access or modify the data.

PostGIS has several features most commercial spatial databases don't, some of which initially draw people to PostGIS as an enterprise spatial database management system. PostGIS is actively developed and supported. Support for PostGIS is built into an increasing number of applications including MapServer, JUMP, QGIS, FME, and more. There are extensive functions for interacting with spatial data, without needing a GIS client application. This has inspired many to use PostGIS.

PostGIS can be considered an advanced spatial database because it has the ability to both store and manipulate spatial data. PostGIS isn't simply a data storage repository, but also an environment for interacting with spatial data. The OGC has created a specification for storing and querying spatial data in an SQL database—the Simple Features Specification for SQL (SFSQL). OGC specifications aren't just nice to have; they are becoming an integral requirement for geospatial data interoperability. When sharing data or enabling open access to geospatial information is required, these open standards become critical.

PostGIS has one of the most robust implementations of the SFSQL specification, according to the OGC resources page at *http://www.opengeospatial.org/resources/ ?page=products*. Because PostGIS implements all SFSQL specifications, you can access standardized functions without proprietary twists and turns over the lifespan of your projects. Some other applications only implement subsets of the SFSQL specification.

The way geographic data is presented in PostGIS (as returned in a query) is very intuitive, as you will see from the examples in this chapter. You can get access to coordinates of spatial features through a variety of methods, depending on your need. You can query from a command-line SQL tool or view them graphically with mapping software. Either way, you aren't bound to using proprietary tools to get access to your information.

Server-Based GIS

PostgreSQL is a database server product. When requests are made to the database, the server processes the request, prepares the data, and returns the results to your application. All the heavy-duty work is done on the server, and only the results are sent back to you. For many applications, this is critical. Even with the horsepower of modern computers, most PCs aren't designed to handle the intense workload of database queries. If all the data had to be sent across a network to be processed by your application on the user's machine, the network and client program would be a major performance bottleneck.

The same problem exists for GIS and spatial data management. Many, if not most, GIS desktop applications have a strong reliance on the user's computer. This may be fine for normal mapping processes (though mapping complex features can be very slow), but when you consider doing more advanced spatial analysis, problems appear.

Consider this example. You have a large number of polygons to merge together based on some attribute. The GIS program loads the required polygons into your computer's memory or into a temporary file. This alone can be a major bottleneck, because it sucks down large amounts of data over the network. However, when the process of merging polygons begins, it isn't uncommon to see major memory and processor used, not to mention major hard-disk activity while churning through all the data.

Another issue is that the desktop GIS program may not have the capability to do the analysis you need. Your options are usually to purchase an add-on software component or use another application to process the data. The same process as in the previous example occurs: there's heavy data copying and processing on the PC, and you often need to convert the data to another format.

PostGIS takes advantage of the server-based database by making an extensive set of GIS functions available on the server. One way to think of this is that PostGIS includes the spatial data storage and also spatial data-manipulation capabilities usually found only in desktop GIS products. This significantly reduces the requirements of client applications by taking advantage of the server's capabilities. This is a key strength of PostGIS.

Future GIS desktop applications will be little more than products for visualization, with the GIS functionality happening in the spatial database. There is already some movement toward this model. With the openly accessible capabilities of PostGIS, application developers can build spatial capabilities into their database applications right now.

PostGIS is an extension of the PostgreSQL database, so having a standard PostgreSQL installation is the place to start. A custom compiled version of PostgreSQL isn't required to use PostGIS. PostGIS consists of three components:

PostGIS libraries
> The core library is *libpostgis.so* or *libpostgis.dll* on Windows. This library is the interface between PostgreSQL capabilities and the spatial abilities of PostGIS.

PostGIS script for functions and types
> There is one main script that loads in the hundreds of PostGIS specific functions and types: *postgis.sql*. Newer versions of PostGIS don't have a *postgis.sql* file; instead you use a file called *lwpostgis.sql*.

Optional script for project support
> An optional script called *spatial_ref_sys.sql* is often loaded that lets you use spatial reference systems or projections with PostGIS data.

The scripts are platform-independent, so getting the libraries you need is the hardest part. You may want to compile your own PostGIS extension to include custom capabilities, though this is increasingly unnecessary.

Documentation from the PostGIS web site is a good starting point for everyone, and walks you through more detail than presented here. Look for the online PostGIS documentation at *http://postgis.refractions.net/docs/*.

 The examples in this chapter are based on PostgreSQL Version 7.4 and PostGIS Version 0.8. At the time of writing PostgreSQL is at Version 8.0 and PostGIS 1.0 is about to be released. More recent versions are available, but there are still some problems being ironed out. Some of the examples will show slightly different results if you use the newer versions.

Downloading PostGIS Install Packages and Binaries

Install packages or binary (precompiled) versions are available for a few different computing platforms.

PostgreSQL and PostGIS are both in active development, and some links and references for getting them installed can become quickly out of date. You should always refer to the main web sites for the latest pointers and instructions:

PostgreSQL (*http://www.postgresql.org*)
PostGIS (*http://postgis.refractions.net*)

PostGIS for Windows

Native Windows versions of PostgreSQL have recently become available. These allow you to install the standard PostgreSQL database and, depending on the package, may also include PostGIS functionality. For packages that don't include all the PostGIS functionality, the PostGIS libraries and scripts need to be installed and run. Some Windows installation packages have been created to help automate this.

The official install package for PostgreSQL is available at *ftp://ftp.postgresql.org/pub/binary/*. Under the most recent version, there is a Windows folder.

One version was developed by Mark Cave-Ayland and is available from his web site, *http://www.webbased.co.uk/mca/*. He includes links to the main PostgreSQL installers as well as his own package containing PostGIS and other spatial libraries such as GEOS and Proj. This package is used by many people who frequent the PostGIS mailing list (which is the place to ask questions when you run into difficulty). See this link to search the archives of the mailing list or to subscribe to it: *http://postgis.refractions.net/support.php*.

PostGIS is also available as a MapServer for Windows package. See the MS4W download page for notes and the package to download: *http://www.maptools.org/ms4w/*. MS4W is easy to install and start using.

Another PostGIS installer is available as part of the DC Maintenance Management System (DCMMS) at *http://dcmms.sourceforge.net/*.

PostGIS for Linux

Different Linux distributions tend to have different easy-to-install versions of PostgreSQL and PostGIS. RPM and Debian packages are probably two of the most common.

French readers may be interested in this page, which describes some installation sources in French: *http://www.01map.com/download/*.

RPM packages

If you are looking for simplicity (and your operating system supports them), RPM packages are probably your best bet. Packages are available from a couple of sources.

As with the Windows sources mentioned previously, you will get the PostgreSQL database package and then either compile your own PostGIS portion or install a PostGIS package. If you just want a PostgreSQL database, try going directly to a PostgreSQL download mirror and searching under the *binary* and *rpms* folders for your platform. RedHat 9 and Fedora Core 1 and 2 are both available at *ftp://ftp. postgresql.org/pub/binary/v8.0.1.*

If you intend to compile your own PostGIS support using these packages, you will need to install the source RPM packages as well. PostGIS compilation needs access to files that come only with the source PostgreSQL packages.

Refractions Research hosts a comprehensive set of RPM packages including a Post-GIS package. They also have packages for Fedora, Mandrake, RedHat, SuSE, and source packages as well. You can find these packages at *http://postgis.refractions.net/ rpms/.*

Debian packages

These sites have several open source GIS-related packages available for Debian Linux:

> *http://agrogeomatic.educagri.fr/debian*
> *http://www.bitdaddy.com/gisdebs*

For more details about how to build PostGIS in a Debian environment, the following document may be helpful: *http://edseek.com/archives/2004/03/31/installing-postgis-on-debian-gnulinux/.*

PostGIS for Mac OS X

There are definitely some people using PostGIS in a Mac OS X environment, but getting access to prepackaged binaries and instructions isn't easy. The best way to get help is to contact users on the PostGIS mailing list at *http://postgis.refractions.net/ mailman/listinfo/postgis-users.*

By searching the mailing list, you should be able to find someone else who is using PostGIS on OS X. Most users are more than happy to help fellow Mac users along in their PostGIS quest. A PostgreSQL package exists on FINK at *http://fink.sourceforge. net/pdb/package.php/postgresql74.*

The development package (which includes files you'll need if you compile PostGIS yourself) is available at *http://fink.sourceforge.net/pdb/package.php/postgresql74-dev.* Note that these packages are slightly older than the current version and may not include the most recent functionality.

Marc Liyanaga's web site also has some packages and instructions for getting started: *http://www.entropy.ch/software/macosx/postgresql/*.

Compiling from Source Code

Compiling PostGIS from source code isn't covered here. Source code can be downloaded from the PostGIS web site at *http://postgis.refractions.net/download.php.* This site includes hourly snapshots of source code from the CVS repository, as well as official releases. Source RPMs are also available.

Compilation instructions are provided as a README file that comes with the source:

> *http://postgis.refractions.net/docs/ch02.html*
> *http://postgis.refractions.net/README.postgis.txt*

Steps for Setting Up PostGIS

The PostGIS documentation is the best source for walking through all the steps of setting up PostGIS. This section provides a very brief run-through of steps. Depending on your skill and understanding of PostgreSQL and SQL scripts, these instructions may or may not be enough. If not, please refer to the main PostGIS documentation at *http://postgis.refractions.net/docs.*

Depending on the method you have used to get the PostgreSQL database set up and PostGIS installed, there will be different steps required to get started. Some installation packages include all the steps required to jump right into using PostGIS. Others don't, which means you still need to set up the final stages of PostGIS functionality. If you compile PostGIS from source code, you will always have the following steps to walk through. In a nutshell, these steps involve:

1. Getting PostgreSQL up and running
2. Enabling pl/pgsql language support
3. Loading the *postgis.sql* (or *lwpostgis.sql*) script
4. Loading the *spatial_ref_sys.sql* script
5. Creating a database

Other steps involving loading and accessing data are covered in later sections.

Getting PostgreSQL Up and Running

You must have a PostgreSQL database service running before setting up PostGIS. PostgreSQL runs in a similar fashion to other enterprise database services (MySQL, Oracle, DB2, SQL Server). It waits for requests to come from a client program and then responds by interacting with databases on the server that the service is running on.

To test that your database service is running, you can use the command-line tool psql with the list parameter to give you a list of available databases:

```
> psql -l
          List of databases
      Name     |  Owner   | Encoding
---------------+----------+-----------
 template0     | postgres | SQL_ASCII
 template1     | postgres | SQL_ASCII
(2 rows)
```

This shows two available databases that are part of every PostgreSQL system. The template1 database is the default used as a template for creating a new database. It is copied, and all settings in it are made available to any new database you create. To enable PostGIS functionality for a database, you load PostGIS settings and functions into that database. If you load them into template1, all the PostGIS functionality will be available in every subsequent database you create. Having every database loaded with PostGIS capabilities isn't always desirable but may be reasonable in some cases.

If you are running the database service on a different computer than the one on which you are running the psql command, you will have to tell psql to connect to that computer. This is done by specifying some further parameters when running the psql command. The most important parameter will be the host name of the computer that is running the service. This is used to direct the psql command to look for the service on that remote computer. The -h option is used, followed by the name of the computer.

```
> psql -l -h myserver.com
```

This lists the databases available on the host *myserver.com*. If a PostgreSQL service isn't running or isn't accepting connections from you, you will get an error:

```
psql: could not connect to server:
    Is the server running on host "myserver.com" and accepting TCP/IP connections on
port 5432?
```

Depending on how your database was installed, you may also need to specify a database username. In the previous example of the psql command, you can see that the user postgres owns the template databases. If you want to connect to the service as the postgres user, you use the -U parameter followed by the username:

```
> psql -l -h myserver.com -U postgres
```

There are other parameters that can be added to the command, as you will see in the following examples.

Enabling pl/pgsql Language Support

PostgreSQL has support for internal programming languages that can interact and be embedded within a database. This is a powerful feature of PostgreSQL and is used by

PostGIS. Its functions are programmed using the pl/pgsql language. This language isn't supported by default and needs to be explicitly enabled by running the command:

```
> createlang plpgsql template1
```

Specify `template1` as the target database to add the language support to.

Loading the postgis.sql Script

With the language support enabled, you can now begin loading the PostGIS functions using the *postgis.sql* or *lwpostgis.sql* SQL script.

 SQL scripts, such as *postgis.sql*, are text files with a list of SQL commands that are used to interact with the database. If you are curious, you can open this file in a text editor or in a web browser and have a look at what commands are being used.

Later you will have to type in some SQL commands to test the database. We'll also use SQL to load geographic features into the database.

Again, the `psql` command is used to do this from the command line. Because *postgis.sql* is a file on the system, you need to know the path to the file or change directories so that it is in the same directory from which you run the command:

```
> psql -f postgis.sql -d template1
```

The first parameter specifies the file to load. The second parameter specifies which database to run the SQL commands in. Loading them into `template1` makes the resulting database functions available in the new database that will be created.

Information notices and warnings scroll up the screen while this script is being loaded. There are warnings you can ignore, and several status statements acknowledging commands that ran successfully. An all-out failure of the script causes it to halt and provide a daunting error report similar to:

```
...
psql:postgis.sql:37: ERROR:  function "histogram2d_in" already exists with same
argument types
psql:postgis.sql:42: ERROR:  current transaction is aborted, commands ignored until
end of transaction block
...
```

These errors are saying that part of PostGIS has already been loaded into this database.

If the command runs properly, there will be many new functions, datatypes, and other settings in the `template1` database. There will also be a table called `geometry_columns`, and another called `spatial_ref_sys`. You will check this in a moment, but first you need to load one more script.

Loading the spatial_ref_sys.sql Script

The other script is *spatial_ref_sys.sql*, which populates the spatial_ref_sys table with projection-related information. PostGIS has reprojection (or spatial reference system transformation) capabilities and relies on the data in this table.

You load this script the same way as the *postgis.sql* script:

```
> psql -f spatial_ref_sys.sql -d template1
```

The script inserts over 1,700 records into the spatial_ref_sys table. While this script is running, you will see several INSERT messages, followed by a number on your screen looking something like:

```
...
INSERT 797517 1
INSERT 797518 1
INSERT 797519 1
INSERT 797520 1
COMMIT
```

The final COMMIT and no error messages confirms that the table was populated successfully.

 Depending on your version of PostGIS, the final message may actually be VACUUM.

You will get error messages if you haven't already run *postgis.sql/lwpostgis.sql* or if you have already loaded *spatial_ref_sys.sql*.

Testing PostGIS Functionality

Before creating your first database, it is worthwhile to test the template1 database to make sure everything is installed properly. Because template1 is used to create your new databases, checking before you create them makes fixes and clean-up easier.

Some simple tests can be done using the psql command to connect to the template1 database. The psql command lists databases and runs scripts, as shown earlier, but it also provides an interface for typing in SQL commands. The program it launches allows interactive typing of SQL commands and shows query results. To do this, you start psql followed by the name of a database to connect to, in this case, template1:

```
> psql template1
Welcome to psql 7.4.2, the PostgreSQL interactive terminal.

Type:  \copyright for distribution terms
       \h for help with SQL commands
       \? for help on internal slash commands
```

```
\g or terminate with semicolon to execute query
\q to quit
```

```
template1=#
```

When `psql` starts up, it tells you the version of the program, gives you a few lines of helpful tips for using the program, and then leaves you with a prompt. The prompt is the name of the connected database followed by `=#`.

The program is now ready for some SQL (or `psql` specific) commands. The first test checks to see that the expected PostGIS-related tables have been created. To list all the main objects in the database, type `\d` or use `\dt` to list just the tables (t):

```
template1=# \dt
                List of relations
 Schema |       Name       | Type  |  Owner
--------+------------------+-------+---------
 public | geometry_columns | table | postgres
 public | spatial_ref_sys  | table | postgres
(2 rows)
```

The first script you ran created these tables. If they don't exist, the script didn't run properly.

If the *spatial_ref_sys.sql* script ran properly, there should be records in the `spatial_ref_sys` table. To check this, you can use an SQL command that counts the number of rows in the table:

```
template1=# SELECT count(*) FROM spatial_ref_sys;
 count
-------
  1785
(1 row)
```

To learn more about SQL commands, see the SQL entry in the Wiki-Pedia at *http://en.wikipedia.org/wiki/SQL*.

Don't be confused by the message: (`1 row`). This just describes the number of lines in the report output. The actual result of the query is `1785`, which tells you the table isn't empty. This looks good. Newer versions of PostGIS will show more entries in this table; for example, v1.0 has 2671 entries.

How do you know if it should be 1785 or something different? Just run a quick check from the operating system command line to see the number of times INSERT is used in *spatial_ref_sys.sql*:

```
> grep -c INSERT spatial_ref_sys.sql
1785
```

The spatial functions added to the database are a large part of PostGIS. To do some further checks, peek at a list of the functions available in template1 to ensure they were loaded properly. Using \df describes all the functions in the database. Supplying a wildcard to search will help show only functions that start with the name *post-gis*. PostGIS functions don't all start with the word *postgis*, but this is a simple way to check that the database has some PostGIS-related functions properly loaded. Newer versions of PostGIS will show different results.

```
template1=# \df postgis*
                List of functions
  Result data type | Schema |            Name            |
 ------------------+--------+---------------------------+
  double precision | public | postgis_gist_sel          |
  text             | public | postgis_version           |
  opaque           | public | postgisgistcostestimate   |
 (3 rows)
```

The function names are listed in the right column under Name. If one of these functions can be run, PostGIS has probably been installed properly. The postgis_version function is a good one to run as a test. It returns information about the PostGIS installation that is available:

```
template1=# SELECT postgis_version();
            postgis_version
 ---------------------------------------
  0.8 USE_GEOS=1 USE_PROJ=1 USE_STATS=1
 (1 row)
```

The output tells what version of PostGIS is being used (0.8). It also shows that it can use the GEOS and PROJ libraries as part of PostGIS. These supporting libraries are used by certain PostGIS functions. Proj libraries are used to reproject or transform coordinates, and GEOS is an advanced geometry engine that allows a whole suite of manipulations and analysis of geometry data types.

To learn more about GEOS, including installation instructions, see the GEOS web site at *http://geos.refractions.net/*.

Creating a Spatial Database

The template1 database is the default system template used when creating new databases. Don't use it as an operational database! Instead, create a new database for your projects. New databases are created using the command-line program createdb, followed by the name that identifies the new database:

```
> createdb project1
CREATE DATABASE
```

In this case, the new database is called project1. The text that is printed out (CREATE DATABASE) confirms that the command ran and finished. Now when existing databases are listed, project1 should be included:

```
> psql -l
        List of databases
    Name    |   Owner   | Encoding
------------+-----------+-----------
  project1  | tyler     | SQL_ASCII
  template0 | postgres  | SQL_ASCII
  template1 | postgres  | SQL_ASCII
(3 rows)
```

The project1 database is now ready for data loading. To quit psql, use the \q command.

Load Data into the Database

There are many ways to put data into a database. One method is to manually type SQL commands with psql to insert data into a table. You can also use programs that convert data into an SQL script that can then be loaded, or you can use a tool that exports data directly to the database.

Using shp2pgsql

PostGIS comes with command-line tools called pgsql2shp and shp2pgsql. These can be used to convert from a PostGIS table to a shapefile and back.

The tool shp2pgsql converts the shapes to a text stream of SQL commands. Therefore, you need to pipe it to a text file for later loading or to the psql command to use it immediately. For example, use one of these methods:

```
> shp2pgsql countyp020.shp countyp020 > mycounties.sql
> psql -d project1 -f mycounties.sql
```

or use this one to load the data immediately to the database:

```
> shp2pgsql mycounties.shp mycounties | psql -d project1
```

By default, the shp2pgsql command puts the geometry data into a field called the_geom, whereas the default for the ogr2ogr command (shown next) puts the geometry data into a field called wkb_geometry. These defaults can be overridden and changed to something more meaningful. To acquire the countyp020 data, see the next section.

Using ogr2ogr

ogr2ogr is an excellent program for putting spatial data into a database. It's part of the GDAL/OGR toolkit included in FWTools and introduced in Chapters 3 and 7. This command-line tool takes any OGR supported data layer and exports it into the database.

This example uses some data taken from the U.S. National Atlas site at *http://nationalatlas.gov/atlasftp.html.* Specifically, it uses the County Boundaries data at *http://edcftp.cr.usgs.gov/pub/data/nationalatlas/countyp020.tar.gz.*

The file is a gzip'd tar file. On Linux, you can expand this file using the command-line program tar:

```
> tar -xzvf countyp020.tar.gz
```

This creates a shapefile named *countyp020*. On Windows, most Zip programs (e.g., WinZip) can decompress this file for you.

The ogrinfo command then provides a summary of how many features are in the file:

```
> ogrinfo countyp020.shp -al -so
...
Feature Count: 6138
...
```

It is a good idea to have a feel for how much data will be converted before running the next step. The more features there are, the more time it will take to load the data to the database.

To translate this shapefile to the project1 database, use the ogr2ogr command:

```
> ogr2ogr -f "PostgreSQL" PG:dbname=project1 countyp020.shp
```

This is one of the simplest examples of using ogr2ogr with PostgreSQL/PostGIS. The first parameter is the target data format. In this case, it is a PostgreSQL database. The prefix PG: provides more detail about the target data source. Here, only the database name is supplied: dbname=project1.

> If the database is on a different computer or requires more user access privileges, further details will be required. Multiple database parameters can be included, and you can quote them like this:
>
> ..`"PG:dbname=project1 host=mypc user=tyler"`..

The source data filename is *countyp020.shp*, a shapefile data layer. The conversion process may take a minute or two to run.

As shown in Example 13-1, check to see that it was loaded successfully by going into the psql interpreter again. You can list the tables that are available and do a simple query to see if all the features came across.

Example 13-1. Checking the results of loading a shapefile into PostgreSQL

```
> psql project1
Welcome to psql 7.4.2, the PostgreSQL interactive terminal.

Type:  \copyright for distribution terms
       \h for help with SQL commands
       \? for help on internal slash commands
       \g or terminate with semicolon to execute query
       \q to quit

project1=# \dt
            List of relations
```

Example 13-1. Checking the results of loading a shapefile into PostgreSQL (continued)

```
 Schema |       Name        | Type  | Owner
--------+-------------------+-------+-------
 public | countyp020        | table | tyler
 public | geometry_columns  | table | tyler
 public | spatial_ref_sys   | table | tyler
(3 rows)

project1=# SELECT count(*) FROM countyp020;
 count
-------
  6138
(1 row)
```

This reports the number of features that are in the table. Each geographic feature, in this case, counties, has a record in the countyp020 table.

 You can specify the name you want the table to have when it is created using the -nln parameter followed by the name. In the previous example, it used the name of the original data layer as the name of the output table. If you want the output table to have a different name (counties) use the ogr2ogr command like this (all one line):

```
> ogr2ogr -f "PostgreSQL" PG:dbname=project1 countyp020.shp
  -nln counties
```

This table has more than geographic data. In the psql interpreter, the columns of data in the table can be listed using the \d parameter followed by the name of the table, as shown in Example 13-2.

Example 13-2. Listing the columns and types in the countyp020 table

```
# \d countyp020
           Table "public.countyp020"
    Column     |      Type
---------------+----------------
 ogc_fid       | integer
 wkb_geometry  | geometry
 area          | numeric(9,3)
 perimeter     | numeric(9,3)
 countyp020    | numeric(9,0)
 state         | character(2)
 county        | character(50)
 fips          | character(5)
 state_fips    | character(2)
 square_mil    | numeric(19,3)
Check constraints:
    "$1" CHECK (srid(wkb_geometry) = -1)
    "$2" CHECK (geometrytype(wkb_geometry) = 'POLYGON'::text OR wkb_geometry IS NULL)
```

Each column is listed and shows the datatype that each column can hold. PostgreSQL databases can handle all these types without PostGIS, except for the geometry data.

Only one column in the table contains geometry data: the wkb_geometry column has geometry listed as its type:

```
wkb_geometry | geometry
```

 You can have multiple columns holding geometry data in your table. You can even store different types of geometries (points, lines, or polygons) in the same table by adding more fields of the type geometry.

The ogr2ogr utility automatically names the geometry column wkb_geometry (which stands for well-known binary geometry, another OGC specification), but it can be called anything you like. The other columns hold standard database information—numeric or character/text data.

Both the shp2pgsql and ogr2ogr methods do some metadata tracking by inserting records into the table called geometry_columns. This table tracks which columns in a table include geometric features. Some applications depend on finding entries in this table, and others don't. For example, MapServer doesn't require this, but the Arc-Map-PostGIS connector (discussed at the end of this chapter) depends on it. It is good practice to keep this table up to date. Here's a sample entry in the table:

```
-[ RECORD 1 ]-----+-------------
f_table_catalog   |
f_table_schema    | public
f_table_name      | countyp020
f_geometry_column | wkb_geometry
coord_dimension   | 3
srid              | -1
type              | POLYGON
attrelid          | 949399
varattnum         | 2
stats             |
```

This is the entry for the countyp020 table, as shown by f_table_name = countyp020. The name of the column holding the geometric data is stored in the f_geometry_column field. PostGIS can hold 3D data. coord_dimension can be set to 2 (2D) or 3 (3D). The SRID field refers to the spatial reference system. In this example, it is set to srid = -1, meaning none is specific. The field type = POLYGON says that the geometry column holds polygon features. Any application that accesses PostGIS data can inspect the geometry_columns table instead of looking for information from each and every table.

Spatial Data Queries

One of the strengths of PostGIS is its ability to store spatial data in a mature, enterprise-level, relational database. Data is made available through standard SQL queries, making it readily available to do analysis with another program without having to import and export the data into proprietary data formats. Another key strength is its ability to use spatially aware PostGIS functions to perform the analysis within the database, still using SQL. The spatial data query examples in this section are the most basic possible. PostGIS boasts of a variety of operators and functions for managing, manipulating, and creating spatial data, including the ability to compute geometric buffers, unions, intersections, reprojecting between coordinate systems, and more. The basic examples shown here focus on loading and accessing the spatial data.

To see what data is in the countyp020 table, you can use any basic SQL query to request a listing. For example, this typical SQL query lists all data in the table, including the very lengthy geometry definitions. Running this query isn't recommended:

```
# SELECT * FROM countyp020;
```

Getting a list of over 6,000 counties and their geometries would hardly be useful. A more useful query might be something like Example 13-3 which limits and groups the results.

Example 13-3. A basic SELECT DISTINCT query to list the counties in New Mexico state

```
# SELECT DISTINCT county FROM countyp020 WHERE state = 'NM';
          county
--------------------------------
 Bernalillo County
 Catron County
 Chaves County
 Cibola County
 Colfax County
 Curry County
 DeBaca County
 Dona Ana County
 Eddy County
 Grant County
 Guadalupe County
 Harding County
 Hidalgo County
 Lea County
 Lincoln County
...
(33 rows)
```

This query lists all the counties in the state of New Mexico (state = 'NM'). This has nothing to do with the spatial data, except that all this information was originally in the shapefile that was loaded. To see some of the geographic data, you must run a query that returns this information.

Example 13-4 shows a query that lists all the information about Curry County, including a list of all the geometric points used to define the shape of the county.

At the beginning of this example the \x command tells psql to list the data in expanded display mode. This is a bit easier to read when there is a lot of data and very few records. Using \x a second time disables expanded mode.

Example 13-4. Querying a table to show all the geometric and tabular data for a particular feature

```
project1=# \x
Expanded display is on.
project1=# SELECT * FROM countyp020 WHERE state='NM' AND county = 'Curry County';

[ RECORD 1 ] -------------------------------------------
ogc_fid      | 4345
wkb_geometry | SRID=-1;POLYGON((-103.04238129 34.74721146,
-103.04264832 34.36763382,-103.04239655 34.30997849,
-103.0424118 34.30216599,-103.73503113 34.30317688,
-103.49039459 34.77983856...))
area         | 0.358
perimeter    | 2.690
countyp020   | 4346
state        | NM
county       | Curry County
fips         | 35009
state_fips   | 35
square_mil   | 1404.995
```

 More recent versions of PostGIS don't display the geometry as text by default. To have it display coordinates in text format, you must use the astext() function with the wkb_geometry column like:

```
SELECT astext(wkb_geometry) FROM...
```

Some of the geometry information has been removed because the list of coordinates is very long; there is one pair of coordinates for every vertex in the polygon. This example shows how you can access spatial coordinate data directly with your queries. No GIS program is required to get this level of information, just basic SQL. The results may not be in the format you need, but you can modify it to suit your purposes. For example, if you are creating a custom application that needs access to geographic coordinates, you can call a PostgreSQL database, access the geometry of a table, then manipulate the data into the form your application needs.

Most people interested in web mapping don't need to create their own custom application for accessing and using the power of PostGIS. MapServer, for example, can query PostGIS for the geometry of these features and display it on a map. You only need to know how to point MapServer to the right database and table. More on using MapServer with PostGIS follows later in this chapter.

Building Spatial Indexes

Before doing spatial queries, some preparation work is needed. To improve spatial query performance, you should build spatial indexes for any tables that hold geometry data. This is done using the CREATE INDEX command with a few geometry options. The command to create an index for the geometry in the countyp020 table looks like this:

```
# CREATE INDEX idx_countyp020_geo ON countyp020 USING GIST (wkb_geometry GIST_
GEOMETRY_OPS);
```

The idx_countyp020_geo keyword is used for the name of the index, which is completely arbitrary. The second parameter countyp020 is the name of the table you are creating the index for. The field that holds the geometry data is identified as wkb_geometry. This is the default name given to the geometry columns of data converted with the ogr2ogr utility. The rest of the command consists of keywords needed for the indexing functions to run and must be used as shown.

Any index creation steps should be followed with the command:

```
# vacuum analyze <table name>
```

This does some internal database housekeeping, which helps your queries run more efficiently. You can also run it without specifying a particular table, and it will analyze all the tables. With large amounts of data, the vacuum process can take a long time. Running it on all the tables takes even longer to complete.

Critical Tabular Indexes

Spatial indexing on its own doesn't ensure high performance in your application. You must generally manage spatial and nonspatial data querying efficiently. To do so, you should create regular table indexes for any fields used in the WHERE clause of your query. To optimize for MapServer data access and querying, you can create an index on the unique ID for the table. However, the unique ID used by MapServer may not be apparent. There are two approaches to consider when using PostGIS layers in MapServer. If you use a simple PostGIS connection statement such as:

```
DATA wkb_geometry from countyp020
```

MapServer uses PostgreSQL's internal object ID. This is accessed by referring to it as a field named oid. There are MapServer examples later in this chapter.

The oid column doesn't appear in the column listing for a table using \dt, but you can use it in a SELECT statement to see what the values are.

If MapServer is using a FILTER setting or being used to query features, building an index for the oid column will improve performance. You can build one using a standard CREATE INDEX statement:

```
# CREATE INDEX idx_countyp020_oid ON countyp020 (oid);
```

When you use a more complex DATA setting, such as the subquery shown later in Example 13-10, you need to specify what unique ID column to use because MapServer doesn't necessarily have access to the oid column. You do this with the USING UNIQUE <column name> statement. An index should be created for this column.

Querying for Spatial Proximity

Normal SQL with tabular data is quite powerful, but using PostGIS functions to query for spatial relationships between data opens up another dimension of analysis. GIS analysis software was once needed to do these kinds of queries, but now you can do it within a PostGIS database. For example, you can query the countyp020 table to give you a list of the counties within a certain distance of your home county. You can also do queries across different tables that have spatial data stored in them. If you have a table with the coordinates for certain points of interest, you can query between that table and the countyp020 table to find which county your points are in. The following examples show some of the basics of PostGIS, in the context of some typical spatial tasks.

Find the county for a given point

This example will take a point that is within the United States and use that coordinate to find what county it falls in. A quick search on the Internet for the location of Mount St. Helens brings up the site *http://www.fs.fed.us/gpnf/volcanocams/msh/faqs/location.shtml*. The site lists the coordinates of the summit as: 46.20 N, 122.18 W. These coordinates can be used in a query of the countyp020 shapes.

Here is the SQL statement, with some description of the parts following:

```
# SELECT county
# FROM countyp020
# WHERE distance( wkb_geometry,
#       'POINT(-122.18 46.20)'
#       ) = 0;

          county
--------------------------------------------------
 Skamania County
(1 row)
```

- SELECT county specifies what column you want to see values from as a result of this query. This example requests the name of the county this point is in.

- FROM countyp020 identifies which table you are querying counties for. This query is pretty simple, using a single table called countyp020.

- Line three is where the spatial capabilities start to kick in. The WHERE keyword begins a section that limits the results you see. In this case, PostgreSQL shows only the counties that meet the criteria specified after the WHERE keyword.

- The WHERE clause contains two parts: the distance function and the criteria to compare the results of the distance function to. The distance function is denoted by distance(.....). This is a PostGIS function for comparing two geometric features. It takes two parameters, and each must be a geometric feature. The first parameter to use is: wkb_geometry—the name of the column that holds the spatial data in the countyp020 table. The second parameter (separated from the first by a comma) is text that was manually put together: 'POINT(-122.18 46.20)'. This is a well-known text (WKT) representation of a geometric point. Here are where the coordinates of Mount St. Helens are used. The have been slightly reformatted so they are in the order:

      POINT(*<longitude>* *<latitude>*)

  or:

      POINT(X Y)

- The coordinates are simply wrapped by the word POINT, to tell PostGIS what kind of geometric feature you are using.

 Quite often these kinds of coordinates are written as latitude, longitude. It is a common mistake to forget that what the database is looking for is the x, or east/west values first and the y or north/south values second. Longitude is x, and latitude is y.

- The final line in the query tells PostGIS to compare the distance between the two features and limits the results to those that are = 0. These are features that are side by side or overlap each other. The query is sent away, and PostGIS returns the results—a list of all the counties that the point falls in. Of course, there is only one because a point can only be in one place at a time.

If you have several points making a line, you can add those points here by adding in more pairs of coordinates separated by commas. The keyword POINT is then replaced by LINESTRING:

      LINESTRING(-122.18 46.20, -122.00 45.00)

All the counties the line went through are now returned:

```
                    county
--------------------------------------------------
 Skamania County
 Multnomah County
 Clackamas County
(3 rows)
```

Querying for nearby county polygons

Shapes within a table can also be compared against each other; this uses the SQL method referred to as a *self join*. One table is joined back to itself to do some comparisons. Example 13-5 compares one particular county with all the other counties in order to see which counties border it.

Example 13-5 is much like the previous section's example, but the WHERE and FROM clauses refer to a second table. In this case, the second table is the same as the first but is given an alias. Both tables are given aliases, a and b, respectively. These can now be thought of as different tables.

Example 13-5. Using a self join to find the neighboring polygons of a given county

```
# SELECT a.county
# FROM countyp020 a,
# countyp020 b
# WHERE b.county = 'Sonoma County'
# AND a.wkb_geometry && b.wkb_geometry;

                        county
------------------------------------------------------
 Sonoma County
 Napa County
 Yolo County
 Lake County
 Mendocino County
 Marin County
 Solano County
(7 rows)
```

Table a is targeted by the query in the SELECT statement. The list of counties is from table a. The results from that query are constrained by values in table b. The first part of the WHERE clause—b.county = 'Sonoma County'—reduces table b to being, in essence, just one polygon. This constraint makes the query much more manageable. The query would be relatively useless if it tried to find all counties and all their neighbors. Don't wait up for the answer!

The final line of the query, a.wkb_geometry && b.wkb_geometry, is where PostGIS comes in. Both the geometry columns are compared using the && operator. This operator compares the bounding box (bbox) of each shape to check for overlaps. The bounding box of a shape is the rectangle that encompasses the extent of the shape, as shown by the dashed rectangular outline in Figure 13-1.

The query in Example 13-5 compares the bounding box of Sonoma County with the shapes of the other bounding boxes. Figure 13-2 shows the shapes and their bounding boxes. Notice how they overlap. When there is an overlap between Sonoma County's bounding box (shown in red) and the shape of another (shown in green), that other county is selected as a match.

Using bounding boxes this way makes spatial querying much more efficient. PostGIS doesn't have to do a lot of complex calculations for every vertex or line of every polygon. Instead, it does a rough check using the bounding box rectangles. This uses less memory and is processed much faster.

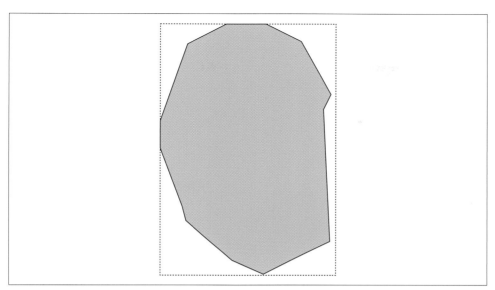

Figure 13-1. A polygon and its bounding box, shown by the dotted rectangle

Figure 13-2. Sonoma County and surrounding county shapes and bounding boxes

This exercise is supposed to show which counties bordered Sonoma County. If you study Figure 13-2, you will notice that one county isn't an adjacent neighbor but its bounding box overlaps Sonoma County's bounding box. This is Yolo County, highlighted in Figure 13-3.

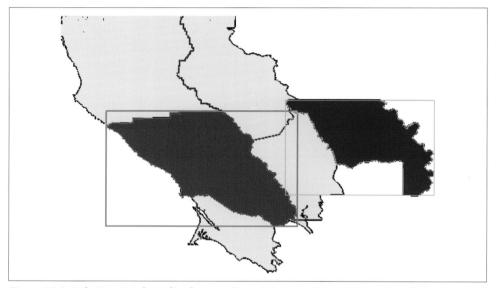

Figure 13-3. Yolo County's bounding box overlapping Sonoma County's even though they aren't adjacent polygons

The && operator is intended to quickly check the general location of shapes. It can't tell you that two shapes are adjacent, but only if they are close to one another. If two shapes don't have overlapping bounding boxes, they will not be adjacent. This function is helpful when doing spatial queries because it allows further analysis by PostGIS to focus only on the shapes that might overlap.

To take the query example one step further, the PostGIS Distance( ) function must be used to determine how close the counties actually are. Example 13-6 is almost identical to Example 13-5 but includes one more WHERE clause.

Example 13-6. Using the distance( ) function to find adjacent polygons

```
# SELECT a.county
# FROM countyp020 a,
# countyp020 b
# WHERE b.county = 'Sonoma County'
# AND a.wkb_geometry && b.wkb_geometry
# AND distance(a.wkb_geometry, b.wkb_geometry) = 0;
```

Example 13-6. Using the distance( ) function to find adjacent polygons (continued)

```
                      county
-------------------------------------------------------
 Sonoma County
 Napa County
 Lake County
 Mendocino County
 Marin County
 Solano County
(6 rows)
```

The only difference is the last line:

```
    AND distance(a.wkb_geometry, b.wkb_geometry) = 0;
```

The distance function requires two sets of geometry features as parameters. PostGIS calculates the minimum distance between the features in the a.wkb_geometry and b.wkb_geometry columns. If there are any shapes that don't share the same border as Sonoma County, they are rejected.

Because the && operator is still being used, the distance function is used only to compare the seven features returned by the query in Example 13-5. The resulting set of features are shown on a map in Figure 13-4. Yolo County is no longer part of the result set.

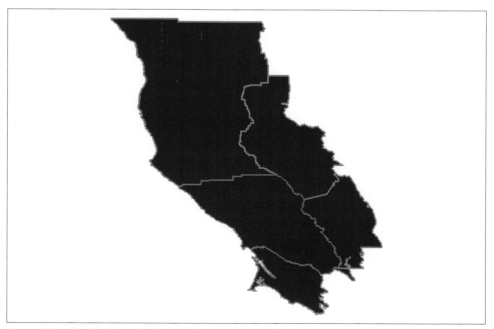

Figure 13-4. The final results show the features selected by the query for counties adjacent to Sonoma County

Planning to visualize query results

If you plan to visualize your results, you can create a view or table with the results of your query. To create a view of the query in Example 13-6, you need to add the `CREATE VIEW <view name> AS` keywords to the beginning of the SQL statement and wrap your command with parenthesis like this:

```
# CREATE VIEW mycounties AS
    ( SELECT a.county......=0 );
```

This view can be accessed just like any table by referring to the name of the view `mycounties`, instead of the name of a table.

You will also need to make sure to include the geometry results in a column of the query. Earlier examples listed only tabular data, but in order to produce graphics, you need to have a geometry column in your query results. For example, you can modify the `SELECT a.county` statement in Example 13-6, by adding the geometry column from table a:

```
# SELECT a.county, a.wkb_geometry
```

Accessing Spatial Data from PostGIS in Other Applications

Visualizing results isn't always the end goal of a spatial query. Often, someone just needs to write a report or provide a statistic. However, figures often help explain the data in a way that a report can't, which is why mapping is such a useful tool for communication.

If you want to visualize the results of PostGIS queries, you have a few options. Depending on what software you use, the simplest method may be to export the data from PostGIS to another format, such as a GML file or an ESRI shapefile. Or you may want to view the data directly in a desktop viewer such as OpenEV or put it in a MapServer web map application.

Exporting PostGIS Data into a Shapefile or GML

You can use the `ogr2ogr` utility to convert from PostGIS into many other formats. As discussed in Chapter 7, it is run from the command line. Here is an example of how to convert the `mycounties` view from PostGIS into a shapefile, though any OGR-supported output format can be used:

```
> ogr2ogr -f "ESRI Shapefile" mycounties.shp "PG:dbname=project1" mycounties
```

The `-f` parameter specifies what the output data format will be. The output dataset name will be `mycounties.shp`. The source dataset is the `project1` database. The final word, `mycounties`, is the name of the layer to request from PostGIS. In this case it is a PostgreSQL view, but it can also be a table.

The shapefile can then be loaded into any GIS or mapping product that supports shapefiles. This format is fairly universal. To create a GML file, it looks almost the same:

```
> ogr2ogr -f "GML" mycounties.gml "PG:dbname=project1" mycounties
```

As noted earlier in the "Load Data into the Database" section, the shp2pgsql and pgsql2shp command-line tools may also be used. Both shapefiles and GML can be used as a data source for a layer in MapServer as discussed in Chapters 10 and 11.

Viewing PostGIS Data in OpenEV

The real power of PostGIS is that the data it holds can be accessed directly by a number of applications. When you export data from PostGIS into another format, it is possible for your data to become out of sync. If you can access the data directly from PostGIS, you won't need to do the exporting step. This has the added benefit of always being able to access the most current data. OpenEV and MapServer are two examples of programs that access PostGIS data directly.

OpenEV can load spatial data from a PostGIS database. This is only possible if you launch OpenEV from the command line and specify the database connection you want to access. For example, to access the project1 database, the command line to start OpenEV looks like this:

```
> openev "PG:dbname=project1 user=tyler host=localhost"
```

You will see a long list of warning and status messages as OpenEV starts up. If it connects to the database properly, you will see a list of the tables to choose from. Figure 13-5 shows the layer list from my project1 database.

 The vertical scrollbar seems to have some problems. You may need to resize the window by stretching it taller, to be able to scroll down to find your layers. More recent layers/tables are listed at the bottom.

When you find the layer you want from the list, click on the check mark beside the layer name. The check mark will become darker. Then press the Accept button to load the data into the OpenEV view. The layer is read-only, and changes aren't saved back into the database.

Viewing PostGIS Data in MapServer

PostGIS is used by many as a data source for MapServer applications. Data management is handled in PostGIS, and MapServer is used as a visualization engine. This combination allows each product to do what it does best.

Appendix B includes examples that use various types of data with MapServer, including PostGIS data. Chapters 10 and 11 describe how to build MapServer

Figure 13-5. The layer selection list for choosing PostGIS layers to load

applications. The global map example used there can be extended to include a layer of the counties of the United States, based on the examples used earlier in this chapter. The layer can be treated like most other layers but with a few more parameters to help MapServer connect to the database.

Basic MapServer layers, like shapefiles, specify the name of the source data using the DATA keyword:

```
DATA <path to source file>
```

A PostGIS data source isn't accessed through a file. Instead, you specify three pieces of database connection information:

```
CONNECTIONTYPE POSTGIS
CONNECTION "dbname=<databasename> host=<host computer name>
        user=<database user name> port=<default is 5432>"
DATA "<geometry column name> from <source data table>"
```

CONNECTIONTYPE tells MapServer what kind of data source it is going to load. The CONNECTION parameter is often called the *connection string*. It includes the same kind of PostgreSQL connection information used earlier in this chapter. Some of the information is optional, but it is a good habit to include all of it even if it is redundant. Port 5432 is the default port for PostgreSQL. Many problems new users run into are related to not having enough information specified here.

The keyword from used in the DATA parameter may cause you grief if it isn't written in lowercase. It is a known bug that gives you errors if you use FROM in uppercase. This bug may be fixed in more recent versions of MapServer.

Example 13-7 shows the full listing of a layer in the MapServer configuration file, based on the county data loaded into PostGIS earlier on.

Example 13-7. A simple PostGIS layer definition in a MapServer configuration file

```
LAYER
  NAME usa_counties
  TYPE POLYGON
  STATUS DEFAULT
  CONNECTIONTYPE POSTGIS
  CONNECTION "dbname=project1 user=tyler host=localhost port=5432"
  DATA "wkb_geometry from countyp020"
  CLASS
    SYMBOL 'circle'
    SIZE 2
    OUTLINECOLOR 0 0 0
  END
  PROJECTION
    "init=epsg:4326"
  END
END
```

This example assumes that you have a SYMBOLSET defined with a symbol named circle available. If you don't, you can ignore the SYMBOL 'circle' line, but your resulting map will look slightly different.

The layer in this example is part of a larger map file called *global.map*, which also includes some global images showing elevation changes. To test the map file, use the shp2img command-line utility from your MapServer installation.

```
> shp2img -e -122.818 37.815 -121.406 41.003 -m global.map -o fig13-6.png
```

See Chapter 10 for more information and some examples using this command. This example draws the layers in the map file, with a focus on a geographic extent covering part of the western United States. The resulting map is saved to an image file called *fig13-6.png* and is shown in Figure 13-6.

This map includes a few city names from a shapefile and an elevation backdrop from some image files. The county boundary layer (black outlines) is from the PostGIS database. Being able to integrate different types of data into one map is an essential part of many MapServer applications.

Highlighting a subset of shapes

With some minor modifications to Example 13-7, you can start to do some basic col-ortheming. Example 13-8 shows how to make one county stand out among the

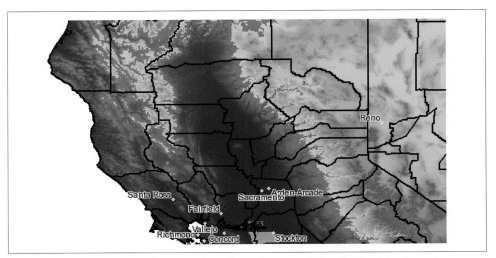

Figure 13-6. A map showing the county boundaries from PostGIS with other MapServer layers

others using multiple CLASS objects in the layer, along with the EXPRESSION parameter. The resulting map is shown in Figure 13-7.

For more information about EXPRESSION syntax, see Table 10-1.

Example 13-8. Emphasizing a county with classes and the expression parameter

```
LAYER
  NAME usa_counties
  TYPE POLYGON
  STATUS DEFAULT
  CONNECTIONTYPE POSTGIS
  CONNECTION "dbname=project1 user=tyler host=localhost port=5432"
  DATA "wkb_geometry from countyp020"
  CLASS
    EXPRESSION ("[county]" = 'Sonoma County')
    SYMBOL 'circle'
    SIZE 4
    OUTLINECOLOR 255 0 0
  END
  CLASS
    EXPRESSION ("[county]" != 'Sonoma County')
    SYMBOL 'circle'
    SIZE 2
    OUTLINECOLOR 0 0 0
  END
  PROJECTION
```

Example 13-8. Emphasizing a county with classes and the expression parameter (continued)

```
   "init=epsg:4326"
 END
END
```

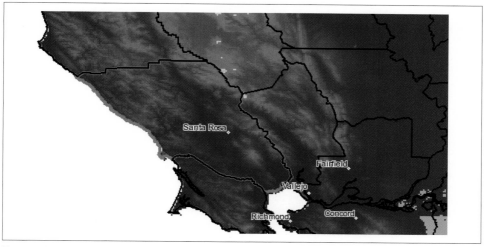

Figure 13-7. Sonoma County highlighted using a second class with a different color, line thickness and expression parameter

Using subqueries for more complex SQL

More sophisticated queries can be used in the DATA line for the layer, but some care is needed to make it work. For example, if you are more comfortable with SQL and want to show only Sonoma County, you might be tempted to use:

```
DATA "wkb_geometry from countyp020 where county = 'Sonoma County'"
```

This won't work. You need to handle any deviation from the most basic DATA parameter as a subquery. Here is an example of a subquery, put onto separate lines for readability only:

```
DATA "wkb_geometry from (
    select wkb_geometry
    from countyp020
    where county = 'Sonoma County')
  as myquery"
```

The subquery is the part in the parentheses and can be much more complex than this example. The myquery keyword is arbitrary but necessary. It can be any name and is simply a placeholder. MapServer needs two more pieces of information to handle subqueries. It needs to be able to uniquely identify each record coming from Post-GIS. To do this, add a using unique <*field name*> clause. If you include a unique number field in your query use that field name: using unique *countyID*. Otherwise you might try using the geometry field because it will probably have unique values for every record: using unique *wkb_geometry*. It may be not be the most efficient choice, but it does work.

MapServer also needs to know what spatial reference system the data will be in. This is specified by adding a using srid = <*SRID #*> clause. If you already have a PROJECTION section for your layer in the map file, you can probably get away with: using srid = -1, which effectively ignores the projection settings.

A working example of this subquery method is shown in Example 13-9.

Example 13-9. A successful subquery with all required parameters

```
DATA "wkb_geometry from ( select wkb_geometry from countyp020 where
        county = 'Sonoma County') as myquery using unique wkb_geometry using srid = -1"
```

A mixture of other PostGIS and PostgreSQL functions can be used in a subquery. For example:

```
DATA "wkb_geometry from ( select wkb_geometry from countyp020 where wkb_geometry &&
'POINT(-122.88 38.52)' ) as myquery using unique wkb_geometry using srid = -1"
```

This example uses the PostGIS bounding box comparison operator (&&) and a manually constructed point geometry. It selects the geometry of the county polygon using the location of the point, just like in earlier examples in the "Querying for Spatial Proximity" section.

PostGIS can also create new spatial features through queries, and MapServer can then map them. For example, you can use the buffer( ) function to create a buffered area around your shape. You can create another layer using the exact syntax as Example 13-9, but then change it so that it uses a buffer( ) to expand the shape. It may also be helpful to simplify the shape a bit so that the buffer is smoother. Here is a complex example that uses both the buffer( ) and simplify( ) functions:

```
DATA "wkb_geometry from (
select buffer( simplify(wkb_geometry,0.01), 0.2)
        as wkb_geometry
from countyp020
where county='Sonoma County ') as foo
using unique wkb_geometry"
```

Both functions require a numeric value as well as a geometry field. These numeric values are always specified in the units of measure for the coordinates in the data. simplify( ) weeds out certain vertices based on a tolerance you provide. In this case it simplifies to a tolerance of 0.2 degrees. That simplified shape is then passed to the buffer( ) function. The buffer drawn around the features is created 0.01 degrees wide.

Many different types of queries can be used, including queries from tables, views, or manually constructed geometries in an SQL statement. For anything other than the most simple table query, be sure to use the using unique and using srid keywords properly and ensure that the query returns a valid geometry.

Using PostGIS attributes to draw labels

As with any MapServer data source that has attribute data, PostGIS layers can also use this information to label a map. Example 13-10 is the same as Example 13-8, but includes parameters required for labeling.

Example 13-10. Specifying LABELITEM and LABEL parameters to draw labels using PostGIS attributes

```
LAYER
  NAME usa_counties
  TYPE POLYGON
  STATUS DEFAULT
  CONNECTIONTYPE POSTGIS
  CONNECTION "dbname=project1 user=tyler host=localhost port=5432"
  DATA "wkb_geometry from countyp020"
  LABELITEM "county"
  CLASS
    EXPRESSION ("[county]" = 'Sonoma County')
    SYMBOL 'circle'
    SIZE 2
    OUTLINECOLOR 0 0 0 #222 120 120
    LABEL
      COLOR 0 0 0
      OUTLINECOLOR 255 255 255
      TYPE TRUETYPE
      FONT ARIAL
      SIZE 14
    END
  END
  PROJECTION
    "init=epsg:4326"
  END
END
```

This example assumes you have a FONTSET specified in the map file, with a font named ARIAL available. If you don't have these, remove the TYPE, FONT, and SIZE lines in the example.

Adding labels to maps is discussed in more detail in Chapters 10 and 11. With PostGIS, there are a couple additional considerations to keep in mind. The attribute specified by LABELITEM must exist in the table that holds the geometry or in the subquery used. While this sounds like common sense, it is easy to forget. Example 13-10 has a simple DATA parameter and doesn't include a subquery. Because it points to an existing table, all the attributes of that table are available to be used as a LABELITEM. However, if a subquery is used as in Example 13-9, the attribute used in LABELITEM must also be returned as part of the subquery. To use the code in Example 13-9, more than just the wkb_geometry column needs to be returned by the subquery. The resulting settings needs to look like:

```
DATA "wkb_geometry from ( select county, wkb_geometry from countyp020 where county =
'Sonoma County') as myquery using unique wkb_geometry using srid = -1"
```

The only addition was county in the subquery. This makes the county attribute available to MapServer for use with labels, in addition to the wkb_geometry attribute which was already part of the subquery.

The other common issue encountered when creating labels is related to the case of field names. In PostgreSQL (as with other relational databases), it is possible to have upper- and lowercase field names, in addition to normal names with no explicit case. All the field names used in the examples so far have been normal, but some tools may create fields that are all uppercase, all lowercase, or (even worse) mixed case. This makes it difficult to refer to field names because the exact case of every letter in the field name needs to be specified throughout your MapServer layer parameters. This is done by using double quotes around field names, which gets confusing when you may already be using double quotes around a field name as in LABELITEM "county" in Example 13-10. If the county attribute is stored as an uppercase field name, then a set of single quotes must be wrapped around the field name. The field name must be written in uppercase, like: LABELITEM '"COUNTY"'.

Using attributes for labeling maps is common, but the two issues related here apply equally to any aspect of the LAYER parameters that refer to PostGIS fields, not just for labeling purposes, for example in the DATA, CLASSITEM, and EXPRESSION parameters, and more.

If you use ogr2ogr for loading data into PostgreSQL, you may need to use another option to ignore uppercase table and field names. The layer creation option -lco LAUNDER=YES ensures that all table and field names are in normal case. By default, ogr2ogr maintains the case used in the data source.

Using PostGIS in Other Applications

Other open source applications that aren't discussed in this book, but are able to access PostGIS data, include Quantum GIS (QGIS), uDIG, Java Unified Mapping Platform (JUMP), Thuban, GeoServer, GRASS GIS, etc. Links to these applications are provided in Chapter 8.

Some commercial vendors have implemented PostGIS support as well. Safe Software's Feature Manipulation Engine supports reading and writing of PostGIS datasets. This powerful tool makes migrating to PostGIS simple and large-scale conversion projects easy. It supports the conversion of dozens of vector and database formats. See *http://safe.com* for more on licensing and using FME.

Cadcorp's Spatial Information System (SIS) also supports PostGIS, starting at SIS v6.1. For more information, see their press release at *http://www.cadcorp.com*.

ArcMap and PostGIS

Even if you're using PostGIS, your organization may still be using ESRI's proprietary tools. A common question for ESRI ArcGIS users is "How can I access PostGIS data in ArcMap?" There is an open source project called the PostGIS-ArcMap Connector, PgArc for short. You can find this project at *http://pgarc.sourceforge.net/*.

PgArc automates the import of PostGIS tables into temporary shapefiles and loads them into ArcMap. Layers can then be edited and put back into PostGIS, overwriting the existing table in the database. There have been some changes introduced with ArcMap 9 that are currently being addressed. More improvements can still be made to strengthen the product; volunteer ArcMap programmers are always welcome.

Another way to access PostGIS data is to use the Web Mapping Server capabilities of MapServer. MapServer can access PostGIS data and create map images using the WMS standard. ESRI has an interoperability extension for ArcMap that allows users to access WMS layers. MapServer is excellent at filling this middle-man role. Chapter 12 is devoted to using MapServer with Open Geospatial Consortium Web Mapping Standards.

For ArcView 3 users, Refractions Research has an excellent WMS connector available at *http://www.refractions.net/arc3wms/*. An ArcIMS emulator is also available that can make MapServer layers available as ArcIMS layers. More information about the emulator is at *http://mapserver.refractions.net/*.

Custom Programming with MapServer's MapScript

If you have programming experience, you may want to do more to customize MapServer, incorporating MapServer capabilities directly into a custom application. Enter MapScript, an application program interface for MapServer.

Introducing MapScript

MapScript exposes the functionality of MapServer to various scripting languages. This reduces programming time for developers who want to add mapping capabilities to an application. Rather than create a custom method for mapping, the MapScript API provides some powerful tools that are robust and ready to use. It also provides a convenient way to interact with mapping data while still using your favorite programming language.

MapScript allows you to load, manipulate, and create map files. For example, you can change layer settings, manipulate map file classes, produce output images, export spatial data, and much more. Because it uses common scripting environments, MapScript functions can be combined with other functions of that language.

Several languages have MapScript support; PHP, Python, Perl, Java and Ruby are readily available. C# and TCL support are under development as well, and these are also included in the MapServer source code tree.

Getting MapScript

How do you get MapScript? There are variety of methods, some easier than others. The common requirement for running MapScript is that the scripting language itself must be available. The header files for the language may also be required if building the MapScript modules from source code.

Building MapScript from Source Code

Building MapScript from source for each language isn't detailed here, but there is a common approach.

To build MapScript for a language, support for that language must have been configured and built into MapServer itself when it was compiled. This sets up the various files in the MapScript language folders that are needed for the next step.

The MapServer source code directory structure includes a folder called `mapscript`. This folder has subsequent folders for each language that has some form of MapScript support. The folder may have a Makefile that is ready to be used by the `make` command, or it may have some setup scripts. Running these produces MapScript modules or libraries (depending on the language), and the scripts can often be used to help install them too. For example, with Python, you build and then install MapScript by running:

```
> python setup.py build
> python setup.py install
```

There are several other files and directories that are part of the Simplified Wrapper and Interface Generator (SWIG) environment. SWIG is used to port MapScript to certain languages. This is now the standard method for producing a MapScript extension for additional languages. If you are familiar with SWIG and want to write a *mapscript_wrap.c* file for a new language, your contributions would be more than welcome. For more information on SWIG, see *http://www.swig.org*.

Compilation instructions are included in *README* files in the specific MapScript language folder. More information can be found in the MapScript and Reference Guides sections of the MapServer documentation page at *http://mapserver.gis.umn. edu/doc.html*.

Obtaining Binary Versions of MapScript

Binary versions of MapScript are also available, depending on the programming language. The best place to get some personal direction is from the MapServer mailing list. These sites distribute various forms of MapScript:

- DM Solutions has PHP MapScript binaries available at *http://maptools.org/php_ mapscript/index.phtml*.

- It is also available as part of the MapServer for Windows (MS4W) environment at *http://maptools.org/ms4w/index.phtml*.

- Frank Warmerdam's FWTools package includes Python MapScript. Windows and Linux platforms are supported. See *http://fwtools.maptools.org*.

- The FGS project at *http://www.maptools.org/fgs/* provides an installer for MapServer and PHP MapScript under Linux.

- Howard Butler's Kitchen Sink build is available for the Windows operating system. It includes Java and Python support as well as several other libraries and utilities. You can find it at *http://hobu.stat.iastate.edu/mapserver*.

Getting Help

Many first-time MapScript users need some hand-holding to get started. The previous links and the MapServer mailing list are good places to go for support. This chapter will show some simple examples to help get you started.

MapScript Objects

For a complete MapScript object, variable, and method guide see the latest on the MapServer documentation web site page or Sean Gillies' reference guide (*http://zcologia.com/mapserver*).

Class diagrams are also available from these web sites:

> *http://www.veremes.com/mapserver*
> *http://www2.dmsolutions.ca/mapserver/dl/mapserver_40_uml.zip*

Classes within the map file can be accessed as objects in MapScript. In fact, there are more objects to handle than you normally see, because MapServer does a lot of the work with them behind the scenes. The main part of a MapScript application is the map object (mapObj). The mapObj can have many layer objects (layerObj) as well as legend (legendObj), scale bar (scalebarObj), and reference map (referenceMapObj) objects. Figure 14-1 shows a diagram of how these objects are hierarchically structured.

The main object is the mapObj. You can add a layerObj, classObj, and styleObj to the mapObj. Other objects should never be explicitly created, such as webObj, scalebarObj, legendObj, and colorObj. These are already part of the mapObj, and constructing new objects for them will fail. If you get segmentation faults from MapScript, this may be the cause.

All the attributes of objects that you normally see in the map file are available for manipulation through MapScript.

Using the MapScript API is best understood by walking through some simple examples.

MapScript Examples

MapServer map files are still a key component to writing a MapScript-based application. If you have a map file ready to use, you can start accessing and manipulating it right away. However, a powerful feature of MapScript is the ability to create maps on the fly without having a map file. In this case, you can build your map from scratch.

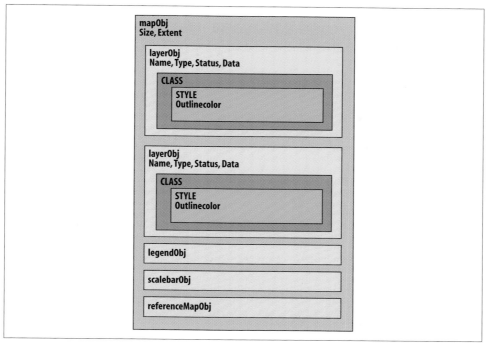

Figure 14-1. The MapScript API's hierarchical object structure

In the first two examples, a simple map file is used, as shown in Example 14-1. In the third example, a custom map file is created using MapScript. To keep the example short and simple, I've removed optional components like the scale bar, legend, and reference map.

Example 14-1. A simple map file used for the examples in this chapter

```
MAP
  SIZE 600 300
  EXTENT -180 -90 180 90
  IMAGECOLOR 180 180 250
  IMAGETYPE PNG

  UNITS DD
  WEB
    IMAGEPATH "/srv/www/htdocs/tmp/"
    IMAGEURL "/tmp/"
  END

  LAYER
    NAME countries
    TYPE POLYGON
    STATUS DEFAULT
    DATA countries_simpl
```

Example 14-1. A simple map file used for the examples in this chapter (continued)

```
  CLASS
    NAME 'Countries'
    OUTLINECOLOR 100 100 100
    COLOR 200 200 200
  END
 END
END
```

 You can download the country boundary data in shapefile format from *http://ftp.intevation.de/freegis/worlddata/freegis_worlddata-0.1_ simpl.tar.gz*.

This compressed file contains a shapefile called *countries_simpl*. The map file example assumes that the *countries_simpl.** files are in the same folder as the map file. This dataset is used elsewhere in this book.

The map file shown in Example 14-1 produces the map shown in Figure 14-2.

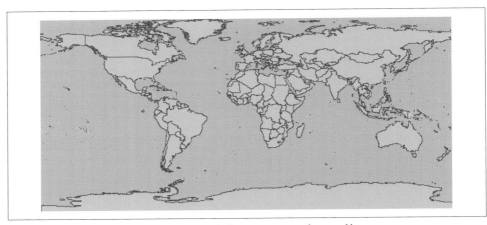

Figure 14-2. A basic map of the world, made from a very simple map file

Multiple programming languages can be used with MapScript. The examples in this chapter use the Python programming language. To show how Python and other languages compare, the same MapScript example is shown in Python, Perl, PHP, Java, and Ruby at the end of this chapter.

 To keep these examples as simple as possible, no error checking, optimization, or modularization is included. These examples aren't intended to be used as-is in a production environment.

Opening the Map File and Drawing the Map

The most basic functionality of MapServer is its ability to read in a map file and create an image showing the map. This can be done with MapScript in only a few short steps, as shown in Example 14-2.

Example 14-2. Opening a map file and drawing a map into an image file

```
# map1.py
# Python MapScript Example 1

import mapscript

# Set the map file to use
mapfile = "global.map"

# Create a mapObj, initialized with the mapfile above
mapobject = mapscript.mapObj(mapfile)

# Create an imgObj that has an image of the map
mapimage = mapobject.draw()

# Save the mapimage to a file
mapimage.save("worldmap.png")
```

In Example 14-2, the lines starting with the pound # symbol are comments that help describe the process. In other languages, comments may be coded differently. As you can see, this is a very short example. Here's a description of each line of code.

```
mapfile = "global.map"
```

This line doesn't use MapScript at all; rather it sets the mapfile variable to a string that points to the *global.map* map file it loads in the next step.

```
mapobject = mapscript.mapObj(mapfile)
```

This line creates an object that becomes the core of the application, the map object or mapObj. Just like a map file (which includes the map object and has layers, projections, and other settings in it), so mapObj is the highest level in the MapScript object hierarchy. All the other objects used in this example are taken from it.

Many attributes and methods are available for the mapObj. In this example, only one method is used.

```
mapimage = mapobject.draw()
```

The draw method of the mapobject returns an image object or imgObj. This object is stored in the variable mapimage.

```
mapimage.save("worldmap.png")
```

The final step uses the save() method to take the map image and save it to a file. The output filename for the image is given as a string directly in the method, but can also be assigned as a separate string variable like mapfile was earlier.

If you provide an empty string for the filename in the save( ) method, MapScript prints the image to stdout. Depending on the language and how the application is being run, stdout may be a terminal, interpreter shell, web page, etc.

That's it! Now you can take this basic example and incorporate some mapping capabilities into your own application.

Manipulating Map Settings

Example 14-3 demonstrates Python MapScript interacting with the map object. It shows how to create a new class that uses a class expression to highlight a certain country.

Example 14-3. Creating a new class, selecting a country, and drawing it in a different color

```
# map2.py
# Python MapScript Example 2

import mapscript

# Set the map file to use
mapfile = "global.map"

# Create a mapObj, initialized with the mapfile above
mapobject = mapscript.mapObj(mapfile)

# Get the first layer and set a classification attribute
layer1 = mapobject.getLayer(0)
layer1.classitem = "NAME"

# Get the first Class in the layer and duplicate it
classCanada = layer1.getClass(0)
layer1.insertClass(classCanada)

# Give the class a meaningful name
classCanada.name = "Canada"

# Set the expression used to limit the features drawn
classCanada.setExpression("Canada")

# Get the Style and modify the Color used
canadaStyle = classCanada.getStyle(0)
canadaStyle.color.setRGB(250, 250, 125)

# Create an imgObj that has an image of the map
mapimage = mapobject.draw( )

# Save the mapimage to a file
mapimage.save("worldmap.png")
```

This example modifies the properties of the layer, adds a new class, and changes its color. Perhaps the most powerful feature it demonstrates is the ability to create or modify expressions that limit what features are drawn. The map produced is shown in Figure 14-3.

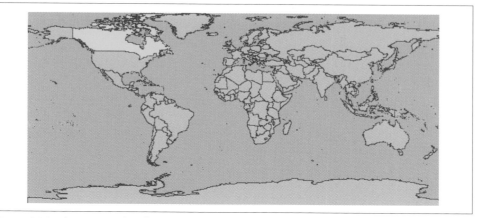

Figure 14-3. The map results of Example 14-3 showing the base map class and a filtered class only showing Canada

The following is a closer examination of Example 14-3.

```
layer1 = mapobject.getLayer(0)
layer1.classitem = "NAME"
```

The setting of the classitem layer property is really the first new line added to this example. Just like setting a CLASSITEM property in the map file, this setting allows the use of an expression that filters the features shown in a class. In this case, the attribute called "NAME" is queried using the value of the expression. This won't be used until the setExpression() function later on.

```
classCanada = layer1.getClass(0)
layer1.insertClass(classCanada)
```

This may look a little obscure. The first line gets the first class (0) defined for the layer. In the map file there is only one CLASS object defined. The insertclass() function creates a second class by copying the original. The purpose of this example is to show Canada highlighted on the world map, therefore we keep the first class in place without modifying and then make a copy of it and filter out all countries other than Canada.

```
classCanada.name = "Canada"
classCanada.setExpression("Canada")
```

Setting the .name property for a class allows it to be used when drawing a legend. In this case, a legend isn't being drawn, but it is a good habit to always name your classes for future reference.

The setExpression() function is the heart of this example. You may have been expecting to see some kind of logical statement such as an SQL clause like:

```
...where country = 'Canada'
```

That style of statement is possible, but this example shows a simple way of doing the same thing. The value set in the expression here is used along with the classitem property for the layer. Therefore, behind the scenes, the statement: [NAME] = "Canada" is used to exclude features that don't meet this criteria.

You can set statements like this in setExpression() too, without having a classitem set for the layer, but getting the syntax right can be tricky and varies depending on the type of data source. The more simple you can keep it, the better. For more information on using expressions with MapServer, see the "Understanding Operators" section in Chapter 10.

```
canadaStyle = classCanada.getStyle(0)
canadaStyle.color.setRGB(250, 250, 125)
```

These final new lines simply change the color of the features (those that meet the expression logic) to a highlighting yellow. The value (250, 250, 125) represents the proportion of red, green, and blue color values to shade the features with.

Creating a Map File from Scratch

The next example, Example 14-4, doesn't use an existing map file but creates its own. The map file it creates is similar to that shown in Example 14-1. The sections are laid out to mimic the structure of the map file in Example 14-1 so that you can easily follow the logic of the program.

Example 14-4. Creating a new map file from scratch using MapScript

```
# custommapfile.py
# Build a custom map file using Python MapScript

import mapscript

# Create the map object, set properties
map = mapscript.mapObj()
map.name = "CustomMap"
map.setSize(600,300)
map.setExtent(-180.0,-90.0,180.0,90.0)
map.imagecolor.setRGB(180, 180, 250)
map.units = mapscript.MS_DD

# Set the web object image properties
map.web.imagepath = "/srv/www/htdocs/tmp/"
map.web.imageurl = "/tmp/"

# Create the layer object, as a child of the map
layer = mapscript.layerObj(map)
```

Example 14-4. Creating a new map file from scratch using MapScript (continued)

```
layer.name = "countries"
layer.type = mapscript.MS_LAYER_POLYGON
layer.status = mapscript.MS_DEFAULT
layer.data = "countries_simpl"
layer.template = "template.html"

# Create the class object as a child of the layer
class1 = mapscript.classObj(layer)
class1.name = "Countries"

# Create a style object as a child of the class
style = mapscript.styleObj(class1)
style.outlinecolor.setRGB(100, 100, 100)
style.color.setRGB(200, 200, 200)

# Write the map object into a map file
map.save("custom.map")
```

The map file that this script creates doesn't look identical to Example 14-1 because MapScript creates several other default values. However, the map file functions in the same manner and produces the same map image as a result.

 The object names used in this example are simple but not necessarily recommended because they are so close to the names of actual MapScript objects. This isn't a problem in this example, but would be a problem if the class1 object had been named class. Because class is a reserved keyword for many programming languages, it produces an error if used as a object name.

Other Resources

For more examples of MapScript, see some of these links. They point to a few different packages and tutorials.

PHP MapScript By Example HOWTO
> http://mapserver.gis.umn.edu/doc/phpmapscript-byexample-howto.html

Chameleon, MapLab and Gmap demo
> Comprehensive mapping systems built with PHP MapScript (*http://maptools.org/*)

Mobile Geographics:
> Simple recipes using PHP MapScript (*http://www.mobilegeographics.com/mapserver/*)

Tom Kralidis
> Example of downloading point coordinates and creating a new shapefile (*http://www.kralidis.ca/gis/eqmapping/index.html*)

Python Cartographic Libary (PCL)
    Mapping tools for Python, not necessarily using MapServer, but similar in features; also includes links to Cartographic Objects for Zope. (*http://zcologia.org/*)

Parallel MapScript Translations

A simple example is shown in this section using multiple scripting programming languages. Examples 14-5 through 14-9 provide a reference point for programmers who want to see how MapScript can be used in various languages. All these examples do the exact same thing—open a map file, draw the map, and save it to an image file. They are meant to be run in the same folder as the *global.map* map file, and they all produce an image file called *worldmap.png*.

Example 14-5. Python MapScript basic example

```
# map1.py
# Python MapScript Example 1

import mapscript

# Set the map file to use
mapfile = "global.map"

# Create a mapObj, initialized with the mapfile above
mapobject = mapscript.mapObj(mapfile)

# Create an imgObj that has an image of the map
mapimage = mapobject.draw()

# Save the mapimage to a file
mapimage.save("worldmap.png")
```

Example 14-6. Perl MapScript basic example

```
# map1.pl
# Perl MapScript Example 1

use mapscript;

# Set the map file to use
$mapfile = "global.map";

# Create a mapObj, initialized with the mapfile above
$mapobject = new mapscript::mapObj($mapfile);

# Create an imgObj that has an image of the map
$mapimage = $mapobject->draw();

# Save the mapimage to a file
$mapimage->save("worldmap.png");
```

Example 14-7. PHP MapScript basic example

```php
<?PHP
// map1.php
// PHP MapScript Example 1

// MapScript extension could also be loaded in php.ini
if (!extension_loaded("MapScript"))
   dl('php_mapscript.'.PHP_SHLIB_SUFFIX);


// Set the map file to use
$mapfile = "global.map";

// Create a mapObj, initialized with the mapfile above
$mapobject = ms_newMapObj($mapfile);

// Create an imgObj that has an image of the map
$mapimage = $mapobject->draw( );

// Save the mapimage to a file
$mapimage->saveImage("worldmap.png");

?>
```

Example 14-8. Java MapScript basic example

```java
import edu.umn.gis.mapscript.*;

 public class map1 {
    public static void main(String[] args) {
       System.loadLibrary("mapscript");

       mapObj mapobject;
       imageObj mapimage;
       String mapfile;

       // Set the map file to use
       mapfile = "global.map";

       // Create a mapObj, initilized with the mapfile above
       mapobject = new mapObj(mapfile);

       // Create an imgObj that has an image of the map
       mapimage=mapobject.draw( );

       // Save the mapimage to a file
       mapimage.save("worldmap.png",mapobject);
   }
 }
```

Example 14-9. Ruby MapScript basic example

```
# map1.rb
# Ruby MapScript Example 1

require "mapscript"
include Mapscript

# Set the map file to use
mapfile = "global.map"

# Create a mapObj, initialized with the mapfile above
mapobject = MapObj.new(mapfile)

# Create an imgObj that has an image of the map
mapimage = mapobject.draw

# Save the mapimage to a file
mapimage.save("worldmap.png")
```

A Brief Introduction to Map Projections

Map projections are a critical component of any mapping application, whether for a hardcopy printout or an interactive web map. If you are new to mapmaking, you may see projections as a confusing and intimidating topic. If so, keep in mind that even some of the more advanced mapmakers have just enough map projection knowledge to do what they need. The theory runs as deep as math itself. With a minimal amount of orientation, you can get started with map projections.

This guide will prepare you for using map projections with MapServer. For more information about MapServer, see the other chapters in this book. In this section, general concepts are discussed, and a few popular projections are introduced. The syntax for setting projections in a MapServer map file is also covered.

The Third Spheroid from the Sun

The Earth is round, or so they say. Video games, globes, and graphic art may depict the Earth as a perfect ball shape or *sphere*, but in reality the Earth is a bit squished. Therefore, we call the Earth a *spheroid*, rather than a sphere. It is sphere-like, but somewhat elliptical.

To take it one level further, we all know that the surface of the Earth isn't perfectly uniform. There are mountains and valleys, bumps and dips. *Geoid* is the term used for a more detailed model of the Earth's shape. At any point on the globe, the geoid may be higher or lower than the spheroid. Figure A-1 shows an example of the relationships among the sphere, spheroid, and geoid.

Figure A-1 is based on a graphic courtesy of Dylan Prentiss, Department of Geography, University of California, Santa Barbara. Further descriptions are available at the Museum's Teaching Planet Earth web site, *http://earth.rice.edu/mtpe/geo/geosphere/topics/remotesensing/60_geoid.html*.

As you can see, when talking about the shape of the Earth it is very important to know what shape you are referring to. The shape of the Earth is a critical factor when

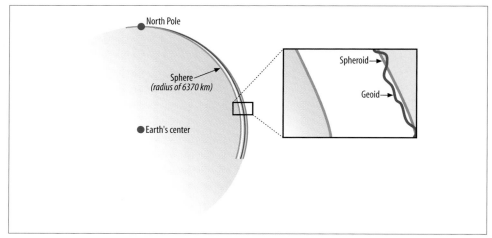

Figure A-1. Illustration of methods for describing the Earth's shape

producing maps because you (usually) want to refer to the most exact position possible. Many maps are intended for some sort of navigational purpose, therefore mapmakers need a consistent way of helping viewers find a location.

Geographic Coordinate System

How do you refer someone to a particular location on the Earth? You might say a city name, or give a reference to a landmark such as a mountain. This subjective way of referring to a location is helpful only if you already have an idea of where nearby locations are. Driving directions are a good example of a subjective description for navigating to a particular location. You may get directions like "Take the highway north, turn right onto Johnson Road and go for about 20 miles to get to the farm." Depending on where you start from, this may help you get to the farm, or it may not. There has to be a better way to tell someone where to go and how to get there. There is a better way; it is called the Geographic Coordinate System.

The increasing use of hand-held Global Positioning System receivers is helping the general public think about the Geographic Coordinate System. People who own a GPS receiver can get navigation directions to a particular location using a simple pair of numbers called *coordinates*. Sometimes an elevation can be provided too, giving a precise 3D description of a location.

A Geographic Coordinate System, like that shown in Figure A-2, is based on a method of describing locations using a longitude and latitude degree measurement. These describe a specific distance from the equator (0° north/south) and the Greenwich Meridian (0° east/west).

From this starting point, the earth is split into 360 slices, running from the North Pole to the South Pole, known as degrees and represented by the symbol °. Half of

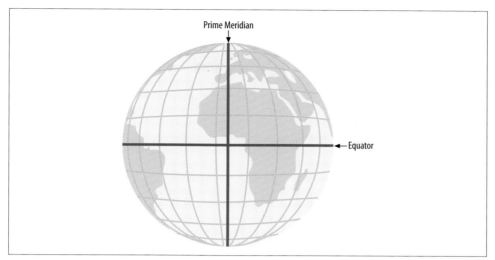

Figure A-2. A Geographic Coordinate System

these slices are to the east of 0° and half are to the west. These are referred to as longitudes or *meridians*. Therefore, the maximums are 180° west longitude and 180° east longitude (see Figure A-3).

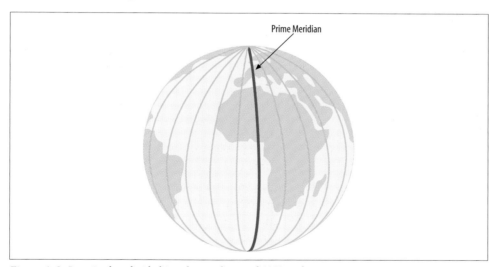

Figure A-3. Longitudes, divided into hemispheres of 180° each

A variant of the basic geographic coordinate system for longitudes is useful in some parts of the world. For example, 180° west longitude runs right through the South Pacific Islands. Maps of this area can use a system where longitudes start at 0° and increase eastward only, ending back at the same location which is also known as 360° (see Figure A-4).

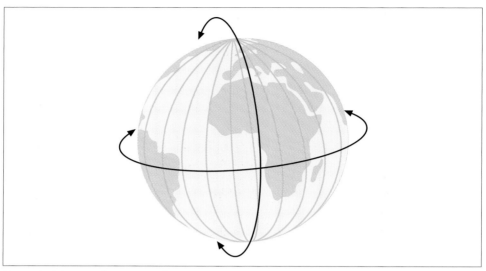

Figure A-4. Longitudes, running from 0 to 360°

The earth is divided into latitudes as well. You can picture these as 180 slices running horizontally around the globe. Half of these slices are north of the equator and the other half are south of the equator. These are referred to as latitudes or parallels. Therefore the values range from 90° south latitude (at the south pole) to 90° north latitude (at the north pole) (see Figure A-5).

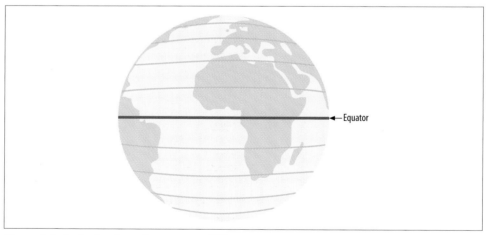

Figure A-5. Latitudes, from the equator to 90°

Decimal degrees versus degrees minutes seconds

Global coordinates can be represented using a couple of different notations. It is hard to say if one of them is more common than the other, but some are certainly more intuitive than others.

One of the more traditional notations is known as Degrees Minutes Seconds (DMS). The coordinates are written as three separate numbers, each representing a degree, minute, and second, respectively.

For example, `122°W` is read as 122 degrees west. Rarely are the degrees alone precise enough for a location; minutes and seconds are subdivisions of each degree and provide more precision. Each minute is 1/60th of a degree. Likewise, one second is 1/60th of a minute. A more precise example would be `122°30'15"W`, read as 122 degrees, 30 minutes, and 15 seconds west.

At the other end of the spectrum is the decimal degree (DD) notation. This notation uses a decimal place in place of minutes and seconds. For example, `122.525°W` is read as `122.525` degrees west. The decimal portion, `.525`, represents just over half a degree.

In between DMS and DD are a couple more permutations. One of the more common is to have a degree and a minute, but the seconds are a decimal of the minute; for example, `122°30.25"`. I find this type of notation difficult to use because it mixes two worlds that don't play well together. It can't be called either DD or DMS, making it tough to explain. I highly recommend using Decimal Degrees as much as possible. It is commonly understood, supported well by most tools and is able to be stored in simple numeric fields in databases.

It is also common to see different signs used to distinguish an east or west value. For example, `122°W` may also be known as `-122°` or simply `-122`; this is minus because it is less than or west of the Greenwich Meridian. The opposite version of it, e.g., `122°`, is assumed to be positive and east of `0°`.

Map Projections: Flattening the Spheroid

The Geographic Coordinate System is designed to describe precise locations on a sphere-like shape. Hardcopy maps and onscreen displays aren't at all sphere-like; hence they present a problem for making useful depictions of the real world. This is where map projections come in. The problem of trying to depict the round earth on a flat surface is nothing new, but the technology for doing so has improved substantially with the advent of computerized mapping.

The science of map projections involves taking locations in a Geographic Coordinate System and projecting them on to a flat plane. The term *projection* tells a little bit about how this was done historically. Picture a globe that is made of glass. Painted on the glass are the shapes of the continents. If you were to put a light inside the glass, some light would come through and some would be stopped by the paint. If you held a piece of paper up beside the globe, you would see certain areas lit up and other areas in shadow. You would, in fact, see a *projected* view of the continents, much like a video projector creates from shining light through a piece of film. You can sketch the shapes on the paper, and you would have a map. Projections are meant for display on a flat surface. Locating a position on a projected map requires the use of a planar coordinate system (as opposed to a geographic coordinate system). This is considered *planar* because it is a simple plane (the flat paper) and can only touch one area on the globe.

This example has limitations. You can map only the portion of the earth that is nearest the paper, and continents on the other side of the globe can't be mapped on the same piece of paper because the light is shining the other way. Also, the map features look most accurate close to the center of the page. As you move outward from the center, the shapes get distorted, just like your shadow late on a summer day as it stretches across the sidewalk: it's you, but not quite right. More inventive ways of projecting include all sorts of bending and rolling of the paper. The paper in these examples can be referred to as a plane: the flat surface that the map is going to be projected on to.

There are many different classes and types of map projections. Here are just a few of the most simple:

Cylindrical projections
> These involve wrapping the plane around the globe like a cylinder. They can touch the globe all the way around, but the top and bottom of the map are distorted.

Conic projections
> These look like, you guessed it, a plane rolled into a cone shape and set like a hat onto the globe. If you set it on the top of the globe, it rests on a common latitude all the way around the North Pole. The depth of the cone captures the details of the pole, but are most accurate at the common latitude. When the paper is laid flat, it is like removing the peel of an orange and laying it perfectly flat.

Orthographic projections
> These look like a map drawn by an astronaut in orbit. Instead of having the light inside the globe, it's set behind the globe; the paper is flat against the front. All the features of the continents are projected onto the paper, which is hardly useful for a global-scale map because it shows only a portion of the globe. However, if the features on the backside are ignored, then it looks like a facsimile of the earth. With the current processing power of computers, rendering maps as spheres is possible, but these realistic-looking perspectives aren't always useful.

The role of mathematical computations is essential to projecting map data. It is the heart of how the whole process works. Fortunately, you don't need to know how it works to use it. All you need to know is that the glass-globe analogy is, in fact, replaced by mathematical calculations.

Each map projection has strong and weak points. Different types of projections are suited for different applications. For example, a cylindrical projection gives you an understandable global map but won't capture the features of the poles. Likewise a conic projection is ideal for polar mapping, but impossible for global maps.

Although there are a few main classes of projections (cylindrical, conic, etc.) there are literally hundreds of projections that have been designed. The details of how each one is implemented vary greatly. In some cases, you simply need to know what map projection you want. In others, you need to know detailed settings for where the *plane* touches the globe or at what point the map is centered.

Planar/Projected Coordinate System

Both *planar* and *projected* are terms that describe the coordinate system designed for a flat surface. The Geographic Coordinate System uses measurements based on a spherical world, or degrees. A projected coordinate system is designed for maps and uses a Cartesian Plane to locate coordinates.

The Cartesian Plane is a set of two (or more) axes where both axes intersect at a central point. That central point is coordinate 0,0. The axes use common units and can vary from one map projection to another. For example, the units can be in meters: coordinate (100,5) is 100 meters east and 5 meters north. Coordinate (−100,−5) is 100 meters west and 5 meters south.

The Y axis is referred to as the central meridian. The central meridian could be anywhere and depends on the map projection. If a projection is localized for Canada, the central meridian might be 100° west. All east/west coordinates would be relative to that meridian. This is in contrast to the geographic coordinate system where the central meridian is the Greenwich Meridian, where all east/west coordinates are always relative to the same longitude.

The X axis is perpendicular to the Y axis, meeting it at a right angle at 0,0. This is referred to as the latitude of origin. In a projected coordinate system, it can be any latitude. If focused on Canada, the latitude of origin might be 45° north. Every projected north/south coordinate is relative to that latitude. In the geographic coordinate, this is the equator, where all north/south coordinates are always relative to the equator.

Using Map Projections with MapServer

The projection settings in a MapServer map file are at two levels: the output map projection and the projection of the input layers of features to be drawn. Example A-1 shows a sample of the projection settings for an output map.

Example A-1. Example settings for the map to be rendered using an Albers Equal Area projection

```
PROJECTION
  "proj=aea"
  "ellps=WGS84"
  "lat_0=10"
  "lon_0=-90"
END
```

The settings may look confusing to anyone unfamiliar with projections, but they have a straightforward purpose. If you can get these four settings clear in your mind, you'll be able to handle most projections with ease.

PROJ.4: Projection Library and Utilities

The terms used in Example A-1, proj, ellps, lat_0, lon_0, are all keywords for the projection library used behind MapServer, called PROJ.4. There are other options (e.g., datum, units, etc.), but these are the most common. PROJ.4 isn't just a set of libraries that MapServer uses. It also comes with some command-line utilities. One of these is a program called proj, which lists the available projections, ellipsoids, etc.

Running the command:

```
> proj -l
```

returns a list of the available map projections, including the abbreviation used in the proj= setting for MapServer.

This utility can also project coordinates interactively by keyboard or from a text file; it's perfect for bulk projection of coordinates.

For more information on PROJ.4 see *http://proj.maptools.org/*.

The first line in Example A-1, "proj=aea", is the most important. It specifies the name of the projection. The abbreviation aea is short for Albers Equal Area projection. Every PROJECTION...END object must have a projection name specified. You should also specify an ellipsoid, e.g., ellps=WGS84. Some functions will not require an ellps parameter to be used, but some will fail without it. If in doubt, use the World Geodetic System WGS84. All the other parameters can be optional. There are 121 projections available through PROJ.4.

The second line, "ellps=WGS84", specifies the *ellipsoid* to use for the projection. WGS 84 is a specific representation of the shape of the earth. Depending on the area being mapped, there may be more or less precise ellipsoids to use. There are 42 in total. Choosing one to use isn't necessarily straightforward, unless you can find one that was generated specifically for your country or region of interest. If you can find such, you will get more accurate projection results. WGS 84 is a generally useful ellipsoid for global applications.

The third line, "lat_0=10", specifies the *latitude of origin* as 10° north. The default latitude of origin is 0° if not specified. The *projected* north/south coordinates will all start at 0 at this latitude.

The final line, "lon_0=-90", sets the *central meridian* as 90° west or –90°. The default is 0° if not specified. The *projected* east/west values all start at 0 at this longitude.

 To learn more about the WGS84 ellipsoid, see *http://www.wgs84.com/wgs84/wgs84.htm*.

EPSG Codes

Depending on the map projection to be used, there may be more or fewer settings required. It isn't always necessary to specify all the settings. There are some short-cuts available. One common method is to use a master spatial reference systems list that comes with PROJ.4. This text file, usually named *epsg*, contains predefined projections, latitude of origins, ellipsoids, etc. You can then refer to a more complex set of options using a single number. These codes are called EPSG codes. They were developed and maintained by the European Petroleum Survey Group (EPSG). See *http://www.epsg.org/* for more information about the group.

Here are two examples from the EPSG definitions:

```
# NAD83 / UTM zone 10N
<26910> +proj=utm +zone=10 +ellps=GRS80 +datum=NAD83
        +units=m +no_defs no_defs
<>

## WGS84 / LCC Canada
<42101> +proj=lcc +ellps=WGS84 +lat_0=0 +lon_0=-95
        +lat_1=49 +lat_2=77 +x_0=0 +y_0=-8000000.0
        +datum=WGS84 +units=m no_defs
<>
```

As you can see, there are several options used in both of these. Both are single lines, but are shown on multiple lines here for clarity. Rather than have to specify each of these, as in Example A-1, you can simply provide the EPSG code number:

```
PROJECTION
  "init=epsg:26910"
END
```

This automatically sets all the projection options to project the map into UTM zone 10N using the NAD83 datum. UTM zones and other projections are described in the next section.

Likewise, "init=epsg:42101" would set it to a Lambert Conformal Conic (LCC) projection, with specific options suitable for mapping Canada. This definition is considered custom, or nonstandard. It was developed independently of the EPSG organization and won't necessarily appear in the default EPSG file. Many of the custom definitions come with PROJ.4 in a separate file. If you can't find the one you need, it is worth asking for it on the MapServer mailing list or IRC channel. Simply append the additional lines of text definition to the EPSG file, and they are instantly available for use.

EPSG versus epsg

When EPSG codes are used in a MapServer PROJECTION object, the text epsg should be in lowercase. When used in other contexts (such as Open Geospatial Consortium Web Map Server requests using MapServer), the text must be uppercase. For example if you have a wms_srs attribute in a METADATA object for a layer, it would be:

```
"wms_srs" "EPSG:26910"
```

This is a common problem when using EPSG codes with MapServer.

 You can specify epsg in uppercase in the PROJECTION object, but on some operating systems, you have to rename the EPSG file to uppercase.

Map Projection Examples

The examples in the following section are based on some global map data that is stored in the Geographic Coordinate System. Each example is one projection at a suitable scale. This section is intended to introduce a few of the more common types of map projections and provide a picture of what they look like. Some brief description is provided, but other books and documents are recommended for learning more about these projections.

The specific MapServer projection settings are included for reference. As long as all your layers have a valid projection set for them, these example projection settings can be used to change the output map projection.

 A global map grid shapefile was used as a layer for the map figures in this section. This shapefile was used instead of the internal MapServer graticule generator (the GRID object). The GRID object produces very simple lines that can't be properly transformed by many projections.

A Python script called mkgraticule.py is included in the pymod folder of the FWTools package. This created the map grid for these maps.

For more on FWTools, see *http://fwtools.maptools.org/*.

Simple Cylindrical Projection

Figure A-6 shows the most basic world map. The global coordinates, latitudes, and longitudes are displayed on a rectangular grid. Each rectangle is the same size on

---

both x and y planes. This is the default projection used with MapServer when you specify the latlong projection. It is commonly known as a Simple Cylindrical projection, more technically known as Plate Carré. It is from the family of Equidistant Cylindrical projections. See the other references listed at the end of this chapter for more information about these types of projections.

This projection is most useful near the equator because the features are distorted as you move away from the equator. The features of Antarctica in Figure A-6 are a good example of how distorted it can be.

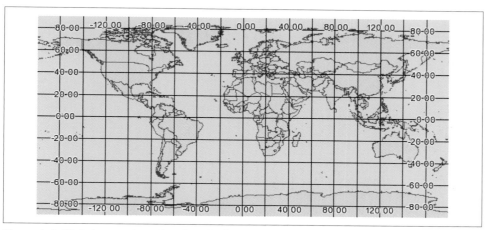

Figure A-6. Global map using a Simple Cylindrical projection

MapServer syntax

Specifying this projection is easy. All you need to set is the projection name and ellipsoid:

```
PROJECTION
    "proj=latlong"
    "ellps=WGS84"
END
```

or:

```
"init=epsg:4326"
```

The extents of this map are set to:

```
EXTENT -180 -90 180 90
```

Orthographic Projection

Figure A-7 shows an example of the orthographic projection mentioned earlier. This projection has some popular appeal because it makes the map look like a globe.

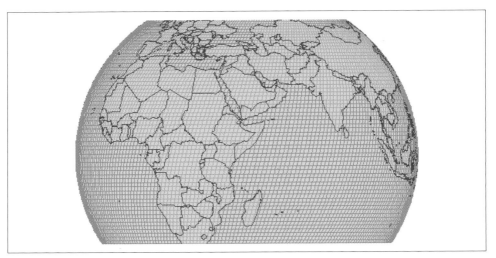

Figure A-7. Map of the Eastern Hemisphere using orthographic projection

MapServer syntax

The projection name is shortened to ortho. Specify a lat_0 and lon_0 to center the map on a particular latitude and longitude, respectively.

```
PROJECTION
  "proj=ortho"
  "lat_0=45"
  "lon_0=45"
  "ellps=WGS84"
END
```

The extents of this map are set in meter units:

```
EXTENT -8710000 -2739000 8710000 4493000
```

The extents are set to be wider than the earth (extents are 17,420 km wide) so you can see the curvature of the sphere. They aren't set to be taller than the earth, so the north and south portions are cut off.

 While orthographic projections look neat, they aren't without problems. Some limitations in MapServer make them difficult to use. Features at the pole or close to the extremes (e.g., near 180 or −180 longitude) may not appear properly or may show gaps. Also, if your features have only a few points along a line, some lines may not be displayed at all. These bugs are known and may soon be corrected.

Mercator Projection

Figure A-8 shows an example of the Mercator projection which may appear common to many. It is most useful near the equator. As you can see, the grid isn't regular looking and it isn't possible to map the northern extremes accurately.

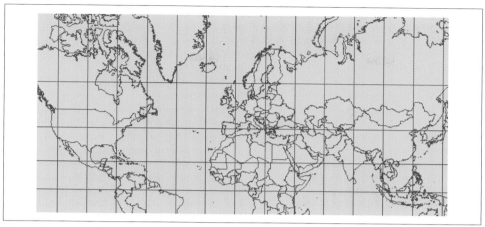

Figure A-8. Example map showing northern latitudes in Mercator projection

MapServer syntax

The projection name is shortened to `merc`:

```
PROJECTION
  "proj=merc"
  "ellps=WGS84"
END
```

The extents of this map are set in meter units:

```
EXTENT -14896048 0 16000000 11779439
```

Transverse Mercator Projection

Figure A-9 shows an example of the Transverse Mercator projection. Like the Mercator projection, it is most useful near the latitude of origin, in this case 10° north.

MapServer syntax

The projection name is shortened to `tmerc`:

```
PROJECTION
  "proj=tmerc"
  "lat_0=10"
  "lon_0=80"
  "ellps=WGS84"
END
```

The extents of this map are set in meter units:

```
EXTENT -500000 -3500000 500000 3500000
```

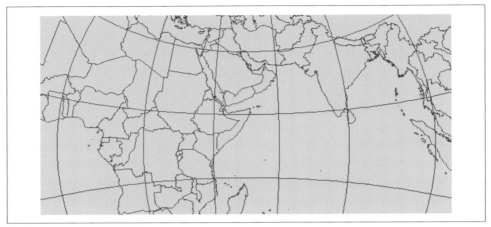

Figure A-9. Map of Africa and south Asia in Transverse Mercator projection

Albers Equal Area Projection

Figure A-10 shows an example of the Albers Equal Areas projection, designed to preserve the relative areas of different parts of the globe.

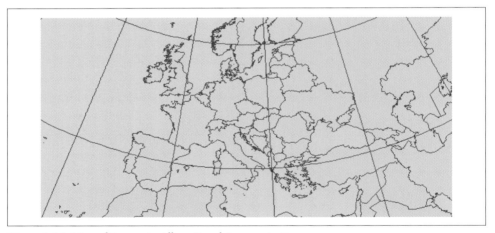

Figure A-10. Map of Europe in Albers Equal Area projection

MapServer syntax

The projection name is shortened to aea. A first and second parallel is specified too, which provides more accurate detail between those parallels. The central meridian, lon_0, is also set.

```
PROJECTION
  "proj=aea"
```

```
   "lon_0=15"
   "lat_0=55"
   "lat_1=35"
   "ellps=WGS84"
END
```

The extents of this map are set in meter units:

```
EXTENT -100861 -2500195 100819 1000195
```

Stereographic Projection

Figure A-11 shows an example of the Stereographic projection.

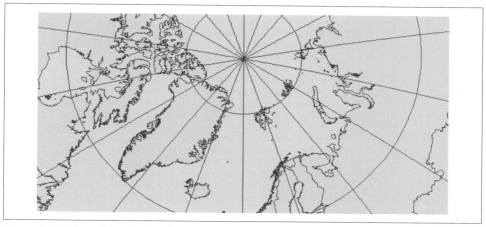

Figure A-11. Map of the North Pole in Stereographic projection

MapServer syntax

The projection name is shortened to stere. The central meridian defaults to 0°, but the first parallel is set to 80° north.

```
PROJECTION
   "proj=stere"
   "lat_0=80"
   "ellps=WGS84"
END
```

The extents of this map are set in meter units:

```
EXTENT -800861 -2000195 800819 2000195
```

Universal Transverse Mercator Projection

The Universal Transverse Mercator (UTM) projection may be the most popular map projection. It uses a global system of 60 predefined zones that are 6° wide and 90° high, from the equator to the poles. The zone number starts at −180° west and increments eastward. North and south designations are defined by the equator. There are zones 1N and 1S (north/south of the equator).

The UTM zones are a regular grid, but there are some irregularities to the grid in northern Europe. The central meridian lies in the middle of the zone and crosses the first parallel, the equator, at the center of the zone. Rather than longitudes and latitudes, the axes are referred to as *northings* and *eastings*, being relative to the center point of the zone: 0,0.

UTM projection is designed for regional or local scale maps. They can't be used globally, for large countries, or even large provinces (e.g., the provinces of western Canada). In theory, if features fall in more than one UTM zone, you should not use UTM projection.

Figure A-12 shows a map of the regular UTM zone grids. This map doesn't include the Northern Europe irregularities of the actual system, but is meant to give the general idea of the UTM zone concept.

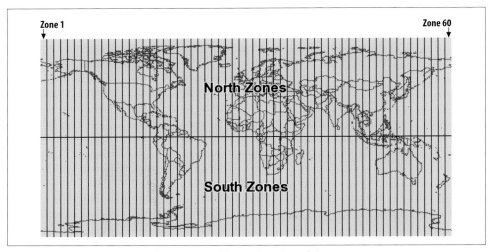

Figure A-12. UTM zone map showing, roughly, the location of the zones

Figure A-13 shows Cuba, using UTM Zone 18N projection. The longitudes are shown as a reference, representing the width of the UTM zone. Because Cuba crosses more than one UTM Zone, using a UTM projection is probably not the best choice.

MapServer syntax

```
PROJECTION
  "proj=utm"
  "zone=18N"
  "ellps=WGS84"
END
```

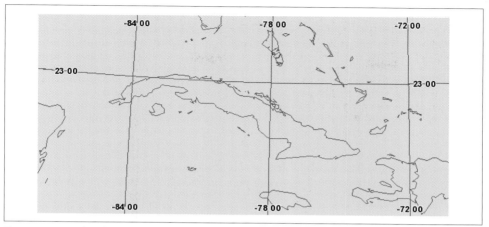

Figure A-13. Cuba shown in UTM 18N projection

The extents of this map are set in meter units:

```
EXTENT -848000 2225000 990000 2565000
```

Using Projections with Other Applications

MapServer is just one application of many that use PROJ.4 to help project coordinates. Two other utilities discussed elsewhere in this book can use the power of PROJ.4 to project data/features into new projections. This is often accomplished using a few command-line options. The gdalwarp and ogr2ogr command-line tools (part of the GDAL/OGR package hosted at *http://gdal.org*) allow you to convert raster and vector data, respectively, between formats. You can also specify a target spatial reference system using the -t_srs option. For example, to convert an image that is referenced to latitude/longitude coordinates, into a Mercator projection, the following command might be used:

```
> gdalwarp -t_srs "+proj=merc +ellps=WGS84" in.tif out.tif
```

There is also an option, -s_srs, that allows you to specify the source SRS. This is essential if the data you have isn't already encoded with projection information.

Here is another example; it uses the ogr2ogr vector conversion utility to convert a shapefile from one SRS to another. The source SRS is also supplied because there was no projection information (or *.prj* file) supplied with the data.

```
> ogr2ogr -s_srs "+proj=latlong" -t_srs "+proj=merc +ellps=WGS84" city_merc.shp city_
in.shp
```

References

This appendix is only an introduction to projections. For more information about map projections, technical specifics, or cartographic principles, please refer to the following online resources:

Museums Teaching Planet Earth web site
    http://www.geog.ucsb.edu/~dylan/mtpe/geosphere/topics/rs/howis.html

PROJ.4: Cartographic Projections Library
    The main PROJ.4 web site includes links to more technical documents that describe the math and parameters involved with specific projections. See the references section at the bottom of the main web page for more links at *http://proj. maptools.org.*

Atlas of Canada's Map Making learning resources
    This resource includes significant information on map projections (*http://atlas. gc.ca/site/english/learningresources/carto_corner/index.html*).

United States Geologic Survey (USGS) projection document
    Check here for an overview of specific projections and theory: *http://erg.usgs.gov/ isb/pubs/MapProjections/projections.html.*

GDAL/OGR libraries and utilities
    Command-line utilities and libraries allow comprehensive access to raster (GDAL) and vector (OGR) data, including projection support; check out *http://gdal.org.*

Spherical trigonometry
    This site has a simple tutorial focused on understanding the trigonometric concepts behind spherical measurements and navigation; find it at *http://www.dynagen.co.za/ eugene/where/sphertrg.html.*

Coordinates, datums and transformations
    Here you find many links to articles, papers and country-specific map projection information *http://www.ferris.edu/htmls/academics/course.offerings/burtchr/geodesy/ datums.html.*

MapServer Reference Guide for Vector Data Access

This document, created by Jeff McKenna and Tyler Mitchell, was presented as part of a workshop given at the Open Source GIS/MapServer Users Meeting in Ottawa, Canada in 2004.

This is a comprehensive reference guide to using different vector data formats with MapServer. This guide is also available on the MapServer web site:

http://mapserver.gis.umn.edu/doc.html

If you have comments, additions or corrections, please contact one of the authors at:

Tyler Mitchell: tylermitchell@shaw.ca
Jeff McKenna: jmckenna@dmsolutions.ca

Vector Data

What is vector data? This quote is a good description of what vector data is:

> Vector: An abstraction of the real world where positional data is represented in the form of coordinates. In vector data, the basic units of spatial information are points, lines, and polygons. Each of these units is composed simply as a series of one or more coordinate points. For example, a line is a collection of related points, and a polygon is a collection of related lines. Vector images are defined mathematically as a series of points joined by lines. Vector-based drawings are resolution independent. This means that they appear at the maximum resolution of the output device, such as a printer or monitor. Each object is self-contained, with properties such as color, shape, outline, size, and position on the screen.
>
> From: *http://coris.noaa.gov/glossary/glossary_l_z.html#v*

MapServer can access vector file formats and database connections. It can also access raster or image data. This is a summary of the vector and database formats with particular focus on how to use them in a MapServer map file and access them using command-line tools such as `ogrinfo`.

MapServer and Vector Data Access

MapServer offers two methods for accessing data:

Using built-in, format-specific, data access capabilities
> The most basic form of data access uses the built-in capabilities that were linked into MapServer when it was compiled. These capabilities are limited to only a few types of vector data, such as ESRI shapefile, PostGIS, Oracle Spatial, and ArcSDE. The default, built-in format for MapServer is the ESRI shapefile format.

Using the capabilities of third-party data access libraries
> One of the most powerful features of MapServer is the ability to use data formats through a pseudo plug-in environment. The most significant third-party library being used is GDAL/OGR. This includes raster (GDAL) and vector (OGR) data.

Using OGR

OGR is used behind the scenes by MapServer when requested. MapServer doesn't require OGR in order to run. Some users may never need the additional capabilities OGR offers, but many users find them absolutely necessary. Because MapServer can access data via OGR, you don't have to program specific types of data format support directly into MapServer. Instead, you can make further additions to OGR and then use MapServer. In essence, the background libraries allow MapServer to bring the data into an internal, memory-based format that MapServer can use. For the most part, using OGR-related formats is seamless and intuitive.

Data Format Types

There are three types of data mapping and GIS data formats. Each type is handled differently. Here are the types and some example formats:

File-based
> Shapefiles, Microstation Design Files (DGN), GeoTIFF images

Directory-based
> ESRI ArcInfo coverages, U.S. Census TIGER

Database connections
> PostGIS, ESRI ArcSDE, MySQL

Each type of data is made up of a data source and (one or more) layers. These two definitions apply to MapServer and OGR:

Data source
> A group of layers stored in a common repository. This may be a file that handles several layers within it or a folder that has several files.

Layer

> A subset of a data source often containing information in one type of vector format (point, line, polygon).

File-based data

File-based data consists of one or more files stored in any arbitrary folder. In many cases, a single file is used (e.g., DGN) but ESRI shapefiles, for example, consist of at least three files, each with a different filename extension: *SHP, DBF, SHX*. In this case all three files are required because they each perform a different task internally.

Filenames usually serve as the data source name and contain layers that may or may not be obvious from the filename. In shapefiles, for example, there is one data source per shapefile and one layer that has the same name as that of the file.

Directory-based data

Directory-based data consists of one or more files stored in a particular way within a parent folder. In some cases (e.g., coverages), they may also require additional folders in other locations in the file tree in order to be accessed. The directory itself may be the data source. Different files within the directory often represent the layers of data available.

For example, ESRI ArcInfo Coverages consist of more than one file with an *ADF* file extension, within a folder. The *PAL.ADF* file represents the Polygon data. *ARC.ADF* holds the arc or line string data. The folder holds the data source, and each *ADF* file is a layer.

Database connections

Database connections are similar to file- and directory-based structures in one respect: they provide geographic coordinate data for MapServer to interpret. That may be oversimplifying what is happening inside MapServer, but in essence all you need is access to the coordinates making up the vector datasets.

Database connections provide a stream of coordinate data that is temporarily stored (e.g., in memory) and read by MapServer to create the map. Other attribute or tabular data may also be required, but the focus of this guide is coordinate data.

One important distinction between databases must be made. The databases discussed here are *spatial* databases, those which can hold geographic data in its own data type. This is opposed to strictly *tabular* databases that can't hold geographic coordinates in the same way. It is possible to store some very simple coordinate data in regular tables, but for anything but the most simple use, a spatial database is required. There are spatial extensions to many databases (open source and commercial). One of the most robust is the PostGIS extension to the PostgreSQL database. This database not only allows the storage of geographic data, but also allows the manipulation of that data using SQL commands. The other open source database with spatial capabilities is MySQL.

Connections to databases usually consist of the following pieces of connection information:

Host
>   Directions to the server or computer hosting the database.

Database name
>   The name of the database you wish to access that is running on the host.

User name/passwords
>   Access privileges are usually restricted by user.

 Some databases (e.g., Oracle) use a name service identifier that includes both the host and database names.

Access to specific pieces of coordinate data usually require:

Table/view name
>   The name of the table or view holding the coordinate data

Geographic column name
>   Where geometry or coordinates are stored

Data Format Guide

The rest of this document is the data format guide. This guide is structured to show the fundamentals of each MapServer-supported data format. Each section discusses one format, ranging from one to several pages in length. The sections typically start with a summary of the most important information about the format, followed by examples of file listings, connection methods, ogrinfo usage, and MapServer map file syntax examples.

Each section has been designed to stand alone, so you may notice that certain warnings and comments are repeated or redundant. This is intentional. Each format is presented in rough order of popular use, based on a survey of the MapServer community.

The following formats are included:

*   ESRI shapefiles (SHP)
*   PostGIS/PostgreSQL database
*   MapInfo files (TAB/MID/MIF)
*   Oracle Spatial Database
*   Web Feature Service (WFS)

- Geography Markup Language (GML)
- VirtualSpatialData (ODBC/OVF)
- TIGER/Line files
- ESRI Arc Info coverage files (ADF)
- ESRI ArcSDE database (SDE)
- Microstation design files (DGN)
- IHO S-57 files
- Spatial Data Transfer Standard files (SDTS)
- Inline MapServer features
- National Transfer Format files (NTF)

 The MySQL spatial database isn't covered in this guide at this time due to lack of familiarity by the authors. Future contributions by MySQL users are welcome in this guide.

ESRI Shapefiles (SHP)

Also known as ESRI ArcView. ESRI is the company that introduced this format; ArcView was the first product to use shapefiles.

File listing

Shapefiles are made up of a minimum of three similarly named files, with different suffixes:

Countries_area.dbf
Countries_area.shp
Countries_area.shx

Data access/connection method

- Shapefile access is built directly into MapServer. It is also available through OGR, but direct access without OGR is recommended and discussed here.
- The path to the shapefile is required. No file extension should be specified.
- Shapefiles hold only one layer of data, therefore no distinction needs to be made.

ogrinfo examples

- The directory can serve as a data source.
- Each shapefile in a directory serves as a layer.
- A shapefile can also be a data source. In this case the layer has the same prefix as the shapefile.

Here's an example that uses ogrinfo on a directory with multiple shapefiles:

```
> ogrinfo /data/shapefiles/
INFO: Open of '/data/shapefiles/'
using driver 'ESRI Shapefile' successful.
```

```
1: wpg_h2o (Line String)
2: wpg_roads (Line String)
3: wpg_roads_dis (Line String)
4: wpgrestaurants (Point)
```

Here's an example that uses ogrinfo on a single shapefile:

```
> ogrinfo /data/shapefiles/Countries_area.shp
Had to open data source read-only.
INFO: Open of 'Countries_area.shp'
using driver 'ESRI Shapefile' successful.
1: Countries_area (Polygon)
```

Here's an example that uses ogrinfo to examine the structure of the file/layer:

```
> ogrinfo -summary /data/shapefiles/Countries_area.shp Countries_area
Had to open data source read-only.
INFO: Open of 'Countries_area.shp'
using driver 'ESRI Shapefile' successful.

Layer name: Countries_area
Geometry: Polygon
Feature Count: 27458
Extent: (-180.000000, -90.000000) - (180.000000, 83.627419)
Layer SRS WKT:
(unknown)
FAC_ID: Integer (5.0)
TILE: Integer (3.0)
ARCLIST: String (254.0)
NAM: String (77.0)
PERIMETER: Real (22.17)
POLYGONCOU: Integer (6.0)
NA2DESC: String (45.0)
```

Map file example

```
LAYER
  NAME my_shapefile
  TYPE POLYGON
  DATA countries_area
  STATUS OFF
  CLASS
    NAME "Countries"
    OUTLINECOLOR 0 0 0
  END
END
```

PostGIS/PostgreSQL Database

PostGIS is Refraction Research's spatial extension to the PostgreSQL enterprise database.

PostGIS support

PostGIS is supported directly by MapServer and must be compiled into MapServer to work.

In most cases, PostgreSQL and PostGIS libraries (*.dll* or *.so*) must be present in the system's path environment for functionality to be present. This includes the `libpq` and `libpostgis` libraries.

Map file example

- Specify `CONNECTIONTYPE POSTGIS`.
- Define `CONNECTION` as:

  `"host=`**`yourhostname`** `dbname=`**`yourdatabasename`** `user=`**`yourdbusername`**
  `password=`**`yourdbpassword`** `port=`**`yourpgport`**`"`

  `CONNECTION` parameters can be in any order. Most are optional. dbname is required. host defaults to `localhost`, port defaults to `5432`—the standard port for PostgreSQL.
- Define `DATA` as: "geometrycolumn from yourtablename". MapServer had a bug related to the keyword `from`. Specify it in lowercase to avoid problems. geometrycolumn can be the_geom if the `shp2pgsql` utility is used to load data, or wkb_geometry if `ogr2ogr` is used.

For example:

```
LAYER
  NAME pg_test
  TYPE POLYGON
  CONNECTIONTYPE POSTGIS
  CONNECTION "host=mapserver.com dbname=gmap user=julio"
  DATA "wkb_geometry FROM province"
  CLASS
    ...
  END
END
```

For more info about PostGIS and MapServer, see PostGIS docs at *http://postgis.refractions. net/docs/*.

MapInfo Files (TAB/MID/MIF)

MapInfo files are also known as TAB or MID/MIF files.

File listing

The *.DAT*, *.ID*, *.MAP* files are also associated with *.TAB* files. Here's an example:

`border.DAT border.ID border.MAP border.TAB`

The term MID/MIF refers to files with *.MID* and *.MIF* extension.

Data access/connection method

- TAB and MID/MIF access is available in MapServer through OGR.
- The `CONNECTIONTYPE OGR` parameter must be used.
- The path to the (*.tab* or *.mif*) file is required, and the file extension is needed.
- The path may be relative to the `SHAPEPATH`

MapInfo files already contain styling information. This styling information can be used optionally by specifying the STYLEITEM "AUTO" parameter in the LAYER object of the map file.

If you use STYLEITEM "AUTO", you must have an empty class in the layer.

ogrinfo examples

Here's an example that uses ogrinfo on a single TAB file:

```
> ogrinfo elev5_poly.TAB
Had to open data source read-only.
INFO: Open of 'elev5_poly.TAB'
using driver 'MapInfo File' successful.
1: elev5_poly (Polygon)
```

Here's an example that uses ogrinfo to examine the structure of the file/layer:

```
> ogrinfo elev5_poly.TAB elev5_poly
Had to open data source read-only.
INFO: Open of 'elev5_poly.TAB'
using driver 'MapInfo File' successful.

Layer name: elev5_poly
Geometry: Polygon
Feature Count: 2236
Extent: (-141.000000, 60.000000) - (-124.403310, 69.300251)
Layer SRS WKT:
GEOGCS["unnamed",
    DATUM["MIF 0",
        SPHEROID["WGS 84 (MAPINFO Datum 0)",6378137.01,298.257223563],
        TOWGS84[0,0,0,0,0,0,0]],
    PRIMEM["Greenwich",0],
    UNIT["degree",0.0174532925199433]]
AREA: Real (0.0)
PERIMETER: Real (0.0)
ELEV5_: Integer (0.0)
ELEV5_ID: Integer (0.0)
TYPE: Real (4.0)
ELEV5: Real (4.0)
...
```

Map file example

```
LAYER
  NAME Elevation_Poly_5
  TYPE POLYGON
  STATUS DEFAULT
  CONNECTIONTYPE OGR
  CONNECTION "./hypso/elev5_poly.TAB"
  STYLEITEM "AUTO"
  CLASS
    NAME "Elevation Poly 5"
  END
END # Layer
```

Oracle Spatial Database

- MapServer can support Oracle Spatial through OGR.
- OGR must be compiled with Oracle Spatial support and MapServer must be compiled to use OGR.
- MapServer also supports Oracle Spatial natively.

For more information about Oracle Spatial and MapServer see the MapServer documentation and reference pages at *http://mapserver.gis.umn.edu/doc.html*.

Map file example using OGR support

```
LAYER
    ...
    CONNECTION "OCI:user/pwd@service"
    CONNECTIONTYPE OGR
    DATA "Tablename"
    ...
END
```

Example:

```
LAYER
    ...
    NAME "Ottawa"
    CONNECTIONTYPE OGR
    CONNECTION "OCI:jeff/blah@ora_cities"
    DATA "CITIES"
    TYPE POINT
    ...
END
```

Map file example using native support

```
LAYER
    ...
    CONNECTIONTYPE oraclespatial
    CONNECTION "user/pwd@service"
    DATA "GEOMETRY FROM tablename"
    ...
END
```

Web Feature Service (WFS)

WFS is an Open Geospatial Consortium specification. For more information about the format itself, see *http://www.opengeospatial.org/*.

WFS allows a client to retrieve geospatial data encoded in Geography Markup Language (GML) from multiple Web Feature Services. GML is built on the standard web language XML.

WFS differs from the popular Web Map Service specification in that WFS returns a subset of the data in valid GML format, not just a graphic image of data.

Capabilities

Requesting capabilities using the GetCapabilities request to a WFS server returns an XML document showing what layers and projections are available, etc.

Example of a WFS GetCapabilities URL

```
http://www2.dmsolutions.ca/cgi-bin/mswfs_gmap
?VERSION=1.0.0
&SERVICE=wfs
&REQUEST=GetCapabilities
```

Example of the resulting XML from GetCapabilties

Example B-1. Resulting XML from GetCapabilities

```
...
<FeatureTypeList>
 <Operations>
  <Query/>
 </Operations>
   <FeatureType>
    <Name>park</Name>
    <Title>Parks</Title>
    <SRS>EPSG:42304</SRS>
    <LatLongBoundingBox minx="-173.433" miny="41.4271" maxx="-13.0481" maxy="83.7466" />
   </FeatureType>
   <FeatureType>
    <Name>road</Name>
    <Title>Roads</Title>
    <SRS>EPSG:42304</SRS>
    <LatLongBoundingBox minx="-148.059" miny="35.882" maxx="-33.7745" maxy="72.5503" />
   </FeatureType>
   <FeatureType>
    <Name>popplace</Name>
    <Title>Cities</Title>
    <SRS>EPSG:42304</SRS>
    <LatLongBoundingBox minx="-172.301" miny="36.3541" maxx="-12.9698" maxy="83.4832" />
 </FeatureType>
 </FeatureTypeList>
...
```

Data access/connection method

- WFS access is a core MapServer feature.
- MapServer currently supports WFS Version 1.0.0.
- The CONNECTIONTYPE WFS parameter must be used.

WFS layers can be requested through a layer in a map file, or you can request the GML directly through the browser with a GetFeature request. You can specify a specific layer with the TypeName request. In a map file, the name/value pairs should be put into a METADATA object.

You can limit the number of features returned in the GML by using the MaxFeatures option (e.g., &MAXFEATURES=100).

Example of a WFS request directly through the browser

The following URL requests the GML for the layer road (see the earlier section, "Capabilities," for the possible layers available on this test server). The URL is all one line, broken up here for readability.

```
http://www2.dmsolutions.ca/cgi-bin/mswfs_gmap
?VERSION=1.0.0
&SERVICE=wfs
&REQUEST=getfeature&TYPENAME=road
```

Map file example

```
LAYER
  NAME "wfs_gmap_roads"
  STATUS DEFAULT
  TYPE LINE
  CONNECTIONTYPE WFS
  CONNECTION "http://www2.dmsolutions.ca/cgi-bin/mswfs_gmap?
  METADATA
    "wfs_version" "1.0.0"
    "wfs_srs" "EPSG:42304"
    "wfs_typename" "road"
    "wfs_request_method" "GET"
    "wfs_service" "WFS"
  END
  CLASS
    NAME "roads"
    COLOR 0 0 0
  END
END  # layer
```

Geography Markup Language Files (GML)

- Also known as Geographic Markup Language and GML/XML.
- GML is a text-based, XML format that can represent vector and attribute data.
- This is an Open Geospatial Consortium specification for data interchange.

File listing

GML files are usually a single text file with a GML filename extension (*coal_dep.gml*). Some may use XML as the filename extension.

XML schema documents often accompany GML files that have been translated from some other format (e.g., using the ogr2ogr utility).

Example of text in a GML file

GML uses sets of nested tags to define attributes and geometry coordinates:

```
<gml:featureMember>
  <Coal_Deposits fid="1">
    <UNKNOWN>0.000</UNKNOWN>
    <NA>0.000</NA>
```

```
    <ID>2</ID>
    <ID2>2</ID2>
    <MARK>7</MARK>
    <COALKEY>110</COALKEY>
    <COALKEY2>110</COALKEY2>
    <ogr:geometryProperty>
      <gml:Point>
        <gml:coordinates>78.531,50.694</gml:coordinates>
      </gml:Point>
    </ogr:geometryProperty>
  </Coal_Deposits>
</gml:featureMember>
```

Data access/connection method

- GML access is available in MapServer through OGR.
- The CONNECTIONTYPE OGR parameter must be used.
- The path to the GML file is required, including a file extension.
- There can be multiple layers in a GML file, including multiple feature types.

ogrinfo examples

Here's an example that uses ogrinfo on a single GML file:

```
> ogrinfo /data/gml/coal_dep.gml
Had to open data source read-only.
INFO: Open of 'coal_dep.gml'
using driver 'GML' successful.
1: Coal_Deposits
```

Here's an example that uses ogrinfo to examine the structure of one layer:

```
> ogrinfo -summary /data/gml/coal_dep.gml Coal_Deposits
Had to open data source read-only.
INFO: Open of 'coal_dep.gml'
using driver 'GML' successful.

Layer name: Coal_Deposits
Geometry: Unknown (any)
Feature Count: 266
Extent: (23.293650, 37.986340) - (179.272550, 80.969670)
Layer SRS WKT:
(unknown)
UNKNOWN: Real (0.0)
NA: Real (0.0)
ID: Integer (0.0)
ID2: Integer (0.0)
MARK: Integer (0.0)
COALKEY: Integer (0.0)
COALKEY2: Integer (0.0)
LONG: Real (0.0)
LAT: Real (0.0)
```

Map file example

```
LAYER
  NAME coal_deposits
  TYPE POINT
  STATUS DEFAULT
  CONNECTIONTYPE OGR
  CONNECTION "gml/coal_dep.gml"
  CLASS
    COLOR 0 0 0
    SYMBOL 'circle'
    SIZE 6
  END
END
```

VirtualSpatialData (ODBC/OVF)

This is an OGR extension to MapServer. It allows you to connect to databases that don't explicitly hold spatial data, as well as flat text files. Your data must have an x and a y column, and the data may be accessed through an ODBC connection or a direct pointer to a text file.

Types of databases

The VirtualSpatialData OGR extension has been tested with the following databases and should, in theory, support all ODBC data sources.

- Oracle
- MySQL
- SQL Server
- Access
- PostgreSQL

Types of flat files

Comma, tab, or custom delimited text/flat files work with VirtualSpatialData.

Create the data source name (DSN)

Specific notes about creating a DSN on Windows and Linux can be found by searching the MapServer reference documents site at *http://mapserver.gis.umn.edu/doc*.

On some Windows systems you *must* create a SYSTEM DSN.

Test your connection

Test your connection with ogrinfo. The syntax for this command is:

```
> ogrinfo ODBC:user/pass@DSN table
```

ogrinfo examples

Here's an example that accesses a comma-separated text file through ODBC; it's a flat text file *coal_dep.txt* containing lat/long points:

```
unknown,na,id,id2,mark,coalkey,coalkey2,long,lat
0.000,0.000,1,1,7,87,87,76.90238,51.07161
0.000,0.000,2,2,7,110,110,78.53851,50.69403
0.000,0.000,3,3,3,112,112,83.22586,71.24420
0.000,0.000,4,4,6,114,114,80.79896,73.41175
```

If the DSN name is *Data_txt*, the ogrinfo command to see a list of applicable files in the directory is:

```
> ogrinfo ODBC:jeff/test@Data_txt
INFO: Open of `ODBC:jeff/test@Data_txt'
using driver `ODBC' successful.
1: coal_dep.csv
2: coal_dep.txt
3: coal_dep_nf.txt
4: coal_dep_trim.txt
5: Copy of coal_dep.txt
6: deposit.csv
7: maruia.asc
8: oahuGISbathy.csv
9: oahuGISbathy.txt
10: on_pts.txt
11: on_pts_utm.txt
12: test.txt
13: utm_test.txt
```

The username and password may be optional, so the following may also be valid:

```
> ogrinfo ODBC:@Data_txt
```

Therefore, the command to see more information about one of the specific layers is:

```
> ogrinfo ODBC:@Data_txt coal_dep.txt
INFO: Open of 'ODBC:@Data_txt'
using driver 'ODBC' successful.

Layer name: coal_dep.txt
Geometry: Unknown (any)
Feature Count: 266
Layer SRS WKT:
(unknown)
UNKNOWN: String (255.0)
NA: String (255.0)
ID: String (255.0)
ID2: String (255.0)
MARK: String (255.0)
COALKEY: String (255.0)
COALKEY2: String (255.0)
LONG: String (255.0)
LAT: String (255.0)
OGRFeature(coal_dep.txt):0
  UNKNOWN (String) = 0.000
  ....
```

Here's an example that creates a virtual data file with an *ovf* extension:

```
<OGRVRTDataSource>
    <OGRVRTLayer name="mylayer">
        <SrcDataSource>ODBC:user/pass@DSN</SrcDataSource>
    <SrcLayer>tablename</SrcLayer>
  <GeometryType>wkbPoint</GeometryType>
        <LayerSRS>WGS84</LayerSRS>
    <GeometryField encoding="PointFromColumns" x="x" y="y"/>
    </OGRVRTLayer>
</OGRVRTDataSource>
```

More information on *ovf* files can be found at *http://www.remotesensing.org/gdal/ogr/drv_ vrt.html.*

Here's an example *ovf* file for *coal_dep.txt:*

```
<OGRVRTDataSource>
  <OGRVRTLayer  name="coal">
      <SrcDataSource>ODBC:Data_txt</SrcDataSource>
      <SrcLayer>coal_dep.txt</SrcLayer>
      <GeometryField encoding="PointFromColumns" x="Long" y="Lat"/>
      <GeometryType>wkbPoint</GeometryType>
  </OGRVRTLayer>
</OGRVRTDataSource>
```

Map file example

Using an *ovf* file, your layer may look like:

```
LAYER
  CONNECTION "coal.ovf"
  CONNECTIONTYPE OGR
  DATA "coal-test"
    METADATA
      "wms_srs"    "4326"
      "wms_title"    "coal-test"
    END
  NAME "coal-test"
  SIZEUNITS PIXELS
  STATUS ON
  TOLERANCE 0
  TOLERANCEUNITS PIXELS
  TYPE POINT
  UNITS METERS
  CLASS
    STYLE
        COLOR 255 0 0
      MAXSIZE 100
      MINSIZE 1
      SIZE 6
      SYMBOL "star"
    END
  END
END
```

You may also specify the *ovf* contents inline this way:

```
    LAYER
        CONNECTION "<OGRVRTDataSource>
<OGRVRTLayer  name='coal-test'>
<SrcDataSource>ODBC:@Data_txt</SrcDataSource>
<SrcLayer>coal_dep.txt</SrcLayer>
<GeometryField encoding='PointFromColumns' x='Long' y='Lat'/>
<GeometryType>wkbPoint</GeometryType>
</OGRVRTLayer>
</OGRVRTDataSource>"
        CONNECTIONTYPE OGR
        DATA "coal-test"
          METADATA
            "wms_srs"    "4326"
            "wms_title"   "coal-test"
          END
        NAME "coal-test"
        SIZEUNITS PIXELS
        STATUS ON
        TOLERANCE 0
        TOLERANCEUNITS PIXELS
        TYPE POINT
        UNITS METERS
        CLASS
          STYLE
              COLOR 255 0 0
            MAXSIZE 100
            MINSIZE 1
            SIZE 6
            SYMBOL "star"
          END
        END
    END
```

TIGER/Line Files

TIGER/Line files are created by the U.S. Census Bureau and cover the entire United States. They are often referred to simply as TIGER files. For more information, see *http://www.census.gov/geo/www/tiger/*.

File listing

TIGER/Line files are text files and directory-based data sources. For example, one county folder TGR06059 contains several associated files:

```
TGR06059.RT1 TGR06059.RT2 TGR06059.RT4 TGR06059.RT5
TGR06059.RT6 TGR06059.RT7 TGR06059.RT8 TGR06059.RTA
TGR06059.RTC TGR06059.RTH TGR06059.RTI TGR06059.RTP
TGR06059.RTR TGR06059.RTS TGR06059.RTT TGR06059.RTZ
```

Data access/connection method

- TIGER/Line access occurs through OGR.
- The full path to the directory containing the associated files is required in the CONNECTION string. The layer number is added to the CONNECTION string, after the path, separated by a comma: for example., CONNECTION "/tiger/data,0".
- The layer number in the map file is actually the ogrinfo layer number, minus one.

ogrinfo examples

Here's an example that uses ogrinfo on a TIGER directory to retrieve layer numbers:

```
> ogrinfo TGR06059 (NOTE that this is a directory)
ERROR 4: Tiger Driver doesn't support update.
Had to open data source read-only.
INFO: Open of 'TGR06059'
using driver 'TIGER' successful.
1: CompleteChain (Line String)
2: AltName (None)
3: FeatureIds (None)
4: ZipCodes (None)
5: Landmarks (Point)
6: AreaLandmarks (None)
7: Polygon (None)
8: PolygonCorrections (None)
9: EntityNames (Point)
10: PolygonEconomic (None)
11: IDHistory (None)
12: PolyChainLink (None)
13: PIP (Point)
14: TLIDRange (None)
15: ZeroCellID (None)
16: OverUnder (None)
17: ZipPlus4 (None)
```

For the CompleteChain Line layer, the ogrinfo layer number is 1. However, when referring to this layer in a map file CONNECTION, the layer number will be one less, 0.

Here's an example that uses ogrinfo to examine the structure of the TIGER layer CompleteChain:

```
> ogrinfo TGR06059 CompleteChain
ERROR 4: Tiger Driver doesn't support update.
Had to open data source read-only.
INFO: Open of 'TGR06059'
using driver 'TIGER' successful.

Layer name: CompleteChain
Geometry: Line String
Feature Count: 123700
Extent: (-118.125898, 33.333992) - (-117.412987, 33.947512)
Layer SRS WKT:
GEOGCS["NAD83",
    DATUM["North_American_Datum_1983",
        SPHEROID["GRS 1980",6378137,298.257222101]],
```

```
    PRIMEM["Greenwich",0],
      UNIT["degree",0.0174532925199433]]
MODULE: String (8.0)
TLID: Integer (10.0)
SIDE1: Integer (1.0)
SOURCE: String (1.0)
FEDIRP: String (2.0)
FENAME: String (30.0)
FETYPE: String (4.0)
FEDIRS: String (2.0)
CFCC: String (3.0)
FRADDL: String (11.0)
TOADDL: String (11.0)
FRADDR: String (11.0)
TOADDR: String (11.0)
FRIADDL: String (1.0)
TOIADDL: String (1.0)
FRIADDR: String (1.0)
TOIADDR: String (1.0)
ZIPL: Integer (5.0)
```

Map file example

```
LAYER
  NAME Complete_Chain
  TYPE LINE
  STATUS DEFAULT
  CONNECTIONTYPE OGR
  CONNECTION "/path/to/data/tiger/TGR06059,0"
  CLASS
    COLOR 153 102 0
  END
END # Layer
```

ESRI ArcInfo Coverage Files

ESRI ArcInfo coverage files are also known simply as coverages and, less commonly, as ADF files.

File listing

Coverages are made up of a set of files within a folder. The folder itself is the coverage name. The files roughly represent different layers, usually representing different types of topology or feature types.

```
> ls /data/coverage/brazil
aat.adf  arc.adf  arx.adf  bnd.adf  lab.adf  prj.adf  tic.adf  tol.adf
```

A folder with the name INFO is also part of the coverage. It sits at the same hierarchical level as the coverage folder itself. Therefore, to copy a coverage (using regular filesystem tools), the coverage folder and the INFO folder must both be copied. The INFO folder holds some catalog information about the coverage:

```
> ls /data/coverage/info
arc0000.dat  arc0001.dat  arc0002.dat  arc.dir
arc0000.nit  arc0001.nit  arc0002.nit
```

Data access/connection method

- CONNECTIONTYPE OGR must be used. The ability to use coverages isn't built into MapServer.
- The path to the coverage folder name is required.
- The layer number is used to specify what type of features to draw (as per the layer number from ogrinfo, but minus one).

ogrinfo examples

- The directory is the data source.
- Layers are found within the directory.

Here's an example that uses ogrinfo on a coverage directory:

```
> ogrinfo /data/coverage/brazil
INFO: Open of 'brazil'
using driver 'AVCBin' successful.
1: ARC (Line String)
2: CNT (Point)
3: LAB (Point)
4: PAL (Polygon)
```

Here's an example that uses ogrinfo to examine the structure of a layer:

```
> ogrinfo -summary /data/coverage/brazil PAL
Had to open data source read-only.
INFO: Open of 'brazil'
using driver 'AVCBin' successful.

Layer name: PAL
Geometry: Polygon
Feature Count: 1
Extent: (1272793.274958, 795381.617050) - (1287078.382785, 807302.747284)
Layer SRS WKT:
(unknown)
ArcIds: IntegerList (0.0)
AREA: Real (18.5)
PERIMETER: Real (18.5)
F_OPER#: Integer (5.0)
F_OPER-ID: Integer (5.0)
OPER: String (2.0)
FCODE: String (10.0)
```

Map file example

```
LAYER
  NAME Brazil_bounds
  TYPE POLYGON
  STATUS DEFAULT
  CONNECTIONTYPE OGR
  CONNECTION "/data/coverage/brazil, 3"
  CLASS
    NAME "Brazil Admin Areas"
    OUTLINECOLOR 153 102 0
    SIZE 2
  END
END
```

ESRI ArcSDE Database (SDE)

ArcSDE is ESRI's spatial plug-in for SQL Server, Oracle, and DB2 databases. It is also known as Spatial Database Engine, but most commonly as simply SDE.

SDE support

- SDE is supported directly by MapServer.
- MapServer 4.4 supports SDE 9, 8, and SDE for coverages on Linux, Windows, and Solaris platforms.
- Recent developments in MapServer (v4.4) have added support for SDE raster layers. Using raster layers is beyond the scope of this guide.

Connecting to SDE

1. Install the SDE client libraries from the SDE CDs.
2. Compile MapServer with SDE support.
3. Define the layer in the map file.

Map file example

1. Specify CONNECTIONTYPE SDE
2. Define the CONNECTION as: *hostname,instancename,databasename,username,password*
3. Define the DATA as: *tablename, geometrycolumn*

For example:

```
LAYER
  NAME test
  TYPE POLYGON
  CONNECTION "sde.dms.ca,port:5151,sde,user,password"
  CONNECTIONTYPE SDE
  DATA "NTDB.WATER,SHAPE"
  CLASS
    ...
  END
END
```

For more about SDE and MapServer, see the MapServer documentation page at *http://mapserver.gis.umn.edu/doc,* or search the reference documentation.

Microstation Design Files (DGN)

These are also known as DGN files.

File listing

Data is encapsulated in a single file, usually with the suffix *.dgn*; for example: *0824t.dgn*.

Data access/connection method

- Access is available in MapServer through OGR.
- The CONNECTIONTYPE OGR parameter must be used.
- The path to the *dgn* file is required; file extension is needed.
- All types of features in a DGN file are held in one "layer" of data. The layer is called elements and is the first and only layer.
- The type of feature to be read from the DGN depends on the TYPE parameter in the map file.
- DGN files typically contain POINT, LINE, POLYGON, and ANNOTATION feature types.
- DGN files contain "styling" information, i.e., how to color and present the data. This is used, optionally, by specifying the STYLEITEM "AUTO" parameter.

 DGN files typically use white as a color for their features and therefore aren't visible on maps with white backgrounds.

ogrinfo examples

Using ogrinfo on a single DGN file

Note that no geometry/feature type for the layer is identified because it can be multiple types.

```
> ogrinfo /data/dgn/0824t.dgn
Had to open data source read-only.
INFO: Open of '0842t.dgn'
using driver 'DGN' successful.
1: elements
```

Using ogrinfo to examine the structure of the file/layer

DGN files aren't really GIS data files. They evolved from drafting formats used by computer-aided drafting/design (CADD) programs.

They carry a few key attributes that are usually consistent across all DGN files. Most of the attributes relate to graphical styling of features for map presentation, such as ColorIndex, Style, etc.

Spatial reference system information isn't always encoded into DGN files. This can be a major problem when trying to adequately reference the DGN data in another mapping program.

Measurement units can be a problem. In some cases the features could be located in kilometers or feet even though it isn't obvious from the output of `ogrinfo`. Sometimes the only way to identify or correct a problem with units is to open the file in Microstation software.

```
> ogrinfo -summary /data/dgn/0824t.dgn elements
INFO: Open of '0824t.dgn'
using driver 'DGN' successful.

Layer name: elements
Geometry: Unknown (any)
Feature Count: 22685
Extent: (-513183.050000, 150292.930000) - (-224583.220000, 407463.360000)
Layer SRS WKT:
(unknown)
Type: Integer (2.0)
Level: Integer (2.0)
GraphicGroup: Integer (4.0)
ColorIndex: Integer (3.0)
Weight: Integer (2.0)
Style: Integer (1.0)
EntityNum: Integer (8.0)
MSLink: Integer (10.0)
Text: String (0.0)
```

Map file example

```
LAYER
  NAME dgn
  TYPE LINE
  STATUS DEFAULT
  CONNECTIONTYPE OGR
  CONNECTION "dgn/0824t.dgn,0"
  STYLEITEM "AUTO"
  CLASS
  END
END # Layer
```

IHO S-57 Files

- Also known as S57. The IHO S-57 format is a vector interchange format used for maritime charts.
- Developed by the International Hydrographic Organization (IHO). For more information about the IHO see *http://www.iho.shom.fr/*.

File listing

Individual S57 data files have an extension of *.000*; for example, *US1BS02M.000*.

Data access/connection method

- S57 access in MapServer occurs through OGR; CONNECTIONTYPE OGR must be used.
- Specify a full path or a relative path from the SHAPEPATH to the *.000* file for the CONNECTION.
- The CONNECTION must also include a layer number (as per the layer number from ogrinfo, but minus one).

Special notes

The underlying OGR code requires two files from your GDAL/OGR installation when reading S57 data in MapServer: *s57objectclasses.csv* and *s57attributes.csv*. These files can be found in the */GDAL/data/* folder. If you receive an error in MapServer such as:

```
msDrawMap(): Image handling error. Failed to draw layer named 's57'. msOGRFileOpen():
OGR error. GetLayer( 9) failed for OGR connection
```

you may have to point MapServer to these files using the CONFIG parameter in the main section of your map file:

```
CONFIG GDAL_DATA "C:\gdal\data"
```

ogrinfo examples

Here's an example that uses ogrinfo on an S57 file to get the OGR index number:

```
> ogrinfo us1bs02m.000
ERROR 4: S57 Driver doesn't support update.
Had to open data source read-only.
INFO: Open of 'us1bs02m.000'
using driver 'IHO S-57 (ENC)' successful.
1: ADMARE (Polygon)
2: CBLSUB (Line String)
3: CTNARE
4: COALNE (Line String)
5: DEPARE
6: DEPCNT (Line String)
7: LNDARE
8: LNDELV
9: LNDRGN
10: LNDMRK
11: LIGHTS (Point)
12: OBSTRN
13: RDOSTA (Point)
14: SEAARE
15: SBDARE
16: SLCONS
17: SOUNDG (Multi Point)
18: UWTROC (Point)
19: WATTUR
20: WRECKS
21: M_COVR (Polygon)
22: M_NPUB (Polygon)
23: M_NSYS (Polygon)
24: M_QUAL (Polygon)
25: C_ASSO (None)
```

Here's an example that uses ogrinfo to examine the structure of an S57 layer:

```
> ogrinfo us1bs02m.000 DEPARE
ERROR 4: S57 Driver doesn't support update.
Had to open data source read-only.
INFO: Open of 'us1bs02m.000'
using driver 'IHO S-57 (ENC)' successful.

Layer name: DEPARE
Geometry: Unknown (any)
Feature Count: 297
Extent: (165.666667, 48.500000) - (180.000000, 60.750000)
Layer SRS WKT:
GEOGCS["WGS 84",
    DATUM["WGS_1984",
        SPHEROID["WGS 84",6378137,298.257223563]],
    PRIMEM["Greenwich",0],
    UNIT["degree",0.0174532925199433]]
GRUP: Integer (3.0)
OBJL: Integer (5.0)
RVER: Integer (3.0)
AGEN: Integer (2.0)
FIDN: Integer (10.0)
FIDS: Integer (5.0)
LNAM: String (16.0)
LNAM_REFS: StringList (16.0)
DRVAL1: Real (0.0)
DRVAL2: Real (0.0)
QUASOU: String (0.0)
SOUACC: Real (0.0)
VERDAT: Integer (0.0)
INFORM: String (0.0)
NINFOM: String (0.0)
NTXTDS: String (0.0)
SCAMAX: Integer (0.0)
SCAMIN: Integer (0.0)
TXTDSC: String (0.0)
RECDAT: String (0.0)
RECIND: String (0.0)
...
```

Map file example

```
LAYER
  NAME s57
  TYPE POLYGON
  STATUS DEFAULT
  CONNECTIONTYPE OGR
  CONNECTION "./s57/us1bs02m.000, 4"
  CLASS
    COLOR 247 237 219
    OUTLINECOLOR 120 120 120
  END
END # Layer
```

Spatial Data Transfer Standard Files (SDTS)

This is a U.S. Geological Survey (USGS) format. SDTS has a raster and a vector format. The raster format isn't supported in MapServer; only the vector formats are supported, including VTP and DLG files.

File listing

SDTS files are often organized into state-sized pieces; for example, all pf the state of Maryland, U.S.A.

Files are also available for multiple types of features including hydrography, transportation, and administrative boundaries.

This example uses transportation data, which consists of 35 separate files, each with the suffix *DDF*.

```
MDTRAHDR.DDF    MDTRARRF.DDF    MDTRCATS.DDF
MDTRDQCG.DDF    MDTRFF01.DDF    MDTRLE02.DDF
MDTRNA03.DDF    MDTRN003.DDF    MDTRSPDM.DDF
MDTRAMTF.DDF    MDTRBFPS.DDF    MDTRCATX.DDF
MDTRDQHL.DDF    MDTRIDEN.DDF    MDTRLE03.DDF
MDTRNE03.DDF    MDTRPC01.DDF    MDTRSTAT.DDF
MDTRARDF.DDF    MDTRBMTA.DDF    MDTRDDSH.DDF
MDTRDQLC.DDF    MDTRIREF.DDF    MDTRNA01.DDF
MDTRN001.DDF    MDTRPC02.DDF    MDTRXREF.DDF
MDTRARDM.DDF    MDTRCATD.DDF    MDTRDQAA.DDF
MDTRDQPA.DDF    MDTRLE01.DDF    MDTRNA02.DDF
MDTRN002.DDF    MDTRPC03.DDF
```

Data access/connection method

- SDTS access is available in MapServer through OGR.
- The `CONNECTIONTYPE OGR` parameter must be used.
- The path to the *catalog* file (*????CATD.DDF*) is required, including file extension.
- There are multiple layers in the SDTS catalog, some of which are only attributes and have no geometries.

ogrinfo examples

Here's an example that uses `ogrinfo` on a catalog file (note that the first seven layers don't have geometries):

```
> ogrinfo /data/sdts/MD/MDTRCATD.DDF
Had to open data source read-only.
INFO: Open of 'MDTRCATD.DDF'
using driver 'SDTS' successful.
1: ARDF (None)
2: ARRF (None)
3: AMTF (None)
4: ARDM (None)
5: BFPS (None)
6: BMTA (None)
```

```
 7: AHDR (None)
 8: NE03 (Point)
 9: NA01 (Point)
10: NA02 (Point)
11: NA03 (Point)
12: NO01 (Point)
13: NO02 (Point)
14: NO03 (Point)
15: LE01 (Line String)
16: LE02 (Line String)
17: LE03 (Line String)
18: PC01 (Polygon)
19: PC02 (Polygon)
20: PC03 (Polygon)
```

Here's an example that uses ogrinfo to examine the structure of the file/layer:

```
> ogrinfo -summary /data/sdts/MD/MDTRCATD.DDF LE01
Had to open data source read-only.
INFO: Open of 'MDTRCATD.DDF'
using driver 'SDTS' successful.

Layer name: LE01
Geometry: Line String
Feature Count: 780
Extent: (-80.000289, 36.999774) - (-74.999711, 40.000225)
Layer SRS WKT:
GEOGCS["NAD27",
    DATUM["North_American_Datum_1927",
        SPHEROID["Clarke 1866",6378206.4,294.978698213901]],
    PRIMEM["Greenwich",0],
    UNIT["degree",0.0174532925199433]]
RCID: Integer (0.0)
SNID: Integer (0.0)
ENID: Integer (0.0)
ENTITY_LABEL: String (7.0)
ARBITRARY_EXT: String (1.0)
RELATION_TO_GROUND: String (1.0)
VERTICAL_RELATION: String (1.0)
OPERATIONAL_STATUS: String (1.0)
ACCESS_RESTRICTION: String (1.0)
OLD_RAILROAD_GRADE: String (1.0)
WITH_RAILROAD: String (1.0)
COVERED: String (1.0)
HISTORICAL: String (1.0)
LIMITED_ACCESS: String (1.0)
PHOTOREVISED: String (1.0)
LANES: Integer (2.0)
ROAD_WIDTH: Integer (3.0)
BEST_ESTIMATE: String (1.0)
ROUTE_NUMBER: String (7.0)
ROUTE_TYPE: String (9.0)
```

Map file example

```
LAYER
  NAME sdts_maryland
  TYPE LINE
  CONNECTIONTYPE OGR
  CONNECTION "data/sdts/MD/MDTRCATD.DDF,14"
  STATUS DEFAULT
  CLASS
    COLOR 0 0 0
  END
END
```

Inline MapServer Features

Inline features refer to coordinates entered directly into the map file. They aren't a file or database format and don't require any DATA or CONNECTION parameters. Instead they use a FEATURE section to define the coordinates.

Inline features can be used to define points, lines, and polygons as if taken from an external file; this requires direct entry of coordinate pairs in the map file using a particular syntax.

Data access/connection method

This is a native MapServer option that doesn't use any external libraries to support it.

Map file example

Each FEATURE..END section defines a feature.

Points

Multiple points can be defined in a FEATURE section. If multiple points are defined in the same layer, they have the same CLASS settings; for example, for colors and styles.

Coordinates are entered in the units set in the layer's projection. In this case, it assumes the map file projection is using decimal degrees.

```
LAYER
  NAME inline_stops
  TYPE POINT
  STATUS DEFAULT
  FEATURE
    POINTS
      72.36 33.82
    END
    TEXT "My House"
  END
  FEATURE
    POINTS
      69.43 35.15
      71.21 37.95
      72.02 38.60
    END
    TEXT "My Stores"
```

```
      END
    CLASS
      COLOR 0 0 250
      SYMBOL 'circle'
      SIZE 6
    END
  END
```

Lines

Lines are simply a list of points strung together, but the layer must be TYPE LINE instead of TYPE POINT.

```
LAYER
  NAME inline_track
  TYPE LINE
  STATUS DEFAULT
  MAXSCALE 10000000
  FEATURE
    POINTS
      72.36 33.82
      70.85 34.32
      69.43 35.15
      70.82 36.08
      70.90 37.05
      71.21 37.95
    END
  END
  CLASS
    COLOR 255 10 0
    SYMBOL 'circle'
    SIZE 2
  END
END
```

Polygons

Polygons are the same as the line example, just a list of points.

They require the TYPE POLYGON parameter, and the final coordinate pair needs to be the same as the first, making it a closed polygon.

National Transfer Format Files (NTF)

NTF files are mostly used by the U.K. Ordnance Survey (OS). For more on the Ordnance Survey, see their web site at *http://www.ordnancesurvey.co.uk*.

File listing

NTF files have an NTF extension.

Data access/connection method

- NTF access requires OGR.
- The path to the NTF file is required in the CONNECTION string. It may be relative to the SHAPEPATH setting in the map file or the full path.
- The CONNECTION must also include a layer number (as per the layer number from ogrinfo, but minus one).

ogrinfo examples

Here's an example that uses ogrinfo on an NTF file to retrieve layer numbers:

```
> ogrinfo llcontours.ntf
ERROR 4: NTF Driver doesn't support update.
Had to open data source read-only.
INFO: Open of 'llcontours.ntf'
using driver 'UK .NTF' successful.
1: LANDLINE_POINT (Point)
2: LANDLINE_LINE (Line String)
3: LANDLINE_NAME (Point)
4: FEATURE_CLASSES (None)
```

For the LANDLINE_LINE layer, the ogrinfo layer number is 2; however, when referring to this layer in a map file connection, the layer number is 1.

Here's an example that uses ogrinfo to examine the structure of an NTF layer:

```
> ogrinfo llcontours.ntf LANDLINE_LINE
ERROR 4: NTF Driver doesn't support update.
Had to open data source read-only.
INFO: Open of 'llcontours.ntf'
using driver 'UK .NTF' successful.

Layer name: LANDLINE_LINE
Geometry: Line String
Feature Count: 491
Extent: (279000.000000, 187000.000000) - (280000.000000, 188000.000000)
Layer SRS WKT:
PROJCS["OSGB 1936 / British National Grid",

    GEOGCS["OSGB 1936",
        DATUM["OSGB_1936",
            SPHEROID["Airy 1830",6377563.396,299.3249646,
                AUTHORITY["EPSG","7001"]],
            AUTHORITY["EPSG","6277"]],
        PRIMEM["Greenwich",0,
            AUTHORITY["EPSG","8901"]],
        UNIT["degree",0.0174532925199433],
        AUTHORITY["EPSG","4277"]],
    PROJECTION["Transverse_Mercator"],
    PARAMETER["latitude_of_origin",49],
    PARAMETER["central_meridian",-2],
    PARAMETER["scale_factor",0.999601272],
    PARAMETER["false_easting",400000],
```

```
        PARAMETER["false_northing",-100000],
        UNIT["metre",1,
            AUTHORITY["EPSG","9001"]],
        AUTHORITY["EPSG","27700"]]
LINE_ID: Integer (6.0)
FEAT_CODE: String (4.0)
...
```

Map file example

```
LAYER
  NAME ntf_uk
  TYPE LINE
  CONNECTIONTYPE OGR
  CONNECTION "./ntf/llcontours.ntf,1"
  STATUS DEFAULT
  CLASS
    NAME "Contours"
    COLOR 0 150 200
  END
END
```

Index

We'd like to hear your suggestions for improving our indexes. Send email to *index@oreilly.com*.

MapServer for Windows (MS4W), 42, 173
    environment, 277
MapServer-supported data format
        guide, 310–336
MapTools.org site, 42
McKenna, Jeff, 307
Mercator Projection, 300
meridians, 291
metadata, mapping, 11
Microstation Design files (DGN), 308, 327
    data access/connection method, 327
    map file example, 328
    ogrinfo examples, 327
MINFEATURESIZE option, 158
Mitchell, Tyler, 307
Mobile Geographics, 285
Museums Teaching Planet Earth web
        site, 306
MySQL, 308

N

NASA Topography, 67
National Geophysical Data Center Interactive
        Map Services web site, 216
National Oceanic and Atmospheric
        Administration (NOAA), 65
National Transfer Format files (NTF), 334
    data access/connection method, 335
    map file example, 336
    ogrinfo examples, 335
ne operator, 164
nl command (Unix), 89

O

oblique air photos, 131
observations
    locating positions of, 13
    quantifying, 13
    visualizing on a map, 14
OGC (see Open Geospatial Consortium)
OGR, 151, 308
    project web site, 30
    utilities, 31
    utilities web site, 184
    vector formats supported, 30
ogr2ogr, 183, 253, 305
    as feature extraction tool, 95
    converting PostGIS data, 266
    CSV files and, 131
    selecting portions of data, 131
    transforming coordinates, 118

using to convert a shapefile into GML
        format, 94
using to convert shapefiles to other
        formats, 96
using with ogrinfo, 159
-where option, 160
ogrinfo, 307
    detailed information about geographic
        data, 73–77
    examples
        ESRI ArcInfo Coverage files, 325
        ESRI Shapefiles (SHP), 311
        GML, 318
        IHO S-57 files, 329
        MapInfo files (TAB/MID/MIF), 314
        Microstation Design files (DGN), 327
        National Transfer Format files
            (NTF), 335
        Spatial Data Transfer Standard files
            (SDTS), 331
    TIGER/Line files, 323
        VirtualSpatialData (ODBC/OVF), 320
    filtering output from, 154
    --help parameter, 75
    listing data in shapefile, 83
    on a single TAB file, 314
    -sql option, 75
    -sql parameter, 77
    -summary option, 77
    using to examine contents of world
        countries shapefile, 152
    using to examine structure of
        file/layer, 314
    using to examine the structure of the
        file/layer, 312
    using with the ogr2ogr conversion
        tool, 159
ogrtindex, 151
online street mapping applications, 132
Open Geospatial Consortium (OGC), 18,
        214
    OGC Transactional Web Feature Server
        (WFS-T), 34
    Open Geospatial Consortium web services
        (OWS), 19
    specification, 315
open source
    GIS and mapping tools, 104
    GIS/mapping products, 21
    software, 4
Open Source GIS/MapServer Users
        Meeting, 307

PostGIS (*continued*)
country polygons, querying, 262
databases, 23, 33
Debian Linux environment, 246
Distance( ) function, 264
documentation web site, 244
drawing labels, 273
find the country for a given point, 260
for Linux, 245
for Windows, 245
functionality testing, 250
install packages, 245
layers in MapServer, 259
Mac OS X environment, 246
MapServer for Windows package, 245
ogr2ogr, using to load data, 254
ogr2ogr utility for converting data, 266
overview, 241
postgis.sql SQL script, loading, 249
PostgreSQL extension, 244
RPM packages, 245
server-based databases, 243
setting up, 247
shp2pgsql tool, 253
source code, compiling from, 247
spatial data queries, 256
spatial querying, 260
subqueries and, 272
Version 0.8, 244
viewing data in MapServer, 267
viewing data in OpenEV, 267
Web Mapping Server, 275
web site, 241, 245
PostGIS-ArcMap Connector (PgArc)
project, 275
PostGIS/PostgreSQL Database, 312
map file example, 313
support, 312
PostgreSQL, 32
converting to, 97
Help, 241
official install package web site, 245
overview, 243
PostGIS extension to, 309
querying, 98
setting up, 247
subqueries and, 272
Version 7.4, 244
Version 8.0, 244
web site, 245
(see also PostGIS)
Prentiss, Dylan, 289

professional versus personal maps, 2
programming, customized (see MapScript)
Proj.4
Projection Library and Utilities, 296
Cartographic Projections Library web
site, 306
project tasks
analysis, 17
conversion, 18
creating and manipulating, 17
sharing, 18
viewing and mapping, 17
projections
defined, 293
(see also map projections)
psql command-line tool, 248
Python MapScript, 277

Q

Quantum GIS (QGIS), 34, 43, 98, 103
query results, visualizing, 266

R

RADARSAT, 78
raster data
gdalinfo command, 78
types of, 61
versus vector, 21
versus vector data, 59
recenter, adding to map web page, 194
reference map
adding to application, 207
files, 235–240
Refractions Research, 44, 58
OGC Services Survey web site, 216
web site, 33
Refractions WMS Extension for ArcView
3, 225
relational database management systems
(RDBMS), 242
reprojecting source data, 187
(see also map projections)

S

s57objectclasses.csv and s57attributes.csv
files, 329
satellite images, 65
viewing statistics for, 78–81
Scalable Vector Graphic (SVG), 34
scale bar
adding, 167–169

TIFF file, 117
TIGER file format (U.S. Census), 24
    TIGER/Line files, 322
        data access/connection method, 323
        map file example, 324
        ogrinfo examples, 323
Tikiwiki web site, 210
tile4ms (MapServer utility), 151
T-MAPY, 58
transforming data between coordinate
        systems, 138
Transverse Mercator (TM) Projection, 301
TrueType fonts, 163
tsort command (Unix), 90
TYDAC, 58

U

uniq command (Unix), 88–90
    -c option, 89
    -d option, 89
United Nations, 65
UNITS keyword, 168
Universal Transverse Mercator (UTM), 303
        projection, 72
Unix commands
    awk, 90
    colrm, 91
    column, 91
    cut, 91
    expand/unexpand, 91
    grep, 91
        using to show only names of
            airports, 84
    head/tail, 90
    join, 90
    look, 91
    nl, 89
    paste, 90
    sed, 90
        finding specific patterns, 85
        reformatting print results, 86
        removing lines and removing front end
            of lines, 86
    sort, 90
        creating list of ordered elevations, 88
    text-processing, 90
    tsort, 90
    uniq, 88–90
        -c option, 89
    uniq-d option, 89
    wc, 85

U.S. Census TIGER (see TIGER file format)
U.S. Geologic Survey, 67
U.S. Geologic Survey (USGS) projection
        document, 306
U.S. Maps and Data, 67
U.S. National Atlas, 67
U.S. National Geophysical Data Center
        (NGDC), 65
    various types of data, 120
U.S. National Geospatial Data
        Clearinghouse, 67
User-friendly Desktop GIS (UDIG), 103
USGS DEM
    Digital elevation models for the United
        States, 120
UTM (Universal Transverse Mercator)
    projection, 72, 135
    zone map showing, roughly, the location
        of the zones, 304

V

Vasudevan, Venu, 211
vector data
    access
        MapServer methods, 308
        reference guide, 307–336
    defined, 307
    types of, 60
    versus raster data, 21, 59
viewers, free, 104
viewing, 21–35
viewing tools, 17
VirtualSpatialData (ODBC/OVF), 319
    creating DSN, 319
    flat files, 319
    map file example, 321
    ogrinfo examples, 320
    testing connection, 319
    types of databases supported, 319

W

Warmerdam, Frank, 277
    (see also FWTools; GDAL/OGR)
WBMP images, 171
wc command (Unix), 85
Web Feature Service (see WFS)
Web Map Service (see WMS)
web mapping, 18
    applications, 5
    servers, 11

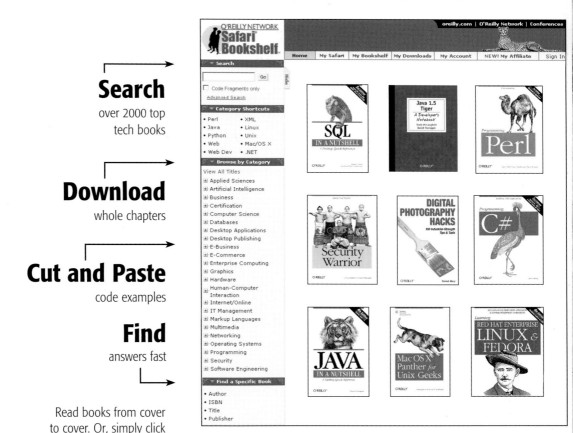

About the Author

Tyler Mitchell is a geographer and open source enthusiast. He works as a Geographic Information Systems (GIS) manager for Timberline Forest Inventory Consultants and lives in beautiful British Columbia, Canada. He is a regular speaker, moderator, and workshop leader at GIS conferences. His foray into the open source world began while looking for alternatives to proprietary mapping tools. He is now a devoted open source GIS advocate.

Colophon

Our look is the result of reader comments, our own experimentation, and feedback from distribution channels. Distinctive covers complement our distinctive approach to technical topics, breathing personality and life into potentially dry subjects.

The animal on the cover of *Web Mapping Illustrated* is a common snipe (*Gallinago gallinago*). Snipe are medium-sized (about 10 inches), wading shorebirds with short legs, pointed wings, and long, straight bills. Both sexes have a strongly patterned back with several buff, longitudinal stripes, a white belly, and dark bars on their flanks.

When flushed, the snipe rises away in a zigzag flight pattern. The flight call resembles a short rasping sneeze. In the spring, males produce an aerial drumming display using outstretched outer tail feathers to generate a low-pitched, whirring sound that attracts interested female partners. Once a female shows interest, the male pursues her and dives with wings held above the body in a V-shape, often rolling and turning upside down. Snipe nest on the ground in thick vegetation on wetlands or pasture where there is easy access to soft ground and small shallow pools. Females produce up to four eggs in 18 to 20 days; the babies are ready to fledge in 19 to 20 days.

Mary Anne Weeks Mayo was the production editor and copyeditor for *Web Mapping Illustrated*. Leanne Soylemez proofread the book. Adam Witwer and Claire Cloutier provided quality control. Peter Ryan provided production assistance. Julie Hawks wrote the index.

Ellie Volckhausen designed the cover of this book, based on a series design by Edie Freedman. The cover image is a loose antique engraving. Karen Montgomery produced the cover layout with Adobe InDesign CS using Adobe's ITC Garamond font.

David Futato designed the interior layout. This book was converted by Keith Fahlgren to FrameMaker 5.5.6 with a format conversion tool created by Erik Ray, Jason McIntosh, Neil Walls, and Mike Sierra that uses Perl and XML technologies. The text font is Linotype Birka; the heading font is Adobe Myriad Condensed; and the code font is LucasFont's TheSans Mono Condensed. The illustrations that appear in the book were produced by Robert Romano, Jessamyn Read, and Lesley Borash using Macromedia FreeHand MX and Adobe Photoshop CS. The tip and warning icons were drawn by Christopher Bing. This colophon was compiled by Mary Anne Weeks Mayo.